Fear and Courage

Fear
and
Courage

S. J. Rachman

Institute of Psychiatry
University of London

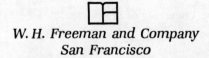

W. H. Freeman and Company
San Francisco

A Series of Books in Psychology

Editors
Jonathan Freedman
Gardner Lindzey
Richard F. Thompson

Library of Congress Cataloging in Publication Data

Rachman, Stanley
     Fear and courage.

     (A series of books in psychology)
     "This book grew out of an earlier analysis entitled
The meanings of fear."
     Bibliography: p.
     Includes index.
     1. Fear. 2. Courage. I. Rachman, Stanley. The
meanings of fear. II. Title.
BF575.F2R29   616.8'522   78-464
ISBN 0-7167-0089-1
ISBN 0-7167-0087-5 pbk.

Printed in the United States of America

9 8 7 6 5 4 3 2 1

For Emily and Tom

Contents

Contents

Acknowledgments

Because I have discussed most of the matters contained in this book with many colleagues and students during the past few years, it is impossible to acknowledge my debt to each of them by name. However, A. Bandura, P. de Silva, H. J. Eysenck, N. Garmezy, A. George, R. Hodgson, P. Lang, B. Melamed, M. Seligman, and J. Wolpe have been especially helpful. I also express my thanks to the following colleagues for help on specific points and/or general advice: S. Grey, R. Hallam, I. Marks, L. Parkinson, G. Roper, G. Sartory, and H. Shackleton.

A large part of this book was written at the Center for Advanced Studies in the Behavioral Sciences at Stanford, where I was a Fellow in 1976 – 77, and I am deeply indebted to the excellent staff, the other Fellows, and the Trustees for a happy and productive year. My particular thanks to Dr. G. Lindzey, Mr. P. Cutler, Mrs. D. Brothers, Mrs. J. Kielsmeier, Mrs. F. Duignan, and Mrs. K. Jencks—and back here in London, to Mrs. P. Levine.

June, 1978   S. J. Rachman

Introduction

This book on fear is the result of recently accumulated information as well as my belated recognition that psychological writings (my own included) on the subject were presenting a lopsided and needlessly gloomy view of human vulnerability. People are much more resilient than most psychologists have implied. Although this work is an expansion of my earlier analysis *The Meanings of Fear* (published in England in 1974),[1] it contains a great deal of new material as well as a new perspective—not only on fear, but on courage.

Although a significant proportion of my working time, both as a research worker and clinician, has been spent on the psychology of fear, my interest in courage is recent. The immediate cause of this interest was the courage shown by severely anxious neurotic patients as they carried out the newly de-

veloped behavioral training programs. Some of these
training programs require the patients to exercise
considerable persistence in the face of intense fear,
and the courageous manner in which these already
fearful people cope with the requirements of the task
is impressive and thought-provoking.

There was little in the scientific libraries to
satisfy my newly aroused curiosity and a search of
the *Psychological Abstracts* —the largest repository of
psychological references—produced a mere hand-
ful of mentions. By contrast, references to fear are extremely common; it is a well researched subject and,
in the past 40 years a multitude of laboratory experiments on animal fears, have been conducted. There
seems to be no rational reason for this disproportionate scientific emphasis, and one wonders
whether it is not merely one more example of our
heightened interest in morbid and distressing events,
in preference to the common, ordinary, constructive
phenomena of everyday life.

Whatever the cause, the fact remains that we
have little scientific information on the nature of
courage. Because it is a fascinating subject, and one
that can be studied with benefit to many, one purpose of this book is to bring the subject of courage
onto the scientific stage. I collected and analyzed information from diverse sources, some scientific and
other historical, journalistic or anecdotal, in an attempt to construct a workable first view of courage. I
was able to facilitate this task by applying some of the
new ideas on the psychology of fear. The concept
originally proposed by Peter Lang and now known as
the three systems model of fear, was especially helpful. If all goes well, interest in courage will increase,
and the present imbalance between the scientific
interest devoted to fear and that devoted to courage
will be corrected.

Because courage, Socrates' "very noble quality," appears to be universally admired, it is pleasing to report that examples of courage are common and easy to collect. Somewhat to my own surprise I was led to the firm conclusion that people are considerably more resilient than is generally recognized. Psychologists in particular have been so preoccupied with fear and anxiety that we have neglected to notice the occurrence of courage and perseverance in the face of stress and adversity. In a small but not insignificant way, examples of human resilience can be seen daily in clinics, counseling centers, and hospitals, as people struggle to overcome their longstanding and severe fears, under the guidance of professional helpers. On a larger scale, people displayed astonishing resilience during wartime, and the courage of ambulance crews, fire fighters, and other service workers was particularly impressive. In all, these observations provide one with a better rounded and more hopeful view of human qualities.

There is at least as much courage as fear, and at least as much resilience as there is vulnerability. Fears do arise however, and that is the main subject of this book. It contains a discussion of *human fears*, their range, genesis, fluctuations, and nature. Although little direct reference is made to the vast literature describing research on fear in animals, my conception of human fears is considerably influenced by such work, particularly where it pertains to the induction and the avoidance of fear. J. A. Gray's interpretation, *The Psychology of Fear and Stress*, is an admirable guide to much of this research and has been of considerable help.

Although the word *fear* is used without difficulty in everyday language to mean the experience of apprehension, problems arise when it is used as a scientific term. It cannot be assumed that people are always able or even willing to recognize and then describe the experience of fear. In wartime, admissions of fear are discouraged. Similarly, boys are usually discouraged from expressing fear. In surveys carried out on student populations, it has been found that the admission of certain fears by men is felt to be socially undesirable.

The social influences that obscure the accurate expression of fear complicate the intrinsic difficulties in recognizing and describing of our own experiences or predicted experiences. For instance, it is regularly found that many people who state they are fearful of a particular object or situation are later seen to display fearless behavior when they confront the specified fear stimulus. Subjective reports of fear also tend to be of limited value in assessing the intensity of the experience because of the difficulties in translating such expressions as "extremely frightened," "terrified," and "slightly anxious" into a quantitative scale with stable properties.

The Three Components of Fear

For these reasons, among others, psychologists have extended the study of fear beyond an exclusive reliance on subjective reports, by including indexes of physiological change and measures of overt behavior. It is helpful to think of fear as comprising three main components: the subjective experience of apprehension, associated psychophysiological changes, and attempts to avoid or escape from certain situations.

When the three components of fear fail to correspond, as they commonly do, problems arise. People can experience subjective fear but remain outwardly calm, and, if tested, they show none of the expected psychophysiological reactions. We also receive reports of subjective fear from people who make no attempt to escape from or avoid the supposedly frightening situation. The existence of these three components of fear, coupled with the fact that they do not always correspond, makes it helpful to specify in scientific exchanges which component of fear one is referring to.

In our everyday exchanges we rely, for the most part, on people *telling us* of their fears, and then we supplement this verbal information by interpreting the significance of this information and mixing it with clues given by their facial and other bodily expressions. Unfortunately, when made in the absence of supporting contextual cues, these interpretations can be misleading. Moreover, the value of observations of facial and related expressions is limited to certain categories of fear, particularly those of an acute and episodic nature. Diffuse and chronic fears are less visible. So we may without difficulty observe signs of fear in an anxious passenger as an aircraft descends, but fail to recognize the fear in a person who is intensely apprehensive about aging.

Although there are many types of fear, certain categories such as neurotic fears have understandably been studied more intensively than others. Among these varieties, a major division can be made between acute and chronic fears. The acute fears are generally provoked by tangible stimuli or situations and subside quite readily when the frightening stimulus is removed or avoided. The fear of snakes illustrates this acute type. A less common type of acute fear is the sudden onset of panic, which seems to have no tangible source. It can last for as long as an hour or more and often leaves a residue of discomfort. On the whole, the chronic fears tend to be more complex but, like the acute, they may or may not be tied to tangible sources of provocation. The fear of being alone is an example of a chronic, tangible fear, but examples of chronic and intangible fears are by their very nature difficult to specify. One simply feels persistently uneasy and anxious for unidentified reasons—it is a chronic state of aching fear that has been described better by novelists than by psychologists.

A distinction is sometimes drawn between fear and anxiety. Then fear refers to feelings of apprehension about tangible and predominantly realistic dangers, and anxiety to feelings of apprehension that are difficult to relate to tangible sources of stimulation. The inability to identify the source of the fear is usually regarded as the hallmark of anxiety, and in psychodynamic theories, the inability is said to be a result of repression; hence the cause of the fear remains unconscious. Although this distinction between fear and anxiety is not without its uses, it will not be retained in this book. The division between tangible and intangible fears relates to another distinction that has proven to be clinically useful, that of focal versus diffuse fears. Generally, focal fears are more easily modified despite the fact that they often are of long-standing duration.

Although it may be of little practical value, the distinction between innate and acquired fears is an intriguing one. The impact of early Behaviorism, with its massive emphasis on the importance of acquired behavior, led to the interment of the notion that some fears may be innately determined. Even the possible existence of such fears in animals was only reluctantly conceded. In recent years, however, the possible occurrence of innately determined fears in human beings has once more come under serious consideration. One of the more prominent and promising accounts of the inherent determinants of fear, M. Seligman's theory of preparedness, is discussed in detail, in Chapter 7.

The fluctuations of fear are of some interest, especially their emergence in early childhood followed by a general decline in frequency and intensity during middle to late childhood. This rise and fall of fears raises questions of causation. What is the cause of fear? Or, to be more precise, what are the causes of fears? The inevitable subsidiary question is, why do fears decline and disappear?

In an introduction, it is possible to give an over-simplified summary of the major causes of fear. Nevertheless it is important to point out the following causes: exposure to traumatic stimulation, repeated exposures to subtraumatic sensitizing situations, observations (direct or indirect) of people exhibiting fear, and transmission of fear-inducing information. For a considerable time, theories of fear acquisition were dominated by the conditioning theory that emphasized the importance of exposure to traumatic stimulation. Recent recognition of the fact that fears can be acquired vicariously, and by the direct transmission of information, has helped to produce a richer and better balanced account of the causes of fear.

Controllability

A more general observation has been the functional connection between our ability to control potentially threatening situations and the experience of fear. If in the face of threats we feel unable to control the probable outcome, we are likely to experience fear. By contrast, if in the same threatening situation we confidently expect that we will be able to control the likelihood of an unfavorable outcome, we are unlikely to experience fear.

Although the concept of controllability is important and enables us to make sense of a considerable amount of information, it is not without difficulties, and a critical examination of its present status is undertaken in Chapter 16 of this book. The idea of controllability is also implied in Bandura's new theory of the basis of behavioral change;[2] the cornerstone of this theory is that modifications of fear are mediated by changes in "perceived self-efficacy," which is an elaborated version of the "sense of controllability." The concept is also prominent in Seligman's theory of learned helplessness. Although this theory is designed primarily to encompass the phenomena of depression, it incorporates aspects of the genesis of fear. In the original statement of the theory published in 1975, he claimed that helplessness, and therefore depression, resulted from an acquired sense of futility: "Helplessness is the psychological state that frequently results when events are uncontrollable."[3] For purposes of his theory, Seligman offered the following view of controllability. He said that when "the probability of an outcome is the same whether or not a given response occurs, the outcome is independent of that response. When this is true of all voluntary responses, the outcome is uncontrollable."[4] He then goes on to postulate that the expectation of uncontrollability "produces fear for as long as the subject is uncertain of the uncontrollability of the outcome," and this may in turn produce depression.[5]

If people perceive that they are in a position to control the outcome of an event, their anxiety is reduced. Although the theory will be gone into presently, at this point it is worth drawing attention to two aspects of Seligman's conception: First, the person's sense of whether or not he can control the situation is a more important determinant of fear than the objective likelihood of his asserting or failing to assert such control; second, although it is not explicit in the theory, it would appear that a perceived absence of control is likely to lead to fear only when the outcome is expected to be aversive. It seems improbable that an absence of control over a desired outcome is likely to induce fear. In short, the absence of perceived control in a potentially aversive condition generates fear, whereas the acquisition of a perceived sense of mastery reduces fear. Repeated experiences of either of these types may have a cumulative effect, as Seligman maintains. "I suggest that what produces self-esteem and a sense of competence, and protects against depression, is not only the absolute quality of experience, but the perception that one's own actions control the experience. To the degree that uncontrollable events occur, either traumatic or positive, depression will be predisposed and ego-strength undermined."[6]

The sense of controllability is related to *predictability* and Seligman presents persuasive evidence to indicate that in most circumstances, people prefer predictable events to unpredictable ones.[7] There is of course a logical connection between predictability and controllability,[8] and the two often coincide. The concept of controllability would seem to entail predictability, but of course there are predictable events that are beyond our control.

Leaving aside these theoretical questions for the present, we can regard the preference for predictability, and the striving to achieve it, as an early stage in the process of attempting to achieve increased controllability over a potentially aversive outcome. The more information we have about the nature of the expected aversiveness, its likely time of occurrence, its probable duration, its premonitory signs, the greater the likelihood that we will find ways of preventing it from occurring or of reducing its consequences if it does occur. An example of the search for predictability in a potentially aversive situation can be seen in the keen curiosity displayed, especially by children, when confronted by a novel situation (e.g., a new animal). If the child's search for relevant information, such as by examining the animal, increases his expectation of controllability any fear that he might have had will subside. But if the new information alters his prediction about the likelihood of the animal behaving aversively, then the fear may increase.

As we shall see, the concept of controllability and the related notion of predictability offer considerable explanatory power and enable one to encompass many aspects of fear. For our purposes, controllability is taken to mean the person's sense of whether or not he is in a position to reduce the likelihood of an aversive event and/or its consequences. In most circumstances the perception of inadequate powers of control will contribute to fear. A perceived sense of substantial control over the probability of reducing the likelihood of an aversive event and/or its consequences—a sense of mastery if you will—reduces fear. Potentially aversive events that are extremely difficult to predict are more likely to produce fear than are predictable events; similarly, behavior or information that increases one's predictability is likely to contribute to a reduction in fear. Extrapolating from these definitions and concepts, it can be argued that people who have a well developed sense of competence, or, in everyday language, who display considerable self-confidence, will seldom experience fear. People with a poor sense of their own competence, those with little self-confidence, can be expected to experience fear rather frequently.

Fears diminish as a result of repeated exposures, especially to mild or toned-down versions of the frightening situation—by a process akin to habituation. The decline in fears as a consequence of repetition can be facilitated by superimposing on the fearful situation an incompatible response such as relaxation.

The complexity of the relations between the emergence and the decline of a fear can be seen from the fact that repeated exposures to the fear-evoking object or situation increase the fear (sensitization) at some times, and at other times decrease it (habituation). In other words, it is posited that fears exist in a state of balance. This balance tilts in the direction of increased or decreased fear depending on the type of exposure, the intensity of the stimulation, the person's state of alertness, and other factors. The tendency to habituate to repeated stimulation is a universal characteristic and one that is probably extremely important in the shaping of our fears—as well as in the growth of courage. As we shall see when we examine the evidence accumulated during time of war, habituation can occur on a massive scale even in the face of repeated exposures to dangerous and intensive, uncontrollable, and unpredictable stimulation. However, there are also instances in which habituation fails to occur. Some fear responses fall into this group of exceptions and therefore can be considered abnormal in the restricted sense of undue persistence despite repeated exposures. They may be regarded as abnormal in the *clinical* sense as well if the fearful reactions are disproportionate and, to some extent, incapacitating.

Individuals of course vary widely in fearfulness, and we also have evidence of individual differences in the ease with which people habituate to repeated stimulation. It is tempting to relate fearfulness to an inability to habituate satisfactorily, and some interesting attempts have in fact been made.

Fear, or its first cousin anxiety, is a major component of most neurotic disorders. As a result, it is a subject that has greatly occupied clinicians, and they and their research colleagues have explored the effects of a variety of therapeutic methods. Although the pharmacological methods are partly successful,[9] they are outside the scope of this book, and we will consider only psychological methods for reducing fear. These can be divided into two main types: those which attempt directly to reduce the fear or anxiety (as in behavior therapy) and those which attempt to modify the putative underlying causes of the fear or anxiety, as in psychoanalysis and related techniques.

The direct methods are comparatively new and largely the products of experimental psychology. Desensitization, the first established and most extensively used direct method, was recently joined by *flooding* and by *modeling*. These newcomers show every sign of exceeding the power of their precursor. Psychoanalysis is of course the most famous and influential of the indirect methods, and has spawned many derivations. Most of them were, like psychoanalysis itself, developed by clinical psychiatrists or psychologists. The most widely practiced form of indirect treatment is psychotherapy (a confusingly wide term covering many types of activity) and not psychoanalysis, which is a much less common form of therapy. Although there are great differences between techniques, the indirect methods are all founded on the assumption that a thorough exploration of matters seemingly unrelated to the pertinent fear is a necessary prerequisite for the reduction of fear.

Before we proceed to the substance of the book, it is perhaps worthwhile mentioning the sources of information on which the arguments and conclusions are based. They include laboratory research on fear and its modification, surveys of the nature and extent of common and uncommon fears, clinical observations of neurotic patients, and data gathered during times of war. Although much of the information on wartime behavior is patchy and unsupported by the usual types of scientific verification process, it is consistent and unusually rich in value. As a good deal of it rests in obscure sources[10] and is little known (and when known, underinterpreted), extended descriptions are given in this book—before the more accessible and familiar survey data and clinical observations described in the succeeding chapters.

Notes

1) The present revision places greater emphasis on the biological significance of fear, the indirect transmission of fear, human resilience, and courage, among other changes and additions.

2) A. Bandura, *Psychological Review* **84**, 1977, pp. 191–215.

3) M. E. P. Seligman, *Helplessness*, 1975, p. 9. A revised, extended version of the learned helplessness theory is soon to appear (L. Abramson, M. Seligman

and J. Teasdale, 1978). It is an enriched, complex development in which the person's attribution of the cause of the uncontrollability, is given a central position.

4) Seligman, 1975, p. 16.

5) Seligman, 1975, p. 56.

6) Seligman, 1975, p. 99.

7) For exceptions, see S. Miller and M. Seligman, in preparation,

8) See S. Mineka and D. Kihlstrom, in preparation; and Miller and Seligman, in preparation.

9) See M. Lader and I. Marks, *Clinical Anxiety*, 1971, for examples.

10) Much of this invaluable information is tucked away in narrowly distributed governmental and military reports. As if to compensate for the narrowness of distribution, some of these reports extend into as many as 17 volumes.

Chapter 1
"Fear Is Not a Lump"

Since the mid 1950s, important advances have been made in our ability to reduce human fears. Much of the research was carried out on selected university students who exhibited strong but circumscribed fears (of snakes, spiders, public-speaking and so on), and it was hoped that the findings would be applicable to other groups and other fears. In particular, it was hoped that a clearer understanding of severe, disabling fears might emerge. The results of the research are described in Chapter 8, but the studies also produced some unexpected spin-off. In order to ensure that the experimental findings were reliable and replicable, it became necessary to develop instruments for measuring degrees and types of fear.

The typical laboratory study, carried out on a sample of female university students with mini-phobias, consisted of comparisons between treated and untreated groups of subjects. In most experiments, the effects of the experimental treatment were measured by a combination of instruments. In the first place, it was necessary to prepare a general questionnaire that could be applied to a large and unselected group of potential subjects in order to select those who reported a substantial degree of fear of the object or situation in question. This initial selection was usually followed by another sorting test, called an "avoidance test" or a "behavioral approach test." In this one, the experimenter assessed the subjects singly by asking them to approach as close as possible to the fearful object and, if they could, to handle it or simply touch it. In the course of this behavioral test, the subjects were asked to give a report of their subjectively experienced fear in terms of a "fear thermometer," which is a simple scale of discomfort ranging from *calm*, which is scored as zero, to *moderately fearful*, which is scored at five, to *terrified*, which is scored at ten. The subjects were instructed in the use of the scale and were requested to use the full range. The subject's success or failure in the behavioral test was graded in some manner, usually in terms of her proximity to the feared object. This information was then combined with the subjective fear estimates provided on the fear thermometer. In a number of studies the behavioral and subjective measures were supplemented by psychophysiological recordings, most typically those of pulse rate, electrical resistance of the skin, muscle tension, respiration, or some combination of these measures. In some, specific characteristics of the subject's behavior during the behavioral tests (e.g., tremors, pallor) were rated by a group of external judges.

Although, as we shall see in later chapters, the various fear-reduction techniques have been impressively effective, some unexpected and complex findings also emerged. Some perplexing occurrences have also been reported in the clinical application of these fear-reducing techniques. Despite the appearance of marked behavioral improvements, such as a claustrophobic person acquiring the ability to travel on underground trains, some patients deny that they have benefited from treatment. In other patients the physiological reactions observed during the real or symbolic presentation of a fearful object diminish after treatment, but the person continues to complain of excessive fear.

Before it became clear that discrepancies between the various measures of fear are fairly common and even to be expected, a certain amount of confusion prevailed in therapeutic circles. It was then also observed that among some patients the improvements apparent in their *behavior* were followed only weeks or months later by subjective improvements as well. Repeated observations of this type led to the recognition that the different indexes of fear might show different *rates* of response to treatment—a type of desynchrony. The recognition that the patient's subjective report tends to be the slowest to change was of some relief to therapists as well as to patients. In general, the order of change in response to therapy is declining physiological reactivity, followed by behavioral improvements, and, finally, by subjective improvements.

The low correspondence between some measures of fear also led to difficulties in interpreting laboratory findings on fear reduction. It even produced difficulties at the very earliest stage of experiments—the selection of suitably fearful subjects. It is a common experience to find that a substantial proportion of potential subjects who rate themselves as being fearful on a questionnaire will display only slight fear, or no fear at all, when exposed to the fearful object in a behavioral avoidance test. Some of them walk in, approach the snake directly, and then lift it without hesitation in spite of having recorded on the questionnaire that they have an extreme fear of snakes. In laboratory research, as in clinical practice, it is often found that subjective reports of fear tend to diminish more slowly than overt signs of fear and avoidance behavior.

An experimental example of a major discrepancy between different types of measure can be illustrated by the work of G. Paul.[1] In a study on university students with a marked but circumscribed fear of public speaking, he assessed fear by a number of self-report measures, two major physiological measures, external ratings of fear, and a behavioral test of public speaking. The outcome of the experiment was therapeutically successful and a good deal of useful subsidiary information was gathered. Paul found a reasonably high correlation between all the self-report measures of therapeutic improvement, but there was little relationship between the physiological indicants of fear, and no relation between the self-report indexes and the physiological ones.[2] There was a modest correlation between the therapist's and the subject's ratings of improvement.[3] It is interesting to notice that despite the lack of agreement between some of the outcome measures, all the major ones (including self-report and physiological indexes) showed that the treated subjects were significantly improved both at termination of treatment and at follow-up.

Peter Lang of Wisconsin University, who has been responsible for some of the most valuable research and theorizing on the subject of fear and fear reduction, expressed the new view of fear extremely well: ". . . fear is not some hard phenomenal lump that lives inside people, that we may palpate more or less successfully."[4] He has argued convincingly that fear responses are related to each other, but only imperfectly; they are partially independent. In many circumstances, however, they do show corresponding changes. In one of Lang's experiments, he obtained a correlation of 0.41 between the subjects' ratings of fear and their avoidance behavior.

The correlation between the subject's report of fear in the test situation and the estimate made by an external observer was 0.48. But, in the same experiment, the correlation between the questionnaire responses and the fear overtly expressed in the avoidance test was only 0.04.

In a study on automated desensitization, a reassuringly high correspondence between fear reports and heart rate was obtained.[5] Respiratory rate, however, showed a disappointingly low correlation with subjective fear—only 0.05. To paraphrase some of Lang's writings, fear comprises a set of imperfectly coupled systems.

Variations

The variations in patterns of the three components of fear are well illustrated in a series of case studies described by H. Leitenberg, S. Agras, R. Butz, and J. Wincze.[6] They made careful observations of the therapeutic progress of nine fearful subjects and were able to show that behavioral improvements and psychophsiological changes in many of them took independent paths. In some subjects the two components changed in synchrony, whereas in others the behavioral improvements preceded or followed the psychophysiological changes. Other studies of desynchronous change have been provided as well. For example, significant reductions in subjective fear are not necessarily translated into improved coping behavior,[7] and they occasionally lag behind behavioral changes.[8] Highly demanding procedures such as flooding (see page 162) can produce desynchronous changes: behavioral improvements occur first and most easily, but the person is left with excessive subjective fear.[9] Other examples of desynchrony, in which subjective fear failed to correlate with the other two components, are given in Hersen's review,[10] patterns of discordance are set out by Lader and Marks, and Borkovec, Werts and Bernstein have provided a useful analysis of the methodological and measurement problems.[11]

Without doing too much injustice to the finer points of this extensive research, we can summarize the present position as follows. Self-reports of fear correlate well with each other; they correlate moderately well with the ratings of fear made by external judges and also with the avoidance behavior observed in a fear test; self-reports correlate modestly with physiological indexes of fear; physiological indices of fear correlate modestly with each other and hardly at all with muscle tension.

Another point worth mentioning is the strong likelihood that *all* correlations between the various measures or response systems are likely to increase at extremes of the scales. In other words, the correspondence between the different measures will be greater in conditions of extreme fear or extreme calm.[12] For example, in a state of deep relaxation it is likely that the self-report of subjects will be one of calm, the physiological response systems will be reasonably quiescent, there will be no avoidance behavior and an external observer would describe the person as seeming calm.

In an investigation of fear in parachute jumpers, W. Fenz and S. Epstein found evidence of both correspondence and lack of correspondence between different measures.[13] In a group of 10 veteran jumpers, discordant results were obtained. The three physiological measures all showed a steady increase during the entire jumping sequence. This was contrary to the pattern observed in the measure of subjective fear, which varied in the following way— increase in fear, then decrease, followed by another increase (see Figure 1). Among the group of 10 novices, however, subjective fear and psychophysiological reactions showed corresponding patterns of increase and decrease. Heart rate, skin conductance, and respiration all built up to a peak shortly before the jump occurred (e.g., the mean heart rate equaled 145 beats per minute) and then subsided quite quickly after the landing. The veterans experienced only mild increases in heart rate, subjective fear, and other measures, whereas the novices displayed extremely strong reactions. These findings support the idea that the correspondence between measures will increase at extreme levels of fear or, at the opposite extreme, will correspond well during states of calm.

Predictions

In 1974, R. Hodgson and S. Rachman attempted to assemble and integrate the disparate findings on desynchrony, and concluded with several hypotheses that include the following.[14] They argued that con-

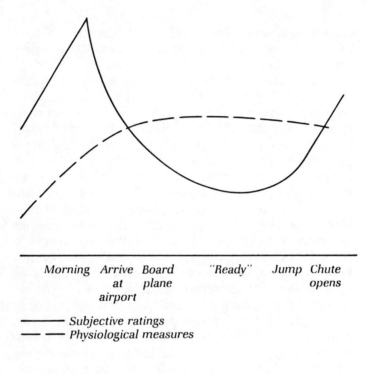

Morning	Arrive	Board	"Ready"	Jump	Chute
	at	plane			opens
	airport				

——— Subjective ratings
— — Physiological measures

Figure 1 *The discordant results obtained in a study of fear in veteran parachute jumpers. The jumpers' subjective fear reports do not correspond to the changes in physiological activity.* [Adapted from S. Epstein and W. Fenz, Journal of Experimental Psychology **70**, 1965, and from Fenz and Epstein, Psychosomatic Medicine **29**, 1967.]

cordance between the three fear components is likely
to be high during strong emotional arousal and that
discordance will be more evident during mild emotional arousal. The first explicit attempt to test these
ideas produced partial support for their value.[15] The
third and fourth hypotheses dealt with the effects of
external demands on the components of fear. The
first test produced partial support for the predictions
that the concordance between components will be
greater under low levels of demand and that high
levels of demand will produce discordance between
components.[16] They also argue that the pattern and
degree of synchronous change produced in the fear
components is a function of the therapeutic procedure employed, but this has not yet been tested. Finally, the prediction that concordance between
components will be found to increase in the followup
period that occurs after a treatment or training program remains to be assessed. If nothing more, the
new analysis of fear provides a basis for fresh predictions and hypotheses of this kind.

In view of the imperfect coupling between systems, what is the best basis for predicting the occurrence of fear? In accord with the advice of Lang and
others, it might be best to avoid reliance on a single
measure. Self-report of experienced fear seems to be
indispensable and, at the same time, potentially misleading. Self-report measures *can* form a useful if
crude basis for prediction of fear and have some practical advantages over more elaborate techniques of
assessment;[17] providing one does not expect too
much of these measures, that is, too great a degree of
refinement, they can be valuable. The inclusion of a
behavioral approach test is highly desirable in almost
all studies, and it will of course provide a valuable
check on the predictive value of a self-report mea-

sure. The ratings of fear made by external judges can be useful but, as we shall see in the next chapter, they are not free of problems. Some physiological indexes, heart rate in particular, can provide useful data for prediction purposes. It has, for example, been shown that heart rate acceleration is frequently correlated with the imaginal rehearsal of fear situations.[18] Measures of skin conductance have sometimes been useful, but individual differences in responsiveness are large, and the index produces technical problems arising out of its rapid adaptation. Measures of muscular tension have not been successful.

Some of the dangers of relying on a single measure include the following. Too great a reliance on self-report can lead one to underestimate a person's degree of courage; too great a reliance on the approach behavior observed in a fear test can lead one to underestimate the degree of a person's *fear*.

This new view of fear as a complex of imperfectly coupled response systems leads us to some novel ideas on the nature of courage (see Chapter 15). As we have seen, a person may be quite willing to approach a frightening object or situation but experience a high degree of subjective fear and even some accompanying unpleasant bodily reactions. This persistence in the face of emotional and physical sensations of fear comes closest to a common view of courage—to continue *despite* one's fear. A psychologist could describe this type of courageous behavior as an example of uncoupling, in which the person's overt behavior advances beyond his subjective discomfort.

Is a person who continues to approach a fearful situation, in the *absence* of any subjective fear or accompanying bodily responses, to be described as courageous or not? Presumably, in psychological parlance, he would have to be described as someone who displays an absence of fear rather than courage itself. Also, how would we describe a person who feels calm when approaching a fearful situation but, when the responses are measured, displays clear (autonomic) physiological disturbances? An autonomic coward? Finally, a person who shows no physiological disturbances when experiencing subjective fear can be said to possess a brave autonomic system.

Perhaps we should reserve the description of "true courage" for those people who are willing and able to approach a fearful situation despite the presence of subjective fear and psychophysiological disturbances. It will be evident that our expanding conception of fear has provoked some entertaining ideas and that more are to come.

Notes

1) G. Paul, *Insight versus Desensitization*, 1966.

2) Paul, 1966, pp. 61—64.

3) Paul, 1966, p. 64.

4) P. Lang, in D. Levis, Ed., *Learning Approaches to Therapeutic Behavior Change*, 1970.

5) P. Lang, B. Melamed, and J. Hart, *Journal of Abnormal Psychology*, **76**, 1970.

6) H. Leitenberg et al., *Journal of Abnormal Psychology* **78**, 1971.

7) A. Hepner and N. Cauthen, *Journal of Consulting and Clinical Psychology* **43**, 1975.

8) H. Becker and C. Costello, *Journal of Consulting and Clinical Psychology* **43**, 1975.

9) B. McCutcheon and A. Adams, *Behavior Research and Therapy* **13**, 1975; Y. Suarez, H. Adams, and B. McCutcheon, *Journal of Consulting and Clinical Psychology* **44**, 1976.

10) M. Hersen, *Behavior Therapy* **4**, 1973.

11) M. Lader and I. Marks, *Clinical Anxiety*, 1971; see also R. Hodgson and S. Rachman, and Rachman and Hodgson, both in *Behavior Research and Therapy* **12**, 1974; S. Rachman, *Behavior Research and Therapy* **14**, 1976; T. Borkovec, T. Weerts, and D. Bernstein, in A. Ciminero et al., Eds., *Handbook of Behavioral Assessment*, 1976.

12) G. Sartory, S. Rachman, and S. Grey, *Behavior Research and Therapy* **15**, 1977.

13) W. D. Fenz and S. Epstein, *Psychosomatic Medicine* **29**, 1967.

14) R. Hodgson and S. Rachman, *Behavior Research and Therapy* **12**, 1974.

15) Sartory, Rachman, and Grey, 1977.

16) G. Sartory, S. Grey, and S. Rachman, *Behavior Research and Therapy* **16**, 1978.

17) D. Griffiths and M. Joy, *Behavior Research and Therapy* **9**, 1971.

18) A. Mathews, *Psychological Bulletin* **76**, 1971; P. Lang, B. Melamed, and J. Hart, *Journal of Abnormal Psychology* **76**, 1970.

Chapter 2
Fear Under Air Attack

Before the outbreak of World War II most authorities expected that air attacks on civilian targets would produce widespread panic, enduring terror, and large numbers of psychiatric casualties. As a noted British psychologist Philip Vernon wrote at the time, "the stimuli presented by a heavy air-raid are far more intense and more terrifying than civilised human beings normally experience ... in the summer of 1940 when raids on a large scale seemed imminent in Britain, many of us were apprehensive lest they should lead to widespread panic and hysteria."[1] These apprehensions were fed by reports of the panicky conduct of the civilian population in Barcelona during raids carried out in the Spanish Civil War, and by similar accounts of frightened crowds fleeing from bombed areas in Flanders and France. A year before the outbreak of World War II, John Rickman, the Editor of the *British Journal of Medical Psychology*, wrote in *The Lancet*, "since air raids may produce panic in the civilian population it is well to consider the factors that facilitate or diminish panic, and what steps, if any, may be taken against it."[2]

Accordingly, in issuing air raid precautions, authorities took into account the psychological as well as the physical dangers. Arrangements were made for the dispersal of city dwellers and special psychological clinics were introduced. However, within a year of the start of the air attacks on Britain, Vernon reached the reassuring conclusion, "fortunately we were wrong." What happened?

To the considerable surprise of almost everyone, the psychological casualties were few, despite the death and destruction caused by the attacks. For example, of 578 civilian casualties admitted to a hospital in a heavily raided area, only two were suffering primarily from psychological disturbance. A report from another heavily bombed area confirmed that only 15 of the 1100 people treated by medical clinics showed psychological disorders. Among 200 admissions to a mental hospital in London during a period of heavy raids, the doctors found that the "air attacks were a major factor in the disorders presented by only five of the total group. Moreover, these five cases responded well to treatment."[3]

Before we describe how most people responded to air attacks and analyze why they did so, it might be helpful to give an account of the kind of disorder that was *expected* to occur on a wide scale, but in fact turned out to be a rare occurrence.

This description of an air raid phobia was provided by Dr. E. Stengel,[4] an experienced clinical psychiatrist: "... a persistent and excessive fear of air raids, which was present all the time but steadily increased toward nightfall. The sound of the sirens precipitated an acute anxiety attack." These phobias, once established, persisted after the air attacks had ceased. The fear of air raids was sometimes accompanied by intense fears of enclosed spaces and/or being alone in public places.

However, as the distinguished psychologist I. L. Janis notes in his valuable study of British reactions to air raids, "the reactions of *most* people generally subsided within one quarter of an hour after the end of the bombing attack."[5] For a minority of people these acute reactions took longer to subside: "... over a period of days and weeks, there is a gradual return to normality, ... characteristic initial symptoms are jitteriness, sensitivity to noise, excessive fatigue, trembling of the hands, and terrifying nightmares in which the traumatic situation is re-experienced."[6]

The resilience that people displayed under air attack was so unexpected and remarkable that the surveys and statistical analyses, to be described later in this chapter, inevitably fail to convey how people managed to cope. The official reports concentrate mostly on reactions that were expected but did not occur. Among the many excellent literary accounts of life during the blitz in Britain, the descriptions provided by Mollie Panter-Downes are among the most vivid, and succeed where the official reports fail.*

Blitz

Her account begins as Londoners prepared for the first air attacks after the declaration of war. "The evacuation of London which is to be spaced over three days began yesterday and was apparently a triumph for all concerned." The BBC provided a Beethoven concert, "interspersed with the calm and cultured tones of the BBC telling motorists what to do during air raids, and giving instructions to what the BBC referred to coyly as expectant mothers who are a good deal more than expectant."[7]

"For the first week of the war the weather was superb." In these early stages, people took the official advice about air raid precautions with seriousness and reacted to the first alarms in a prompt manner. "Even Miss Chupp, one of our sub-wardens found that she had not yet been provided with the tin hat promised by a benevolent government for such a contingency. Nothing daunted, she found an aluminium pudding basin, which fitted to a nicety, mounted her bicycle and shot round her section blowing blasts on a whistle with a violence that shook the pince-nez on her mild nose." After repeated alarms, followed by very little action, the population quickly adapted and apparently showed little concern. The mood is conveyed in this anecdote: "On these fine mornings, London bus-drivers hail each other sardonically by saying, 'Nice day for the blitzkrieg, Bill,' but so far nothing has happened."

It should not be thought however that the people were unaware of the dangers ahead of them. Panter-Downes describes, for example, the anxiety of parents who were hoping that their children might be evacuated to the safety of America. "The one hope these worried people hang on to is that the overwhelmingly generous offer of hospitality from America may be followed up by the sending of American ships to fetch the children. Britons still have an immense faith in America and the workings of her national conscience, but they hope that such gestures will not be delayed much longer. Over here, one gets a new conception of time. It doesn't march on; it hurtles like a dive-bomber."

When in the summer of 1940 the big raids started, people continued to display calm behavior. They quickly adapted their daily style of living to the repeated raids and the disturbance of the nights. On the frivolous side, there were discussions about the best places to take shelter during a raid. "Shoppers prefer Harrods where chairs are provided and first-aid workers unobtrusively but comfortingly hover about. In the public shelters it is usually a case of standing room only, which becomes hard on the feet after an hour or so ..." By September, there were many casualties and a great deal of damage had been done. Newspaper announcements of air raid deaths were covered by the euphemistic phrase, "died very suddenly."

"Life in a bombed city means adapting oneself in all kinds of ways all the time. The calm behavior of the average individual continues to be amazing. Commuting suburbanites, who up to yesterday had experienced worse bombardments than people living in Central London, placidly bragged to fellow passengers on the morning trains about the size of bomb craters in their neighbourhoods, as in a more peaceful summer they would have bragged about their roses and squash." But the continuing raids began to have their effects. "For Londoners there are no longer such things as good nights; they are only bad nights, worse nights and better nights. Hardly any one has slept at all in the past week." Large numbers of people were obliged to sleep each night in the air raid shelters and on the morning after raids, "thousands of dazed and weary families patiently trundled their few belongings in perambulators away from the wreckage of their homes."

"The Nazi attack bore down heaviest on badly nourished, poorly clothed people—the worst equipped of any to stand the appalling physical strain, if it were not for the stoutness of their cockney hearts. Relief workers sorted them into schools and other centers to be fed, rested, and provided with billets. Subsequent raids killed many of the homeless as they waited."

More and more people were forced by the dangers of the bombing or by the destruction of their homes, to seek shelter in the underground railway stations. "Each morning more are leaving their underground sanctuary to go back and find a heap of rubble and splinters where their houses used to be. The bravery of these people has to be seen to be believed. They would be heart-rending to look at if they didn't so conspicuously refuse to appear heart-rending." And so it went on, with loss of sleep continuing to "be as menacing as bombs (and) the courage, humor and kindliness of ordinary people continued to be astonishing under conditions which possess many of the features of a nightmare."

Panter-Downes, like so many other observers, paid particular tribute to the people who continued to provide essential services during the raids. Firemen, wardens, home guards, and nurses alike were killed while on duty. "Nurses have been under fire constantly, for several hospitals have been hit more than once. St. Thomas's on the river opposite the Houses of Parliament . . . is a tragic site, its wards ripped open by bombs." By general agreement, these workers performed extraordinarily well despite the dangers and fatigue. Very few of them developed psychological disorders, or even undue fear reactions.

Surveys

Now to return to the official and professional observations made during the raids, Philip Vernon systematically gathered reports from 50 doctors and psychologists (including the young H. J. Eysenck). Although people reacted fearfully to the early threats and raids, "before the end of 1940 Londoners were generally taking no notice of sirens at all unless accompanied by the noise of planes and gunfire or bombs...."[8] This rapid *habituation* to the intense stimulation that signaled the imminent appearance of danger is one of the most striking findings to emerge from these dreadful experiences. Continuing his professional analysis of the data, Vernon argued, "it might be possible to arrange members of the population along a uni-dimensional continuum according to their degree of habituation to raids. The average position would be highest in places like London, Merseyside, Bristol and Birmingham and lowest in country villages." He said that some evidence suggested that emotionally unstable people found it harder to adapt to the raids, as did those who had undergone a particularly intense raid. Furthermore "a reversion occurs also when there is a long spell of immunity from raids" (probably an example of dishabituation). He also concluded, "there is no doubt that being with others helped the majority of people and that those who live alone tend to find raids much more trying."[9] Like Panter-Downes, Vernon was sure that people with a job to do, "such as civil defense workers, mostly recover their poise readily and set about rescuing casualties, fire-fighting, etc. immediately." Even when people were exposed to intense bombing and near misses, "a good deal of habituation occurs, even to such extreme stimulation." Vernon understandably concluded that "the extent to which people have become habituated to conditions and to noises which were almost unthinkable a year ago still strikes one as extraordinary."[10]

Most of the information gathered during World War II has been ably reviewed by Janis, and his major conclusions are discussed in the following pages. But first, two reports by British doctors are of unusual interest. Dr. Henry Wilson, working in the London Hospital, wrote in 1942 that "the small number of psychiatric casualties that have followed aerial bombardment has been a matter of surprise."[11] Of the 619 civilian casualites brought to first aid posts after the air raids, 134 were suffering from acute effects of fear. Within 24 hours it was possible to discharge all of them, and of these only six returned for further help. Wilson also carried out an interesting comparison between those people who had severe reactions to the air raids and a comparable group that had little or no adverse reactions. As he says, the most surprising feature of the comparison subjects (i.e., those who had few adverse reactions) was the large number who suffered from mild fears of an unrelated kind, such as a fear of enclosed spaces. He also mentions that almost no people employed in essential services required help for adverse psychological reactions. Not one regular policeman was included, and the divisional police surgeon for the district reported only one case among the 900 regular policemen under his care. Wilson himself found it necessary to treat only one fireman among a group of 63 within his catchment area—despite the fact that they were repeatedly exposed to great danger and intense stimulation. In his wide-ranging survey of neurotic responses to air raids, Sir Aubrey Lewis,[12] one of the deans of British psychiatry, also remarked on the comparative invulnerability of firefighters and other people engaged in essential services. Moreover, the few men who required some assistance after exposure to heavy raids and were suffering from exhaustion also showed a rapid recovery after they had rested. Lewis suggests that engaging in a socially useful occupation might have provided a form of inoculation against stress. Some people who were previously of poor mental health were said to be considerably *improved* after taking up some socially necessary work—"they have a definite and satisfying job." He also adduced some evidence to show that a proportion of chronic neurotics attending outpatient clinics "had improved, since the war has given them interests previously lacking."[13]

Lewis's report, prepared at the request of the British Medical Research Council, is authoritative and thorough. From the information he gathered from different parts of the country he concluded, "air raids have not been responsible for any striking increase in neurotic illness." After a period of intense raids, a slight rise in neurotic illness was observed but this occurred chiefly among those who had been disturbed before the raids began.

Much of what he found can be summed up by the fact that, although doctors in Liverpool "trained 18 volunteers as auxiliary mental health workers for service in and after raids but none of the 18 has been required; there was no such work for them to do." In Manchester, which suffered severe raids, there was no "increase in the number of patients attending psychiatric outpatient clinics," nor was there an increased demand for help among the adult evacuees in the quieter areas around Manchester. Various psychiatric departments in the London area confirmed that the number of neurotic illnesses had not increased significantly.

Concerning the effects on children, he concluded, "there is a consensus of opinion that children show great adaptability and recover well from air raid effects, if simple sensible measures are taken. ..." Moreover, information coming from different sources confirmed the view that "frightened mothers communicated their fears to the children."[14]

The British reactions to repeated air attacks—widespread habituation, unexpected resilience, reasonably few phobic reactions, slight or no increases in psychiatric disorders, the exceptionally competent performance of essential service workers—have been described fully and frequently, but they were not particular to this population. Although evidence demonstrates that the British were, in fact as in heroic recollection, exceptionally stoical and persevering, data collected in Japan and Germany after the war shows that on the same indexes of resilience (e.g., displays of fear and incidence of psychological disorders) those civilians too exhibited strong perseverance.

Janis concluded from his review of the evidence accumulated during and after World War II that "psychiatric reports on civilian reactions to bombing indicate that heavy air attacks produce a sizeable incidence of emotional-shock cases with acute anxiety symptoms. Most of these cases appear to be capable of fully recovering, either spontaneously or in response to simple forms of psychiatric treatment, within a period of a few days up to a few weeks."[15] It was more common for air raid victims to display an excessive docility that seems to have verged on depressive reactions. Contrary to expectation, exposure to air raids had little effect on psychosomatic functioning. As Janis concludes, although air raids "contributed to the wartime increase in various types of psychosomatic disorder, the proportion of the bombed population displaying such reactions was probably not very large."[16] Surveys carried out in postwar Germany confirmed that psychosomatic cases were infrequent.

Critics who are skeptical of the significance of psychological stress factors in producing a range of so-called psychosomatic disorders, will not find this observation surprising. Even if the full effects of these wartime events may not have become evident until many years after they took place, it is nevertheless remarkable that such distressing experiences were not followed by an epidemic of psychosomatic illnesses. Certainly most theories of psychosomatic etiology would have led one to predict the occurrence of extensive and intensive problems. Enthusiastic proponents of psychosomatic theories would however be justified in objecting that the evidence shows, albeit surprisingly, that the raids did not in fact produce much distress!

Reports on the reactions of children "agree that chronic behavioral disturbances following air raids were extremely rare,"[17] although transient symptoms often occurred during the air attacks themselves. Although the evidence on this point is less than satisfactory, comprising mainly anecdotes, the fear reactions of the children were attributed to the ex-

citement and other indications of emotional disturbance displayed by parents or other nearby adults.
For example, in his study of the reactions of San
Francisco children to blackouts and alerts, the psychiatrist J. Solomon concluded that whatever fear
was observed, was largely the result of "the contagion
of anxiety from their parents."[18] Without providing
supporting evidence, he concluded that the relationship between the fear displayed by the adults and
the behavior of the observing children was very close.

Information of this kind led Janis to formulate a
general (but premature) conclusion: "The incidence
of acute emotional disturbances among young children in a community exposed to air raids will tend to
vary directly with the incidence of overt excitement
and emotional upset among the adults in that community."[19]

Hiroshima

The extraordinary resilience demonstrated by people
who were subjected to repeated and severe bombing
raids is exceeded by the endurance of the victims of
the atomic bomb attack on Hiroshima, the single
most traumatic event in human history. The death,
destruction, injuries, and illness caused by this ex-
plosion were of a magnitude and intensity without
precedent. Given the scale of the trauma, the adverse
psychological effects were astonishingly, almost un-
believably, small in extent and intensity. After the
disaster, sustained apprehension and shock were experienced. Nevertheless, and remaining aware of the
fact that they had few practical alternatives, large

numbers of the survivors returned to Hiroshima shortly after the attack.

According to Janis, within three months the population was back to about 140,000 people; "... although apprehensiveness about another attack and fears of contamination may have been fairly frequent, such fears evidently were not so intense as to prevent resettlement in the target cities. From the fact that very large numbers of survivors promptly returned to the destroyed areas, it appears that avoidance of the disaster locale did *not* occur on a mass scale." The very low incidence of psychiatric disorders was equally remarkable. "Psychoses, traumatic neuroses, and other severe psychiatric disorders appear to have been a rare occurrence following the A-bomb attacks. A small percentage of survivors probably developed some minor neurotic symptoms that were evoked or precipitated by disaster experiences, such as excessive fatigue, recurrent bodily complaints and persistent phobias."[20] I can think of no psychological theory, naive or sophisticated, commonsensical or scientific, that would have predicted the prompt return of the Hiroshima survivors, or their extraordinary psychological resilience.

Habituation

Some of the strongest evidence pointing to the tendency of fears to habituate with repeated exposures to the fear-provoking situation, comes from these observations of people exposed to air raids. The data on the British are clearly summarized by Janis. "One important point which emerges very clearly is that there was a definite decline in overt fear-reactions as the air blitz continued, even though the raids became heavier and more destructive."[21] The bombed population displayed increasing indifference towards the air attacks, and warning signals tended to be disregarded unless attacking planes were in the immediate vicinity. Given that the person did not suffer any injuries or near misses, emotional adaptation was the rule rather than the exception. This evidence on the British population is consistent with that collected from bombed populations in Japan and Germany. It is particularly interesting that urban people, who of course experienced more air raids, became better adapted as their experiences increased. In contrast, rural civilians, who had less direct and less frequent experience, became more afraid. Two further observations are also in keeping with the habituation account. In the first place, "variable and wide intervals between successive raids tend to have a more disturbing effect than regular, short intervals." Under most circumstances habituation is facilitated by regular and short presentations of the stimulus. Second, "during prolonged quiet intervals between dangerous raids, there tends to be a loss of emotional adaptation (or spontaneous recovery of former fear reactions)."[22] This observation is entirely in keeping with what we know of that habituation process, and is termed "dishabituation."

In all, the information assembled by Janis provides support for a habituation interpretation of the widespread adaptation displayed by people subjected to air raids. Fear reactions are indeed subject to the recognizable process of habituation (and probably of the associated process of sensitization) and what is more, habituation can occur even when the fearful stimulation is intense. For some time it has been assumed that habituation to fear-provoking stimuli, if it occurs at all, is confined to those stimuli which provoke only the mildest degrees of fear. Indeed, this assumption, which is almost certainly erroneous, was put forward as one of the major reasons for discounting the possibility of explaining how the newly developed clinical techniques of fear-reduction produce their effects.

The progressive habituation of fear reactions, despite repeated exposure to intense stimulation, is in contradiction to the expectations generated by a conditioning theory of fear acquisition (see Chapter 10). From that theory it would be deduced that repeated exposure to air raids should result in an increase, not a decrease, in fear reactions. The point is emphasized by Janis's comment that "among a large proportion of the British population, exposure to a series of relatively dangerous raids during the air blitz evidently produced a gradual extinction of fear reactions, just as occurred in the earlier period when the population experienced a series of relatively non-dangerous alerts."[23] Nor could the differing reactions of urban and rural civilians have been predicted. According to this theory the urban population, having endured more frequent exposures to the putatively conditioning experiences, should have experienced *more*, not less, fear than the rural population who underwent fewer exposures.

It must be remembered, however, that the evidence does not point to a uniform process of habituation. Although the majority of people appear to have adapted astonishingly well to repeated bombing raids, a proportion (according to Janis, 26% of a German sample) reported that they became *more* frightened as the number of raids increased. The increase in fear is of course deducible from the conditioning theory, but it is by no means incompatible with habituation explanations. Given exposure to intense fear-provoking situations one would anticipate that some people might well become sensitized rather than habituated. Bearing in mind these exceptions, we can accept Janis's conclusion: "There may be a general tendency toward emotional adaptation under conditions of repeated danger exposures."[24]

We also have some information about the conditions which might interfere with the more usual pattern of increasing habituation to danger. Or to put it another way, sensitization to fear stimuli might be facilitated by "prolonged fatigue, hunger, and other incessant deprivations. . . . What is most often singled out as the primary source of emotional stress, however, is a type of traumatic event that corresponds closely to the *near miss* experiences described in connection with air raid reactions."[25]

J. MacCurdy also drew attention to the powerfully reinforcing effects that arise from exposure to a near miss.[26] Proximity to an extremely dangerous situation generates fear, whereas "remote misses" appear to reduce fears. Among those people who were exposed to remote misses, there was an immense relief experienced at the conclusion of the raid. MacCurdy attributes great importance to this experience—what he calls "successful escape." People who are exposed to remote misses develop an increased tolerance for the emotional stress of subsequent air raids. As noted, this process of gradual adaptation can be disrupted by exposure to a near miss. Other potentially disruptive factors include fatigue, heightened arousal, and irregularity of stimulation.

Precautions

Some evidence suggests that people who regarded the protection and relief measures as inadequate experienced greater fear than those who considered the measures adequate—this finding is, of course, in keeping with the controllability theory. Similarly, the majority of German civilians reported that they were more frightened by night raids than by those which occurred in the daytime—assuming of course that one has a greater sense of perceived control during the daytime. And the reasons given for fearing night raids are compatible with this explanation. The victims complained that at night it is more difficult to flee from fires and destruction because orientation is hampered. It is also conceivable that people psychologically exaggerate the flashes and noises of the bombs. Perhaps the reason is the contrast effect. Noises and flashes of bombs perceived against a dark and silent nighttime background will be more intense, and will produce more fear.

Janis also concluded that "people who face danger tend to feel less fearful if they are able to engage in some form of useful overt activity."[27] Assuming that this view can be substantiated, the controllability theory suggests that if people engage in activities they interpret as increasing their control over the possibility (or effects) of an aversive event, such a pastime should be particularly helpful in controlling fear. A distraction theory might lead us to predict that the fear-controlling value of the activity will be proportional to its distracting powers, rather than to the extent to which it is felt to contribute to one's potential control.

Another factor is the claim, partly supported by a recent experimental study, that work undertaken as part of one's responsibility towards other people is particularly valuable in reducing one's own fears. R. Rakos and H. Schroeder showed that snake-phobic subjects who were required to help other phobics overcome their fear of snakes, benefited from the experience.[28] The significant reductions in the fears of these helpers were attributed to the demands of their helping role and to the beneficial effects of modeling the appropriate coping behavior. This finding is of considerable interest, and further exploration of the phenomenon of therapy through helping is recommended.

In sum, the wartime observations support the view that fear reactions can be controlled to an extent if, during exposure to stress, the person engages in some form of activity. Furthermore, activities of taking responsibility for other people appear to have particularly useful fear-reducing or fear-preventing properties.

Outstanding Problems

The factors of controllability and predictability appear to play an important part in determining fear. It must be admitted, however, that some of the information gathered during the war is not easily accommodated by explanations that rest on these two concepts. For example, as Janis points out, "the high degree of uncertainty and suspense characteristic of periods when air attacks are expected, probably elicits acute fear symptoms in only a relatively small proportion of the population." He goes on to argue that the widespread occurrence of habituation implies that the factors of uncertainty and suspense are "not generally effective in producing tense and prolonged fear reactions."[29] The information leading to this justifiable conclusion presents an unsolved problem for theories that rest on the factors of controllability and predictability.

Seligman's theory of *depression*,[30] with its emphasis on feelings of uncontrollability, might lead one to predict that depression rather than fear can be expected after repeated exposures to the uncontrollable events of an air raid. As we have seen, some of the evidence is indeed consistent with such a prediction. Among many victims of bombing raids, the emotional consequences were *apathy and docility* rather than fear. To quote Vernon, "there is widespread lethargy and lack of energy, even after lost sleep has been made up, and pessimistic feelings about the future."[31] Then Janis points out that, in Japan as well as in England, there was "a high incidence of excessive docility among air raid victims which suggests that acute apathy ... may occur fairly often."[32]

Of course it is not enough merely to point out how and where the available theories of fear fall short. Any and all of them would have predicted that people subjected to the dangers and uncertainty of air raids will develop intense fears, and the failure of this prediction leaves a vacuum. M. Seligman's theory of prepared fears (see Chapter 6) provides some insight.[33] He divided fears into prepared and nonprepared categories; the prepared fears are said to be of biological significance, to show ease of acquisition and unusual stability. Our information on reactions to air raids does not fit this description. For the most part, the fears that were provoked by air raids were acute but short-lived. Enduring fear reactions that generalized widely, did not emerge and we are therefore obliged to conclude that air raids are, in Seligman's terms, nonprepared (fear) situations.

Seligman maintains that prepared fears are survivals from pretechnological times, so that their biological significance has to be seen in evolutionary terms. Air raids, based as they are on sophisticated modern technology, have no evolutionary history, and for this reason human beings are not predisposed to acquire fears during exposures to bombs released from sky-borne craft.[34] Whether this approach offers satisfaction or not, it does at least provide some unusual perspectives on the subject of fear. For me, it emphasizes the curious composition of a species that readily displays fear of spiders and snakes, but possesses a psychological resilience that enables it to endure the dangers and destruction of bombing attacks, repeated by day and by night.

Notes

1) P. Vernon, *Journal of Abnormal and Social Psychology* **36**, 1941.

2) J. Rickman, *The Lancet* **1**, 1938.

3) Vernon, 1941, p. 463.

4) E. Stengel, *British Journal of Medical Psychology* **20**, 1946.

5) I. L. Janis, *Air War and Stress*, 1951, p. 99. An invaluable source book.

6) Janis, 1951, p. 83.

7) Mollie Panter-Downes, *London War Notes*, 1971.

8) Vernon, 1941, p. 459.

9) Vernon, 1941, p. 460.

10) Vernon, 1941, p. 474.

11) H. Wilson, *The Lancet* **1**, 1942, p. 284.

12) Aubrey Lewis, *The Lancet* **2**, 1942, p. 179.

13) Lewis, 1942, p. 179.

14) Lewis, 1942, p. 181.

15) Janis, 1951, p. 87.

16) Janis, 1951, p. 92.

17) Janis, 1951, p. 93.

18) J. Solomon, *American Journal of Orthopsychiatry* **12**, 1942.

19) Janis, 1951, p. 94.

20) Janis, 1951, p. 65.

21) Janis, 1951, p. 111.

22) Janis, 1951, p. 124.

23) Janis, 1951, p. 111.

24) Janis, 1951, p. 113.

25) Janis, 1951, p. 114.

26) J. MacCurdy, *The Structure of Morale*, 1943.

27) Janis, 1951, p. 120.

28) R. Rakos & H. Schroeder, *Journal of Counseling Psychology* **23**, 1976.

29) Janis, 1951, p. 124.

30) M. Seligman, *Helplessness*, 1975.

31) Vernon, 1941, p. 467.

32) Janis, 1951, p. 88.

33) M. Seligman, *Behavior Therapy* **2**, 1971.

34) A small but fascinating piece of experimental evidence supports this possibility. Hodes, Öhman and Lang are preparing a report of their recently completed study, which revealed that subjects establish more stable conditioned autonomic reactions to pictures of snakes or spiders than to those of rifles or revolvers. How, one wonders, will people respond to reconstructions of prehistoric threats (e.g., extinct animals)?

Chapter 3
Combat Fears I

During World War II, a great deal of information about the nature of fear and of courageous behavior was gathered from studies carried out on many thousands of troops serving in theaters of war, from Southeast Asia to North Africa. As L. Shaffer observed at the time, "This unparalleled opportunity to interrogate a large group of healthy young men who faced the imminent danger of death should yield some general ideas on the nature of fear itself."[1] Although the importance attached to this unusually consistent information is not misplaced, some reservations are in order. Because the troops did not constitute a random sample of the population, one cannot make broad generalizations from the data. Most of the combat troops were young, healthy, highly trained, and vigorous people. They were selected in the belief that they would be resistant to breakdown under stress. Moreover, a large part of their training was specifically intended to increase their tolerance for fear and stressful experiences. Thus the resilience most of them displayed might be attributed to a combination of their youthful strength and effective training. Although their capacity and specialized training certainly did help them to control their fear, their resilience cannot be ascribed solely to these two factors. As we have already seen, untrained civilians of all ages and states of health showed a degree of resilience that matched that of combat troops. Although both civilians and soldiers exhibited this strength, it is probable that their inherent qualities and specialized training enabled the troops to do more than "heroically endure." They were prepared for carrying out skilled activities under great danger and encouraged to do so even while attempting to secure their own protection.

In his introduction to the 17-volume report on the performance of U.S. combat air crews, John Flanagan—who was responsible for organizing and coordinating much of this remarkable research—offers a piece of military understatement: "It was definitely a hazardous business."[2] In some theaters of the war, an airman's chances of completing a tour of operational duty were little better than 50 percent. In the most dangerous theaters, the chances of survival were as low as one in four. Flanagan goes on to say, "In the face of this it was encouraging to find that morale in these groups was generally high and that there was very little breakdown of personnel."

The single most striking fact to emerge from these combat studies is that people, these healthy and highly trained young people, were capable of performing extraordinary feats of skill and enterprise even after repeated and prolonged exposures to danger, stress, and injury. Most of the information also testifies to the overwhelming psychological importance of social bonds and approval. Thousands of people repeatedly risked serious injury or death rather than ostracism. It seems that the most important source of motivation was the small social group of which each soldier or airman became a part. To quote Flanagan again, "The primary motivating force which more than anything else kept these men flying and fighting was that they were members of a group in which flying and fighting was the only accepted way of behaving. The air crew combat personnel were closely knit together. First, because they flew, and second, because they fought. In combat operations they lived together and had little contact with people outside the groups ... The individual identified himself very closely with the group and took great pride in his membership in the group...."[3] As we shall see, ideology was an inconsequential motive for the combatants.

An important theme in much of this information is the significance of a person's sense of controllability and personal competence. Fear seems to feed on a sense of uncontrollability: it arises and persists when the person finds himself in a threatening situation over which he feels he has little or no control. But a sense of personal competence, self-confidence if you will, appears to provide protection against fear.

The data also illustrate the superiority of a three-system analysis of fear over the lump theory. Although combat fears were ubiquitous, avoidance behavior was rare. These observations are a clear demonstration of the independence of subjective fear and attempts to escape from or avoid the threatening situation. The persistence of these soldiers and airmen, despite the frequent and often intense subjective fear, exemplifies courageous behavior.

As we shall see, some of the information conflicts with prevailing psychological theories of fear. In retrospect it can be said that one of the major weaknesses of these theories is the assumption that people are far more vulnerable than they are. The theories were designed for creatures more timorous than man.

Flanagan's One Percent

As part of Flanagan's series, Shaffer and others administered a fear questionnaire to 4500 airmen who had combat experience in the European theater of war in 1944.[4] The major part of this study was then repeated on an additional 2000 experienced fliers. All but one percent of the airmen reported that they experienced fear on at least some combat missions. Moreover, a third to half reported that they experienced fear on almost *every* mission. Although there was a relationship between the objective dangers of the missions and the amount of fear experienced, other factors were influential. For example, fliers who took part in the 1945 compaign, during which the combat missions were less severe and less dangerous, experienced greater intensity and frequency of fear than the fliers who took part in the most punishing period, 1944. Sheer exposure to danger is not the sole determinant of fear; the greater fear experienced by the 1945 cohort can probably be understood as reflecting the approaching end of the European battle. Although the air crews agreed that a time-limited tour of operational duty helped them to persevere in their dangerous tasks, it was also observed that fear increased as the crews approached the concluding missions of their operational tour. Although the majority of the airmen reported that having a commitment to fly a circumscribed number of missions or hours, was helpful in reducing combat fear in general, their specific fears increased as they approached the end of their tour of duty. This well-supported finding of a kind of "negative emotional goal-gradient" is interesting, but poorly understood.

The symptoms of fear experienced during combat included palpitations, dryness of the mouth, sweating, stomach discomfort, excessive urination, trembling, tension, and irritability. The most persistent of these symptoms were tension, tremor, and sleep disturbance. The most prominent cumulative effect of repeated exposure to danger was a curious mixture of fatigue coupled with restlessness. Many of the airmen experienced ruminations and bad dreams. Although Shaffer provided no details of the content of the dreams, we know from other sources, such as R. Grinker and J. Spiegel, that the theme of helplessness was common.[5] According to T. Lidz, the theme was strong and repetitive: "The soldier is helpless in the face of an attack and if he attempts to defend himself he is impotent. While attempting to flee he awakens with a terrified scream."[6] A survey of 6000 airmen showed that the factors of helplessness and hopelessness were responsible for major increments in fear. "Being in danger when one cannot fight back or take any other effective action, being idle, or being insecure of the future, were the elements that tended to aggravate fear in combat."[7] The three factors that were rated as most fear-provoking were: being fired upon when you had no chance to shoot back, a report of an enemy aircraft that you could not see, the sight of enemy tracer bullets.

The fliers also reported an interesting change in the content of their fears as combat experience increased. On the first mission their greatest fear concerned their ability to carry out their functions satisfactorily, and specifically, fears of being a coward. This finding is consistent with the common belief that many people anxiously yearn for reassurance that they will not behave in a cowardly manner under test. On later missions, however, fears of personal failure were surpassed by fears of being killed or wounded.

Breakdown

Despite a tendency to overinterpret some of their material, Grinker and Spiegel's detailed clinical accounts of how U.S. air crews reacted to combat provide a useful source of information. Their illustrative case excerpts are vivid, distressing, sometimes horrifying, and usually illuminating. Their major argument is that air combat constituted an extremely stressful experience and that, upon sufficient exposure, most of the air crews began to show adverse psychological effects. Their case descriptions demonstrated that major breakdowns can be precipitated by exposure to a traumatic event, by repeated exposure to minor stress, or by a combination of these conditions in which prolonged combat experience is finally terminated after exposure to a particularly distressing event.

The onset of intense anxiety after exposure to an extremely traumatic event is illustrated by the experience of a 22-year-old American air gunner. On his twelfth bombing mission the aircraft sustained a direct hit and his fellow gunner received a mortal wound. After trying unsuccessfully to save his friend,

> he went to pieces ... and began to tremble all over ... he swung his loaded gun back into the plane and tried to bail out ... but the tail gunner ... caught him just in time to save him from jumping out over the target...."

His immediate reactions were intense and uncontrolled.

> He sat down and began to smoke one cigarette after another. Thoughts tumbled through his mind without any order. He thought of his home and then began to pray with tears running down his face. He again wanted to bail out and was restrained by the tail gunner. He felt he would never get back alive and ... when the plane at last landed, he swung his legs out of the gun hatch and had to be prevented from jumping out of the aircraft before it had come to a stop. He explained afterwards that he was afraid of an explosion and couldn't get out of the aircraft fast enough. When it finally halted he jumped up, ran a short distance, and then stopped, trembling all over.

The gunner's posttraumatic reactions are described as follows:

> During the days following his return to his base he continued to have intense anxiety. He seemed to be afraid of everything, especially of the dark. He could not shake off a feeling that someone was following him. There was severe insomnia, with terror dreams in which he saw the dead turret gunner with blood pouring from his neck. During one nightmare he dreamed that someone, an unknown figure, was standing stooped over the end of his bed.[8]

As in a number of comparable cases, the anxiety reactions were finally superseded by depression.

The most common pattern was for air crew members to show a gradual accumulation of adverse effects, such as insomnia, loss of appetite, tremor, extreme startle reactions, irritability, and tension. These reactions appeared to follow a cumulative pattern, and although the great majority of fliers were able to retain enough control to complete their prescribed tour of duty, a few were unable to do so.

The psychological significance of their declining control, both over their own physiological reactions and the dangers to which they were being repeatedly exposed, is well described by Grinker and Spiegel. "With the growing lack of control over the mental and physical reactions came a grouchiness and irritability that interfered with good relations among men."[9] They describe how good muscular coordination was replaced by uncontrollable tremors, jerky manipulations, and tension. Their "anxiety may be related for a time only to a reaction limited to the most dangerous moments over the target, but it has a tendency to spread until it is continuous or is stimulated by only trivial sounds." Their ability to sleep was impaired and they started to have disturbing nightmares. Their appetite decreased and various gastric symptoms, such as nausea, vomiting and diarrhea, appeared. They also began to report pains and aches, headaches and backaches being particularly common.

In terms of M. Seligman's learned helplessness theory,[10] it is to be expected that fliers' diminishing control over their own reactions and over the objective dangers to which they were exposed, would result in predictable motivational, emotional, and cognitive deficits. Motivational shifts were manifested as enthusiasm was replaced by weariness of battle, which the fliers endured because they recognized they had no other choice. Emotionally, temporary fears changed to constant apprehension, and anxiety spread ever more widely. Cognitively they experienced a growing pessimism about the chances of surviving a complete tour of duty. The following are examples of extreme reactions: some airmen became depressed and secluded themselves from their friends. Thinking and behavior seriously altered. Forgetfulness, preoccupation, and brooding became more frequent, and ultimately even the most purpose ful activity was disrupted.

Although these are extreme examples, the fact remains that most combatants experienced at least moderate fear during the fighting. In addition to their apprehensiveness, they generally experienced certain bodily reactions. For example, the fear symptoms reported by combat infantry troops in the Pacific theater of action (based on a survey of 6000 soldiers) were, in this order, palpitations, sinking feeling in the stomach, trembling, nausea, cold sweat, and feelings of faintness.

A distinction was made between what became known as combat fatigue and anxiety neuroses. Combat fatigue, manifested by excessive tiredness, irritability, and restlessness, generally cleared up after a comparatively short period of rest and recuperation. Anxiety reactions on the other hand were more intense, affected a wider range of psychological functions, and persisted. Quite commonly the onset of an anxiety condition was preceded by an episode of combat fatigue.

Vulnerability to Breakdown

In an attempt to determine the nature of the vulnerability to breakdown, D. Hastings, D. Wright, and B. Glueck collected data on 150 successful airmen who had completed a tour of severe combat duty. Entirely contrary to expectation, they found that nearly half of these successful airmen had family histories of emotional instability. Moreover, their own life patterns gave evidence of emotional instability in half of these 150 airmen, and psychoneurotic tendencies in nearly a third of them. However, "their life patterns are not marked by asocial acts ... but are characterized by vigor, persistence and physical health."[11] All of these successful airmen experienced subjective tension before and during combat, and 94 percent of them said they had experienced fear during combat. A large majority of these successful airmen reported they had suffered from combat fatigue, some of them severely. They also said that during the period of their operational tour of duty, they had become more aggressive outside of combat operations. They also claimed, almost without exception, that their accumulated tension was relieved by the action of combat.

In confirmation of the resilience of these men, no less than 35 percent of the sample of successful airmen had been wounded and/or had crashed during their duty. Eighty percent of them had flown in severely damaged aircraft and/or members of their crew had been wounded. Nearly two-thirds of them came from squadrons that had suffered very heavy losses (in some of these heavy bomber squadrons, the losses ran as high as seven out of ten men killed or lost in action!).

After enduring a traumatic incident, the flier could abort the potential neurotic consequences if he was put to sleep for a period of 12 to 24 hours. It was assumed that it is easier to adjust to a terrifying experience days after its occurrence rather than face it immediately afterward. Incidentally, a large propor-

tion of the men experienced ruminations after carrying out a raid.

This survey undermines the belief that the relationship between emotional instability and the likelihood of breakdown under combat stress is simple.
Doubts about this belief are fed by W. Lepley's finding
that the correlation between combat ratings and
emotional stability was low—ranging between 0.14
and 0.49, with most correlations in the 20's.[12] The
characteristic that correlated most highly with combat ratings was flying skill. Among a group of fighter
pilots, the correlation between flying skill and combat
rating was 0.77, among heavy bomber pilots it was
0.94, and among transport pilots, 0.83.

In light of these findings it is not surprising that
attempts to predict which airmen would be vulnerable to breakdown were almost wholly unsuccessful.
For example, Frederic Wickert was unable to find any
significant relationships between the precombat test
records of the airmen and the occurrence of anxiety
reactions during or after combat.[13] Neither were the
officer selection test results related to the subsequent
development of anxiety reactions. In assessing the
significance of these failures, however, we should
remember that the air combat crews on whom these
ideas were tested were scarcely representative; it may
be that the relationship between these predictive
measures and the emergence of anxiety was
obscured by the fact that the airmen were highly
selected in the first place. If tests of this kind were
applied to a more representative and larger sample,
they might prove to have some predictive value.

To quote Wickert, "There is no relationship between anxiety reaction and conventional printed
tests of aptitude and achievement, whether the tests

are given before combat or after combat ... there was also no relationship between anxiety reaction and pre-combat psychomotor tests, even though both these and the pre-combat printed tests were given under somewhat stress-provoking conditions."[14] It is nevertheless of some interest that "men with greater intellectual ability are better able to control their emotional reactions."[15] A relation between general intellectual ability and specific types of military competence is also seen in the results of a study on paratroop training reported by S. Stouffer. Whereas 60 percent of the trainees from the group with the highest intelligence scores completed the parachute jumping course without error, only 11 percent of the recruits who formed the group with the lowest intelligence scores achieved errorless performance. In addition, whereas only 14 percent of the brightest recruits failed the course, the failure rate among those in the lowest group was 44 percent.[16]

In all, studies showed that both flying and combat skills depend heavily on aptitude and motivation. The anticipated problems of personality, temperament, and adjustment were found to be comparatively minor.

Adaptation

Three of the major changes to occur in response to repeated exposures to combat were an alteration in the content of fears, some adaptation to fear, and the accumulation of symptoms of combat fatigue. According to J. Flanagan, the major fears expressed by airmen before their first combat mission were those of personal failure—worries that they wouldn't perform adequately and/or that they would be cowardly.[17] These fears rapidly diminished to be dominated by the fear of being killed or wounded; this fear increased from 12 to 30 percent with repeated exposures. The fear of cowardice declined from 17 percent on the first mission to 6 percent on subsequent missions. A similar change in content was reported among infantrymen.[18] Before going into action for the first time, 36 percent were frightened of being cowardly, a percentage that dropped to 8 as they accumulated combat experience. Like the airmen, their fears of being wounded or killed became more prominent with increased exposure. Among the infantrymen, 64 percent experienced decreasing fear (habituation?) with increasing exposure, while a much smaller number (14 percent) reported increased fear or sensitization, upon repeated exposures to battle. Other factors being equal (e.g., an absence of traumatic experiences), the majority habituate to combat conditions and experience decreasing degrees of fear. The occurrence of a traumatic episode, a decline in physical condition, or the accumulation of excessive levels of combat fatigue may all contribute to increasing sensitization, to a reversal of the usual pattern of decreasing fear. Indeed it is important to remember that mild fear may improve efficiency. For example, in one of the U.S. Air Force studies, it was found that 50 percent of the airman reported that fear sometimes improved their efficiency, so they were more accurate in their work. A large number of the airmen (37 percent) reported that even *strong* fear increased their efficiency, and only 14 percent claimed that it had an adverse effect on their efficiency.[19]

The Control of Fear

There are no absolute standards, nor even satisfactory comparative ones, against which one can judge the courageous performance of battalions, divisions, squadrons, and still less entire armies, but most people will agree that the U.S. military forces performed well during World War II. Although the policy for preventing and controlling disruptive fear under combat seems justified, in the light of our present understanding, we are unable to evaluate the particular measures taken to combat fear. What we can say is that the information accumulated in the decades since the war's end is for the most part consistent with the three major policies adopted by the military authorities at the time. First, the soldiers were encouraged to be permissive about their own fear symptoms in the face of actual danger. In addition, care was taken to exclude men who were thought to be psychologically unfit for combat. Last and, perhaps most important of all, specific training and instruction were provided. The soldiers were drilled in the appropriate actions to take under combat conditions and their training generally included exposure to realistic battle conditions.

On the first of the three elements in this policy, the adoption of a permissive attitude, there is little evidence on which to base a judgment. The information gathered during the war seems to be equivocal. The evidence pertaining to the second element, the exclusion of vulnerable people, shows it to have been successful. We have grounds for believing that if one observes someone else displaying excessive fear reactions, similar reactions are induced in the observer. Like courageous behavior, fearful behavior can be acquired by a process of observational learning, by modeling (see page 78).

The belief that training can play an important part in preparing people to endure combat and other forms of stress is probably as old as the institution of martial combat itself. If the present emphasis on the value of controllability in coping with fear turns out to be justified, the traditional belief in the utility of simulated combat training will receive modern support. Although there is no danger that combat training would have been dispensed with in the absence of support from the psychologists, modifying the training procedures in an attempt to achieve more controllability over anticipated dangers may well prove to be of value in teaching people to cope with a range of dangerous jobs. Indeed, recent findings from clinical research into the reduction of fear (Chapter 9) point out the advantage to be gained from encouraging fearful people to practice coping with situations that contain the realistic dangers, instead of from teaching them to cope with remote representations of these dangers.[20] So we find that in a survey carried out on infantry troops in the Pacific theater, a positive correlation between their perceived adequacy of combat training and their observed fear reactions during combat was obtained. In a comparable study carried out during the North African campaign in 1943, the troops themselves attached special importance to obtaining training under realistic battle conditions. In a third study, carried out in the Italian theater, no less than 81 percent of the troops gave realistic combat training as the most important type of preparation to provide for new recruits.[21]

In 1977, Professor Albert Bandura of Stanford University, a leading scientist and former President of the American Psychological Association, proposed that therapeutic behavioral changes result from an improved sense of self-efficacy.[22] Almost as if anticipating Bandura's theory, the military authorities based their combat-training policy on two major premises. It was believed, in Stouffer's words, that "the general level of anxiety in combat would tend to be reduced insofar as the men derived from their training a high degree of self-confidence about their ability to take care of themselves and to handle almost any kind of contingency that might threaten them with sudden danger; and the intensity of fear reactions in specific danger situations would tend to be reduced once the man began to carry out a plan of action in a skilled manner."[23] The data gathered by Stouffer and his colleagues provide support for these propositions. But as we shall see, some of their data cast doubt on the *general applicability* of these two major premises. As in a number of other studies, this one revealed a high correlation between the troops' self-confidence expressed before going into combat and the self-reported index of fear reactions experienced during actual combat.

Some of the findings, however, were awkward. For example, 38 percent of the troops who expressed a great deal of self-confidence before combat nevertheless experienced a high degree of fear in it. The converse was also noted. Six percent of the troops who rated themselves as having little or no self-confidence beforehand experienced little or no fear during battle. Even more puzzling is that, 18 percent of the soldiers who said they were losing self-confidence with increasing exposure to combat continued to report low fear reactions. The converse was also observed: 17 percent of the troops who reported they had gained in self-confidence as combat experience increased reported high fear reactions during the event. Thus, although the general trend of the data is consistent with the policy adopted, and indeed with the views recently expressed by Bandura, a substantial minority of the troops described experiences that seem to contradict those views founded on a direct relationship between self-confidence and experienced fear. In sum, troops who expressed a high degree of self-confidence before combat were more likely to perform with relatively little fear during battle; however, a minority who expressed little confidence in themselves also performed well. Then, another minority, about whom one would feel special concern, were those who expressed a high degree of self-confidence before combat, but experienced strong fear during it.

In my opinion, some of the seemingly mysterious observations made during the war are more easily understood if one dispenses with the lump theory of fear and substitutes a three-system analysis. Though recognizing that the three major components of fear are loosely coupled, and that they frequently correspond, we must expect independent trends; then most of the "awkward" examples quoted, cease to be unpredictable. During battle, two of the three major components—subjective fear and physiological disturbances—are commonly observed, whereas the avoidance behavior generally associated with subjective fear is inhibited. In the most interesting minority of cases, however, there is a discordance between the subjective experience of fear (especially the anticipation of these feelings) and the psychophysiological disturbances characteristic of fear. If, as is argued elsewhere in this book (page 277), the physiological aspects of fear are most susceptible to habituation training, it can be expected that this component will decline as combat experience increases, provided the soldier succeeds in avoiding traumatic exposures. The cognitive component of fear is largely, but not solely, modified by the person's perceived self-efficacy—a combination of his actual competence and his confidence in this competence. The growth of perceived self-efficacy is likely to be facilitated by skillful instruction and training and, given a few exposures to combat, should reach its maximum level and then remain reasonably stable. So, providing that other factors remain reasonably constant, one can predict that major desychronous changes in the components of fear will take place in the middle stages of a soldier's combat career.

The results of the extensive study of the control of fear conducted on U.S. air crews is admirably summed up by Shaffer. "The study suggests that there is no royal road and no shortcut toward the control of fear. The greatest factor that reduces fear is confidence in equipment, in fellow crew members, and in leaders. Good equipment is a material problem, but confidence in it is psychological. The study suggests that deliberate training procedures be set up to create confidence ... Next to confidence, concentration on effective activity is the best antidote to fear. Men can be trained to keep busy while in the air, with meaningful tasks that are pertinent to the difficulties encountered. Social stimulation is also of great value. An airplane commander can help to control fear by being calm himself, and by keeping all of the crew in touch with what is going on."[24] In short, studies suggest that the seven most prominent factors for reducing fear are: confidence in equipment, confidence in crew, confidence in leaders, continued activity, observation of a calm model, circumscribed tour of duty.

The factors that were thought to be of less value in controlling fear are equally interesting. Pay, promotion, hatred of the enemy, ideological commitment were found not to be helpful. Also only 60 percent of the airmen felt that praying helped them to any extent. In contrast, more than three quarters of infantrymen who were surveyed found that prayer helped a great deal when they were in combat; indeed, they found it to be the *most* helpful psychological device for coping with fear under the most frightening conditions.

Before we examine the role of ideology and of modeling in greater detail, it is worth emphasizing the importance of *competence* in coping with potentially fearful situations. It will be noticed incidentally that, insofar as fear is a product of a sense of uncontrollability in a potentially aversive situation, the competence of the person in danger is a major determinant of whether or not fear will arise. There is a close, but not absolute, correspondence between self-confidence and fear experienced during combat. We have also seen that the factor which correlated most highly with air combat performance was flying skill. Evidence gathered from studies of astronauts (see Chapter 15) confirms the value of confidence in one's own skill. One of the major conclusions of the large air force study carried out during World War II was that "if adequate aptitude and motivation are assured," the problems of personality, temperament, and individual adjustment are comparatively minor.[25] Although the skills concerned were mostly to do with the ability to fly and navigate with competence, "the findings also suggest that men with greater intellectual ability are better able to control their emotional reactions." The possibility of a correlation between general intellectual ability and competence in the skills that are likely to be required in dangerous situations, is strengthened by the study on the Mercury astronauts—they were men of superior intelligence and broad competence.[26]

Before we examine some of the other determinants of fear and its control, it may be helpful to summarize some of the major points discussed so far. In the face of the dangers and discomforts of combat, U.S. soldiers and airmen were resilient and performed extremely well, even when they experienced subjective fear reactions—as most of them did at some time. Despite repeated exposures to dangers, stress, and even injuries, their fears underwent habituation. Airmen showed a similar pattern but with some variations. Although subjective fear was common, avoidance behavior was not. A small minority of the combatants developed persisting fears of pathological intensity or quality; attempts to identify indexes of vulnerability were unsuccessful. Among the methods of fear-control, improving the soldier's real and perceived efficacy under realistic training conditions, was especially helpful.

Notes

1) L. Shaffer, *Psychological Studies of Anxiety Reactions to Combat*, USAAF Aviation Psychology Research Report No. 14, 1947, p. 143.

2) J. Flanagan, USAAF Aviation Psychology Research Report No. 1, 1948, p. 207. The 17 volumes of this series contain a large amount of important psychological information ranging from fear and courage

to sophisticated analyses of psychomotor behavior. The psychologists recruited by Flanagan and his colleagues were unusually talented, and many of them went on to make distinguished contributions to civilian psychology. They included Bijou, Ghiselli, Irion, Jensen, Neal Miller, Rotter, etc. It must be remembered that the information on fear, much of it gathered by questionnaire and interview methods, was subject to distortion by the pervasive social pressures that encouraged courageous behavior. On the other hand, most of the material was provided anonymously, and for the first time in military history troops were given permission, and on occasion encouragement, to admit their fears and discuss them with their officers, and with inquisitive, jumped-up army psychologists.

3) Flanagan, 1948, p. 208.

4) Shaffer et al., 1947, Vol. 14.

5) See R. Grinker and J. Spiegel, *Men Under Stress*, 1945.

6) T. Lidz, *Psychiatry* **9**, 1946.

7) Shaffer, 1947, p. 131.

8) Grinker and Spiegel, 1945, p. 67.

9) Grinker and Spiegel, 1945, p. 54.

10) M. Seligman, *Helplessness*, 1975.

11) D. Hastings, D. Wright, and B. Glueck, *Psychiatric Experiences of the Eighth Air Force*, 1944, p. 153.

12) W. Lepley, *Psychological Research in the Theaters of War*, USAAF Aviation Psychology Report No. 17, 1947, pp. 197−198.

13) F. Wickert, *Psychological Research on Problems of Redistribution*, USAAF Aviation Psychology Program Research Report No. 14, 1947, p. 121.

14) Wickert, 1947, p. 186.

15) Shaffer, 1947, p. 249.

16) S. Stouffer et al., *The American Soldier: Combat and Its Aftermath*, Vol. 2, 1949. This work, carried out on some hundreds of thousands of U.S. troops during World War II, includes over 200 surveys, and is published in four large volumes. From this mass of data I have attempted to extract those trends that are relevant to the subject of fear. In order to simplify the exposition I have not maintained their careful distinctions between army units, between officers and men, between theaters of campaign and so on, unless distinctions are of importance for the point in question.

17) Flanagan, 1948, p. 215.

18) J. Dollard, *Fear in Battle*, 1944.

19) Shaffer et al., 1947, pp. 130−131.

20) See for example the analysis by A. Bandura, *Psychological Review* **84**, 1977.

21) Stouffer et al., 1949.

22) Bandura, 1977.

23) Stouffer, 1949, p. 22.

24) Shaffer, 1947, p. 136.

25) Shaffer, 1947, p. 249.

26) S. Korchin and G. Ruff, in G. Grosser et al., *The Threat of Impending Disaster*, 1964.

Chapter 4
Combat Fears II

Objective Danger

There is, of course, a relation between the objective dangers encountered during battle and the degree of fear experienced. However, fear is not determined *solely* by objective threats. Combat fliers operating under the safer conditions of the 1945 campaign experienced more fear than their 1944 comrades who were in great danger. In a survey of infantry veterans carried out in the Pacific theater, high levels of fear were reported by 20 percent of those soldiers who had experienced comparatively little stress in combat. However, only 40 percent of troops who had been in dangerous battles and observed a large number of casualties, reported a high degree of fear in battle. Observations of high numbers of casualties in one's group, coupled with the death of one or more friends, were very important determinants of combat fear, but almost as powerful a contributor was witnessing the enemy carrying out atrocities.

Among these infantrymen, however, 22 percent of those who had been exposed to the worst battle experiences remained relatively unaffected, and reported low levels of fear during combat. So, although the relationship between objective dangers and the amount of combat fear experienced is firm, exceptions are found at either end. Some troops experienced considerable fear in the relative absence of danger, and others had little fear even under the most threatening conditions.[1]

Information gathered from airmen who took part in combat during the 1944 compaign in Europe confirms the importance of objective danger in determining fear. The men themselves were of course acutely aware of the direct relationship between the danger of the combat mission and their experience of fear. Moreover, the crew members of heavy bomber squadrons reported significantly more fear than the airmen in medium bomber crews or of fighter pilots. As the dangers posed by flying heavy bombers were extremely high, especially during the first six months of 1944, it is understandable that they should have been more frightened than their comrades. During this period the casualty rate among heavy bomber crews reached the appallingly high figure of 70 percent.[2]

However, even though the casualty rate among the crew members of medium bombers was substantially lower (23 percent), they reported more fear than the fighter pilots whose casualty rate was extremely high (48 percent). This evidence, while confirming the important relationship between danger and experienced fear, indicates the influence of other factors as well. As we have already seen, the fighter pilots might have experienced less fear, despite the greater dangers facing them, because of the enhanced degree of controllability which they exercised during combat. They were, after all, a group of highly trained, self-confident men who had sole control over their machines. Unlike the heavy bomber crews, they were not under instructions to maintain an unchanging course regardless of the actions of the enemy. Rather, they were encouraged to act with initiative and independence. Whether this explanation is satisfactory or not, the astonishing fact is that despite the horrifying casualty rate, according to which their chances of survival were no better than five out of ten, they experienced comparatively little fear during combat.

The Influence of Ideology

One of the more surprising findings to emerge from the extensive study of U.S. infantry soldiers during World War II was the comparative insignificance of ideological factors in their combat fears and their performance generally. The most important combat incentive was a desire to get the war over with, coupled with a wish to return home. The second most important incentive was the need to support and assist one's immediate comrades. Idealistic and patriotic reasons were not regarded as important. So for example, a mere 5 percent of infantry combat veterans reported that a belief in war aims was an important combat incentive. A sample of officers returned a slightly higher percentage of idealistic replies (10 percent), but their primary motivation was similar to that of the enlisted men.

Even among some soldiers saturated with ideological propaganda, political and ethical convictions appeared to have little impact in determining their fears or their conduct before or during combat. Studies of German troops carried out by E. Shils and M. Janowitz during the European campaign of World War II show that "the solidarity of the German army was ... based only very indirectly and very partially on political convictions or broader ethical beliefs."[3] The information was gathered from repeated opinion polls carried out on large numbers of prisoners of war, interrogation of recently captured prisoners, the use of captured documents, and so on. Despite the evident fact that in the closing stages of the war they were being defeated, the German soldiers persevered in the face of increasing casualties and danger, and also maintained a high degree of integrity and fighting effectiveness. Desertion and surrender were uncommon. On the basis of the data they gathered, Shils and Janowitz dispute the view that the "extraordinary tenacity of the German army" can be attributed to the Nazi convictions of the German soldiers. They argue that the integrity of the army was "sustained only to a very slight extent by the National Socialist political convictions of its members, and that the more important motivation of the determined resistance of the German soldier was the steady satisfaction of certain primary personality demands afforded by the social organization of the army." The most important group was what they call the primary unit, consisting of that small group of fellow soldiers, headed by a noncommissioned officer, with whom one spent most of one's time, in and out of combat. When this primary group "developed a high degree of cohesion, morale was high and resistance effective ... regardless in the main of the political attitudes of the soldiers. The conditións of primary group life were related to spatial proximity, the capacity for intimate communication, the provision of paternal proctectiveness by NCOs and junior officers...." The effectiveness of this primary unit was supported by the firm structure of the larger army unit. In the German army, an important additional factor was the widespread devotion to Hitler. As Shils and Janowitz point out, devotion to Hitler "remained at a very high level even after the beginning of the serious reversals in France and Germany." In monthly opinion polls of German prisoners of war, carried out from D-Day until January 1945, in all but two samples, over 60 percent expressed confidence in Hitler. They go on to point out, however, that this was confidence in Hitler the powerful leader, rather than adherence to the political views he expressed.

The evidence shows that, with the exception of Nazis, German soldiers were only slightly influenced by political or ethical considerations. The few criticisms made of Hitler's conduct were technical, not moral. Very few men expressed any repugnance at the massacres carried out, the atrocities committed, or the initiation of destructive, aggressive war. For example, the attitude of the average German soldier to the SS troops was not unfavorable, despite the fact that they were known to commit atrocities on civilians and military opponents. As Shils and Janowitz say, the Waffen-SS units were highly esteemed, not for their Nazi connections, but because of their excellent fighting capacities. The ordinary soldiers felt safer when there was a Waffen-SS unit on their flank.

The significance of these findings on ideological factors is illuminated by comparing the data collected from World War II recruits with that collected by John Dollard from veterans of the Spanish Civil War.[4] The majority of these 300 volunteers had spent more than six months in the front line and no less than 58 percent of them had been wounded at least once. They differed from the regular U.S. soldiers studied by S. Stouffer and his colleagues in a number of important respects. In addition to volunteering for the considerable dangers of warfare, by fighting for a foreign country (and one embroiled in an ideologically divisive civil war at that), they were also risking official and unofficial disapproval. Their training and material were inferior, they were demographically different from the ordinary U.S. troops, and they formed an exceptional part of the poorly organized, poorly equipped, and often ramshackle Republican army. Above all, however, they volunteered on ideological grounds. It is not surprising that they attributed considerably more importance to ideological beliefs. For example, in reply to the question of what they considered to be the most important factors to help a man overcome his fears in battle, 77 percent endorsed "a belief in war aims." The comparable question put to the U.S. regular troops produced the much smaller percentage of 6 percent.[5] Even the more highly motivated airmen studied by F. Wickert and colleagues regarded ideological commitment as a relatively minor determinant of their combat performance. In the responses to a questionnaire on factors that help to overcome fear, ideological commitment was not among the first twenty items, although it did feature prominently as a "broad motivation."[6]

Like the regular airmen and soldiers studied in World War II, approximately three-fourths of the Spanish Civil War volunteers experienced fear when going into battle for the first time. They also showed the same pattern of habituation with repeated exposure to battle. They confirmed the predominantly anticipatory nature of battle fears and the occurrence of postcombat disturbances, including nightmares.

The overwhelming majority of the men felt that they "fought better after observing other men behaving calmly in a dangerous situation."[7] However, 75 percent of them expressed the view that fear can be contagious, that it can be transmitted from one soldier to another.

As many other studies have shown, it was reported that concentrating on a task was helpful in counteracting fear. Interestingly, the soldiers reported that trying to set an example of courage was a useful way of reducing one's own fears. Their attitudes towards veterans who finally cracked up were, like those of the regular soldiers in World War II, lenient. However, for volunteers who espoused idealistic aims, the Civil War veterans expressed harshly punitive attitudes towards deserters; 70 percent of the respondents felt that a man who deserts several times should be shot. By comparison only 2 percent of U.S. combat fliers recommended such a penalty.[8]

Where the regular airmen and soldiers attached special importance to the quality of training and equipment, these volunteers attached twice as much importance to the value of ideological beliefs in overcoming fear. They also attached far more importance to the value of hatred. No less than 83 percent of the Spanish Civil War volunteers said that a strong feeling of hatred for the enemy enabled them to fight more effectively. Expressions of hatred for the enemy were far less common among U.S. regular troops, and they attached less importance to them. Only 7 percent of the 5000 U.S. airmen questioned expressed significant hatred of the enemy.[9]

It seems then that, despite its mass, the evidence collected during World War II is not universally applicable. In certain conditions ideological factors are significant in stimulating courageous behavior. The evidence collected by Alexander George from Chinese soldiers captured during the Korean War suggests that the intensive, indeed unrelenting, barrage of political indoctrination successfully motivated the troops of this Communist army.[10] They performed with exceptional persistence under extremely adverse conditions, but finally when they suffered major defeats, morale disintegrated rapidly and large numbers of soldiers began to surrender. It would seem that the substantial effects of their political indoctrination were eventually eroded by combat defeats. It may also be of some significance that following these defeats, the policy makers in the Chinese Communist army shifted the emphasis from political indoctrination to the development of professional military skills. In his discussion of this and related material, George aptly remarks that in many circumstances there is an indivisible connection between allegiance to and trust in the primary military unit, and shared political beliefs. It remains possible that the ideological determinants of the behavior of, say, the U.S. regular troops were active but embedded in other factors, and that expression of them was inhibited by resistance to conspicious displays of patriotism and other sentiments. Nevertheless, the available evidence does indicate that *explicit* attempts at political indoctrination are of no more than slight value in promoting courageous behavior—at least in Western armies. This somewhat unexpected conclusion is worth further consideration. Is it merely another example of the observation that the immediate antecedents (at least) of our behavior are to a large extent governed by our relations with a fairly small number of familiar people, rather than by our broad associations with or allegiances to larger groupings?

Fear and Courage by Contagion

The concept of modeling, recently reintroduced and creatively elaborated by A. Bandura,[11] is valuable in helping to interpret information on battle contagion. The powerful impact of fearful or fearless leaders was repeatedly demonstrated during World War II. In a survey of 1700 infantry veterans in the Italian theater of war, it was found that 70 percent of them had a negative reaction to seeing a comrade "crack up."[12] Half of the total sample added that it increased their susceptibility to fear. Similarly high figures on the contagious effects of fear were obtained by Dollard; 75 percent of his combat respondents reported susceptibility to fear-contagion. Most of the information shows that the troops placed considerable importance on personal leadership in helping them to cope with dangerous situations. They reported that a courageous example encouraged them to imitate that behavior, and boosted their self-confidence. Recent laboratory research has indicated that the sight of a live, courageous model is more effective than hearing about one; in keeping with this finding, the troops benefited most from what the officers *did* rather than what they said.[13] As we shall see in Chapter 15, the troops rated courageous behavior as the most important characteristic to look for in their comrades.

Increases in fear or in courageous behavior through social contagion were not confined to active combatants. As mentioned in Chapter 2, observers of the behavior of civilians during air attacks frequently commented on the power of modeling. In particular, parental models were important in determining whether children reacted fearfully to air attacks.

The power and pervasiveness of observational learning underline the importance of courageous leaders. Skilled models are of great value both in the preparation for difficult and dangerous tasks, and in their successful execution. Also, the importance of modeling is yet one more reason for excluding from such tasks those people who are likely to display uncontrolled fear reactions.

Controllability and Uncontrollability

In a substantial cross-sectional survey carried out in the Pacific area, Stouffer and colleagues found that combat air crew had four times as many satisfied members as were found among the infantry divisions. The airmen consistently had higher morale and expressed more favorable attitudes, by comparison with men in other combat units. Among the air crews, fighter pilots had the highest percentage of satisfaction (93 percent). In all three categories of bomber crew, the pilots were always top of the list of satisfied members. Light bomber crew pilots scored the highest percentage of satisfaction (91 percent) and heavy bomber pilots the lowest (70 percent).[14]

In another survey by Stouffer, the average number of awards for combat air crew was more than 10 times greater than that for ground troops.[15] One has to remember, however, that the actions of air crew members were more easily recognized. In the midst of a large ground battle the contributions of individual participants are seldom clear. In addition, the air crews participated in discrete episodes of combat, and this made it easier to rate their performance under stressful conditions. Morevoer, it has been suggested that the air force was more generous in awarding decorations. Despite these considerations, it seems likely that a higher proportion of combat air crew displayed acts of courage than did their counterparts on the ground. The courage of air crews may be due to a number of factors such as the highly selected composition of the crews, their high morale, and the fact that they fought in small, close-knit groups with strong group identity.

These considerations aside, however, the factor of controllability may well have played its part. Some of the findings such as the comparative distress experienced by bomber and by fighter crews, and the differences between pilots, navigators, gunners, and so on can be interpreted in terms of controllability theory. If we allow that a person's sense of controllability in a potentially or actually dangerous situation is an important determinant of his fear reactions, then those combatants who had appropriate competence and confidence should have suffered less disruption from fear. As we have seen, the variation in degree of fear experienced by the different members of an air crew can be summarized, in ascending order; fighter pilots, light bomber pilots, heavy bomber pilots, heavy bomber gun crews. Discussing these findings, Stouffer and colleagues postulated that the heavy bomber crews experienced more fear because "the necessity to fly in rigid formation and the restrictions upon evasive action when exposed to flak and enemy fighter attacks, are conditions which probably tended to augment anxiety reactions in all of the members of the crew."[16] This ascending order of fearfulness corresponds roughly to the descending order of perceived control in intensely dangerous conditions. Fighter pilots, in sole control of highly maneuverable machines, were encouraged to operate with a high degree of autonomy. By contrast the pilots of heavy bombers had incomplete control of their large and cumbersome aircraft; furthermore, they often were under instructions to fly in a direct and unchanging path regardless of enemy attacks.

The gunners in heavy bomber crews were subjected to the same exposure to danger, with evasive actions proscribed and with even less control over the impending dangers. There was also evidence that "prolonged inactivity ... may have tended to augment the feelings of helplessness on combat missions."[17] The crew members themselves complained of the immobility enforced by long flights in cramped aircraft. During these flights they were in danger for several hours at a time and with little possibility of reducing the threats surrounding them. They complained that in addition to the emotional strain, they developed considerable muscular tension, and their flying conditions precluded the release of this accumulating tension. If the hypothesis that the release of motor tension is one way of achieving a reduction of fear is correct, their cramped conditions may have contributed to the persistence of their fears.

This can be at best only a partial explanation, for as we have already seen, fighter pilots reported less fear than other members of the crew, even though their conditions were equally cramped. We have to look for an additional factor or factors. One suggestion is that, in addition to the importance of releasing motor tension, concentration of attention upon a distracting task in a situation of stress reduces anxiety. In his analysis of the results obtained in the U.S. aviation psychology research program, J. Flanagan reached a similar conclusion: "Engaging in effective activity is a frequently indicated factor reducing fear ... Even activities that merely keep a man busy, although they may not be very effective in avoiding the real danger, tended to decrease fear."[18] D. Hastings and colleagues reported similar findings. The overwhelming majority of the pilots whom they studied complained of combat fatigue and high levels of tension. They reported that aggressive acts carried out between combat operations, increased during the course of their operational tour of duty. Moreover, they claimed their tension was relieved by the action of combat.[19]

Although these findings are related, we must not confuse the preventive possibilities inherent in carrying out acts that ensure increased controllability with the execution of acts that relieve tension and fear that has already accumulated. This distinction notwithstanding, it is significant that the prevention of activity is a potent contributor to fear. As Stouffer and colleagues pointed out, "During combat the person's mobility may literally be reduced to zero, as when a soldier was pinned in his foxhole for hours or days. . . . Many men have testified that the severest fear-producing situation they encountered in combat was just such immobilization under artillery or motar fire."[20] Immobilization usually precludes any possibility of achieving control and it also precludes the achievement of a release from tension through activity.

To resume the main theme, most but not all of the military information is consistent with the view that a perceived sense of uncontrollability in a potentially aversive situation contributes to fear. In light of the exceptions (e.g., examples of a lack of concordance between self-confidence and experienced fear) and the identification of other factors that contribute to fear (e.g., contagion), an explanation founded solely on the concept of controllability is unlikely to succeed. Nevertheless, given the information currently available, it seems certain that in potentially aversive conditions the person's sense of controllability or uncontrollability is a major determinant of fear.

Trauma and Avoidance Behavior

Despite the fact that the casualty rate was extremely high, fighter pilots were "significantly more willing than any other group to accept another tour of combat duty."[21] Whereas 48 percent of the unmarried fighter pilots expressed a wish to return to combat duty, only 17 percent of the navigators and bombardiers expressed such a preference. Although pilots were more willing than other crew members to return to combat, those who flew fighter aircraft were markedly more willing to volunteer than were the pilots who flew bombers. Unmarried officers and men were more favorably disposed towards returning than married ones.

This evidence of a significant minority of airmen who were willing to return to combat despite the dangers, fears, and fatigue emphasizes that there is no simple connection between fear and avoidance behavior. Persisting with a difficult and dangerous task despite subjective fear, an example of the discordance between the components of fear, is of course our present definition of courageous behavior. Equally remarkable is the fact that the pilots' willingness to return to combat was not related to the severity of their combat experience, that is, to crash landings, injuries, bail-outs, or fatalities among fellow crewmen. However, airmen who had suffered a severe bout of combat fatigue, did show a greater reluctance to return to combat. Although there was a correlation between the frequency and strength of combat fear and a willingness to return to combat, the relationship was not strong. For example, among those airmen who were afraid on every combat mission, as many as 72 percent were willing to return to combat if required. The willingness of wounded and injured fliers to return to combat exemplifies the resilience of these airmen and also provides us with another example of the shortcomings of contemporary theories of fear: there is far more courage and far less fear than our theories permit.

Fears in Solitude

With a few interesting exceptions, most people appear to be more susceptible to fear when they are alone. When they were isolated, even experienced combat veterans performed badly and were far more inclined to surrender. Prolonged isolation had the effect of reinforcing the soldiers' fears and lessened their resistance.[22] As mentioned earlier, civilians experienced more fear when caught alone during air raids. Even such a tried veteran as the war historian

S. L. A. Marshall, who specializes in providing a worm's eye view of battles, experienced panic when he was isolated for a brief period during the Korean War. "So I took off afoot across the stretch with not another person in sight. Halfway, three mortar shells came in, exploding within fifty or so yards of me. The terror I knew was almost overwhelming. I ran until I was exhausted. It always happens that way. Be a man ever so accustomed to fire, experiencing it when he is alone and unobserved produces shock that is indescribable. Whether the difference comes of some atavistic fear or is more truly a reflex of the purely selfish, though human, feeling that if one must die one should at least get public credit for it, is a question for the psychiatrists. I don't know the answer, I only know what happens."[23]

Harold Macmillan, noted for his courageous behavior in World War I, interpreted his own experience of isolation panic in terms of the social demand for courageous behavior. He had been wounded and was making his way towards the nearest dressing station, accompanied by another injured officer. However, "in the darkness, and the confusion of the bombardment, we became separated. At that point, fear, not to say panic, seized me. I suppose that courage is mainly, if not wholly, the result of vanity or pride. When one is in action—especially when one is responsible for men under one's command—proper behavior, even acts of gallantry, are part of the show. One moves and behaves almost automatically as a member of a team or an actor on the stage. But now it was all over; I was alone and nobody to see me. There was no need to keep up appearances, and I was frightened."[24]

Although Macmillan's explanation of his near-panic—the loss of socially restraining influences—is probably significant, it seems unlikely to provide a full account of isolation fears. Instead we can encompass more information by applying the test of controllability. In many instances the presence of another person increases the possibility of control. Even if the key person is himself unable to reduce the probability of an aversive outcome, his companion may be able to do so, or at least to contribute to reducing the odds. Failing that, the presence of another person may be of critical value in attenuating the effects of the aversive event itself, and/or in dealing with the consequences of the event. To take a concrete example, many agoraphobic patients who are unable to venture beyond the garden gate when alone can move freely if they are accompanied by a trusted person. Most often, however, their freedom of movement is not enhanced by the company of a child or a stranger. Their usual explanation for this discriminative behavior is that if the worst happens (e.g., a heart attack or a fainting spell) the trusted companion will take steps to ensure that the patient is protected and returned to safety. In terms of the controllability explanation, the companion increases the probability of controlling *at least* the consequences of the fear reactions. Along these lines, most people who participate in programs intended to desensitize their fears (see Chapter 9) report that even *imagining* a feared situation is more distressing if they think of themselves as being alone rather accompanied. Whatever the explanation, it seems that the presence of another person often serves to inhibit fear.

Besides the additional controllability offered by a companion, the presence of other people may have a directly inhibiting effect on the fear reaction itself. Even when the presence of someone else is unlikely to increase one's potential control of the aversive event—for example when one is watching a frightening television program—a compatible companion may lower or dampen the fear reaction, including the psychophysiological components. The powerful fear-reducing effects of parental presence are self-evident. The possibility that the presence of other people exercises a directly inhibiting effect on fear reactions is strengthened by the observation that *pain reactions* can also be partly inhibited by the presence of another person—even when the factor of controllability is excluded. Although Macmillan was undoubtedly correct in pointing out that social influences modify the overt expression of fear (and the converse, that full-blown fear reactions occur when social restraints are absent), our analysis must include the factor of increased controllability offered by another person and the directly dampening effect that other people have on our fear experiences. If we allow that people are in their most psychologically isolated state in the early hours of the morning, new light is cast on Napoleon's famous remark: "I have very rarely met with two o'clock in the morning courage." It also emphasizes the importance of situational determinants on fear experiences—we fear a lion approaching, but our reactions promptly subside if we see a safe barrier. The fear of lions is not unconditional and unchanging, but contextual. And the same is true of most of our human fears.

To return to the exceptions, some people experience little fear when confronting extremely dangerous situations alone—and indeed prefer to meet them alone. The great majority of U.S. fighter pilots studied in World War II preferred their solitary role, and performed extremely well. They also reported experiencing the least fear of all air combat personnel. As we have seen, they were a particularly self-confident and competent group of young men, and it seems likely that their own confidence in their flying and combat skills—coupled with a sense of control over events—blocked excessive fears. By contrast, the gunners and heavy bomber crewmen who had far less control of events, reported greater fear. The difference can be illustrated by the experience common to most of us that driving a car under difficult road conditions is less frightening than being a passenger. The ability to exert at least some control in a potentially dangerous situation appears to help inhibit fear reactions.

For certain purposes, it might prove worthwhile to distinguish between solitary and group fear on the one hand, and solitary and group courage on the other. Presumably, those people who are most strongly influenced by social approval will show the largest variations in their conduct in solitary and in group situations. But people who are reasonably unresponsive to social influences should show little difference in the fearful or courageous behavior they display alone or in company. So, we are more susceptible to fear when alone; but earlier it was pointed out that, when in a group, we are open to fear by contagion. Even though we have the capacity to collect fears, alone or in company, fortunately it remains one of our under-used capacities.

In summary, most troops experience fear in combat. Nevertheless, the overwhelming majority perform their tasks satisfactorily, and serious breakdowns are uncommon. The discordance between fear and avoidance behavior fits our definition of courage and is best construed in terms of a three-systems analysis. There is a close but imperfect relationship between the presence of danger and the experience of fear, with several important exceptions in which the covariance between danger and fear does not prevail (consider, for example, the fearlessness of highly vulnerable fighter pilots). The soldier's sense of control, his confidence, is an important determinant of fear and courage; fear is generally greater where control is weak or absent.

With some exceptions, ideological factors had little influence in generating or controlling combat fear. Surprisingly weak avoidance behavior was generated by repeated and prolonged exposures to danger and/or by the repeated experience of fear in combat. Individual differences in vulnerability to excessive combat fear are difficult to predict. Most soldiers, however, were more vulnerable to intense fear when alone.

Notes

1) S. Stouffer et al., *The American Soldier*, 1949, pp. 80–82.

2) Stouffer et al., 1949, p. 407.

3) E. Shils and M. Janowitz, *Public Opinion Quarterly* **12**, 1948.

4) J. Dollard, *Fear in Battle*, 1944. This short report proved to be influential and formed the basis for some of the extensive research into fear that was carried out by teams of psychologists during World War II.

5) Stouffer et al., 1949, p. 1107.

6) F. Wickert, Ed., *Psychological Research on Problems of Redistribution*, USAAF Aviation Psychology Program Research Report No. 14, 1947, pp. 134, 217.

7) Dollard, 1944, p. 28.

8) J. Flanagan, *Aviation Psychology Program Research Report, No. 1*, 1947, p. 217.

9) Wickert, 1947, p. 134.

10) A. George, *The Chinese Communist Army in Action*, 1967.

11) A. Bandura, *The Principles of Behavior Modification*, 1969, and *Social Learning Theory*, 1976.

12) Stouffer et al., 1949.

13) Stouffer et al., 1949, p. 125.

14) Stouffer et al., 1949.

15) Stouffer et al., 1949, p. 345.

16) Stouffer et al., 1949, p. 408.

17) Stouffer et al., 1949, p. 409.

18) Flanagan, 1948, p. 135.

19) A. Hastings, D. Wright, and B. Glueck, *Psychiatric Experiences of the Eighth Air Force*, 1944.

20) Stouffer, 1949, p. 83.

21) L. Shaffer, *Psychological Studies of Anxiety Reaction to Combat*, USAAF Aviation Psychology Research Report No. 14, 1947, p. 173.

22) E. Shils and Janowitz, 1948.

23) S. L. A. Marshall, *Battle at Best*, 1963, p. 72.

24) H. MacMillan, *Winds of Change*, 1966, pp. 89–90.

Chapter 5

The Expression and Recognition of Fear

Do our bodies, and especially our faces, convey accurate information about our emotional feelings and in particular, the experience of fear? If fear *is* manifest in our physical appearance, can other people "read" us correctly? Can other people recognize when we are frightened even if we refrain from telling them? And can we in turn gauge when other people are fearful, even without their informing us of their feelings? Is fear expressed in the same manner by people living in different parts of the world?

Darwin was one of the first scientists to tackle these questions and his views are still of considerable interest. In *The Expression of Emotions in Man and Animals*, he argued that although most forms of emotional expression are "innate" or inherited and cannot be said to depend on the will of the individual, those actions which are followed by satisfactory events will become habitual. One of his "principles of expression" has a surprisingly modern flavor for psychologists: "The first of these principles is that movements which are serviceable in gratifying some desire, or in relieving some sensation, if often repeated, become so habitual that they are performed, whether or not of any service, whenever the same desire or sensation is felt, even in a very weak degree."[1]

He presented a systematic account of the gradation from "mere attention to a start of surprise," turning into fear and finally, "into extreme terror and horror." Although some of his descriptions of the gestures supposedly expressive of emotion are extravagant and occasionally border on the comical, his account of the characteristic manifestations of fear is vivid and in keeping with modern accounts:

The frightened man first stands like a statue motionless and breathless ... the heart beats quickly and violently ... the skin instantly becomes pale ... perspiration immediately exudes from the skin and as the surface is then cold, [we have what is termed] a cold sweat ... the hairs also on the skin stand erect and the superficial muscles shiver ... in connection with the disturbed action of the heart, the breathing is hurried ... the mouth becomes dry ... one of the best marked symptoms is the trembling of all of the muscles of the body and this is often first seen in the lips.

Later in the same chapter Darwin described the transition from fear into terror:[2]

The heart beats wildly or may fail to act and faintness ensue; there is a death-like pallor; the breathing is labored; the wings of the nostrils are widely dilated ... there is a gulping of the throat, protruding eyeballs, dilated pupils, rigid muscles. [In the final stages] as fear rises to an extreme pitch, the dreadful scream of terror is heard. Great beads of sweat stand on the skin. All the muscles of the body are relaxed. Utter prostration soon follows, and the mental powers fail. The intestines are affected. The sphincter muscles cease to act, and no longer retain the contents of the body.

He believed that the expression of fear, and other emotions, is deeply rooted in our biological heritage. "We may likewise infer that fear was expressed from an extremely remote period in almost the same manner as it now is by man."[3] Moreover, we can detect the survivals of these earlier forms of behavior in contemporary expressions of fear. Even though they no longer are of obvious biological value, the earlier expressions of fear persist in modern man—"the same results tend to re-appear". He argued that early men had to escape from their enemies or from danger by "headlong flight or by violently struggling with them; and such exertions will have caused the heart to beat rapidly, the breathing to be hurried, the chest to heave, and the nostrils to be dilated."[4] These and related signs of fear-produced exertion are still to be seen in modern man, even though nowadays "when the emotion of fear is strongly felt," it rarely leads to violent struggles or other exertions. The remnants of the formerly useful patterns of behavior and expression are still evident.

Interest in the biological significance of fear and its expression was recently renewed by the publication of M. Seligman's theory of preparedness.[5] Where Darwin concentrated on the biological and evolutionary significance of the expression of fear, Seligman has speculated on the biological-evolutionary significance of the stimuli and situations that provoke the fear. Starting from his rejection of the belief that what we fear is determined by random factors, Seligman postulated that we are highly prepared to acquire certain fears with speed and ease. These "prepared phobias" and fears are said to be of particular biological significance and like Darwin's expressions of fear they are, in part at least, survivals from early periods of human history. Because the preparedness theory will be discussed in the next chapter, here we need only place it in context and note that Seligman's views on the biological significance of fears do not conflict with Darwin's.

Although Darwin's beliefs about the extent to which the facial expression of emotions, such as fear, are universal to all mankind have received only partial support, he seems seldom to have gone badly wrong. Furthermore, some of the types of evidence and means of collection he employed (e.g., judgments of pictorially displayed emotions, cross-cultural comparisons) are still in use today. No one would quarrel with his view that both nature and nurture contribute to the expression of emotions, and the few advances that have been made since Darwin's day are mainly in the analysis of facial displays of emotion. On the question of universal forms of emotional display, which Darwin believed to exist, there has been a slight increase in knowledge. As we shall see, some types of expression are probably universal (e.g. in happiness) whereas others, as in fear, appear to be somewhat confined culturally. Incidentally, Darwin was especially astute in acknowledging that an emotional display may occur universally but not be recognized universally. To take a hypothetical example: if joy were universally expressed by a twitch of the left ear, it would not necessarily follow that everyone would recognize either the twitch or its meaning.

For a period, particularly in the 1920s, experimental psychologists devoted a great deal of attention to these questions. One of the most prominent investigators, Professor Carney Landis, carried out some extraordinary experiments and the conclusions which he drew from these studies were discouraging.[6] This well known research, later supported by the work of M. Sherman,[7] led to pessimistic conclusions and more or less closed this chapter in experimental psychology. During the past decade, however, the vigorous attempts of P. Ekman, W. Friesen, P. Ellsworth, and C. Izard[8] to revive interest in the nonverbal expression and recognition of emotions have helped to prise open the door once more.

The pessimists, led by Landis and Sherman, concluded that we cannot accurately identify someone else's emotions, including that of fear. It was argued that our occasional successes in identification were largely the result of our knowledge of the circumstances that had led up to the behavior under observation. Without excavating the detailed findings of this research, it is worthwhile considering the *type* of experimental evidence on which their conclusions were founded. In his most remarkable experiment, Landis took a large number of photographs of the facial expressions of 25 volunteers who were subjected to each of 17 provoking experiences. Until this time most psychologists had relied on photographs of the posed facial expressions of actors as their test material; in order to overcome the objections to this artificiality, Landis attempted to obtain material derived from genuine and spontaneous expressions of emotion. He went to great lengths and his subjects were exposed to some extremely unpleasant situations, including one or two of dubious character. The subjects were deceived into taking a breath of ammonia, given an electric shock without warning and—most extraordinary of all—required to decapitate a live rat. (Happily, this kind of experiment is now recognized to be unacceptable and cannot be repeated.)

The results showed that there were no facial expressions characteristic of any of the situations and there were no expressions that were consistently correlated with the subject's verbal report of how he felt at the time. Furthermore, external judges were unable to identify the significance of the expressions with any accuracy or guess what the provoking circumstances might have been. In all, Landis argued that facial expressions convey little useful information about emotional states. In fear, for example, he argued that one cannot tell from a person's facial expression whether he is frightened or not.

Landis was persuasive and it was only after contrary findings had been reported on a number of occasions in later years that his experimental methods were subjected to closer scrutiny and for a number of reasons found to be unsatisfactory. As the subjects were passed from one provoking situation to the next without much delay, it is probable that Landis was photographing the consequences of a cumulative disturbance rather than the responses to 17 discrete provocations. It has also been pointed out that the provoking situations are unlikely to have elicited the same emotion in all of his subjects and there is internal evidence that the men and women, for example, were responding differently. It is also clear from internal evidence that many of the experimental conditions failed to elicit any emotional reaction whatever. For these and a number of other reasons, it is not entirely surprising that Landis was unable to obtain clear evidence of characteristic forms of emotional expression in the faces of his subjects.

The views of Landis received support from the findings reported by Sherman to the effect that nurses, psychologists, and medical students had little success in identifying the emotional reactions of very young infants. The observers were shown a series of babies immediately after they had been stimulated by each of four types of stimulus that were intended to evoke the reactions of hunger (missing a feeding period), fear (being dropped), anger (being restrained), and pain (being pricked). Some of the observers were shown filmed recordings of the babies reactions, while others observed them *in vivo*. In neither condition were the observers successful in identifying the hypothetical emotions. However, when the stimuli causing the reactions of the infants were shown to observers, the degree of success in identifying the various emotions was far greater. When the emotion was fear, for example, the success rate increased from 20 percent without the antecedent information to as high as 70 percent when the infants were seen to be dropped. Rather more importance was attached to these findings than might have been justified. At the most, his conclusions should have been restricted to the expression and recognition of emotional behavior in young infants—they were in fact less than eight days old and the differentiation of emotional reactions does not emerge clearly until a later stage of development. Later research by F. Goodenough, carried out with photographs of a one-year-old infant, produced a much higher success rate in the recognition of emotional reaction.[9] Although the 68 observers were correct in judging astonishment in 94 percent of their attempts, their assessment of fear produced a disappointingly low figure of 21 percent correct.

The methods of studying the expression of fear continue to rely to a large extent on the judgements made by selected observers of the emotions presumed to be portrayed, either spontaneously or artifically, in still photographs, motion films, and videotapes. However, in order to assemble the judgements of the observers, it is necessary to classify them in some manner, and this has led to the construction of *categories* of emotion. Most of the schemes extend to between four and seven classes and they generally include happiness, sadness, anger, disgust, fear, and surprise. The last two categories—fear and surprise—often prove to be inseparable. In passing, it is a little cheering to note that the most easily distinguished and recognized of all forms of emotional expression is happiness.

Another way of classifying observed emotions is to use *dimensions* rather than categories, and here the most useful scales appear to be, pleasant-unpleasant and passive-active. In this sort of dimensional scheme, fear tends to lie towards the unpleasant and active ends of the dimensions. This classification of judgements of emotional reaction has been used in research into the behavior of blind and sighted children, and in the best known of these studies the observers had a fair degree of success. However, in all instances the fears portrayed by the blind children were less accurately recognized than those of the sighted children. In both groups of children, the observers were better able to recognize "happiness" and "sadness" than "fear." These findings,[10] taken in conjunction with those from cultural comparisons mentioned below, suggest that the nonverbal expression of fear is determined by both innate and acquired factors, with the acquired predominating. On the other hand, the nonverbal expression of happiness seems to be determined more by innate factors than by acquired ones. We might expect, therefore, that a Chinese baby brought up in Denver would show happiness in a similar way to his cousin reared in Chungking, but they may well display fear in dissimilar ways.

On the question of whether or not forms of emotional expression are universal, Darwin's views are still serviceable and current assessments tend in the direction of recognizing limited instances of universality. In plain language, a few types of emotional expression seem to be common to all cultures. In the nature of the matter, a conclusive statement will never be possible because of the insuperable practical and technical problems involved; nevertheless, some small measure of agreement in both emotional expression and recognition is reported from cultures as diverse as the United States and remote areas of Borneo. The greatest agreement is generally found in the recognition of "happiness" and, as before, "fear" and "surprise" cannot be disentangled. "Fear" is sometimes confused with "anger" and/or "disgust." The findings from cross-cultural studies show interesting similarities to those reported on blind children and in general support the view that the nonverbal expression of fear is largely a matter of learning.

Attempts have also been made to specify which *components* of facial expression are involved in specific emotions but little progress has been made, perhaps because it is premature to go into details before the broader forms of expression are better understood. We are not in a position to say that particular muscle movements are involved in the expression of, say, "disgust," and yet others involved in the expression of "anger," but we are within sight of means by which we may detect small component differences in the expression of pleasant and unpleasant emotions. It is of course recognized that the eyes are important in the expression of fear (and sadness) while the mouth is important in signifying happiness, anger, or disgust.

As we have seen, a good deal of effort has gone into attempts to isolate the crucial, *nonverbal* expressions of fear and other emotions. In practice, however, the expression of fear is rarely restricted to nonverbal communication. Moreover the display almost inevitably occurs in an understandable context and this greatly assists in the identification of the emotion being experienced. All of this means that in everyday life we are faced with a far easier task than that presented to the experimental observers. Consequently we should, and probably do, make fewer errors of judgment.

At the risk of oversimplifying a lot of data, it seems that we are more likely to recognize general categories rather than specific types of emotional expression, assess happiness more accurately than fear or surprise, interpret better in context and make fewer errors when a person responds verbally as well as physically. Errors of judgment concerning fear are greater when subjects differ widely in backgrounds, or when they are very young or silent.

Judgments made out of context will have a higher error rate. Errors of judgment also arise as a result of deceptions—the "actor" may control his overt reactions or transform them (e.g., feign sadness rather than display happiness). It is often assumed that people devote a lot of effort to disguising their emotional experiences—a process aptly called *"denial."* There is no doubt at all that at times we prefer not to convey our emotional feelings. Indeed the absence of such restraints would result in chaos. It may be, however, that the frequency and importance of the phenomenon of denial has been exaggerated. An extension of the concept of denial to include emotional feelings of which we are not conscious, as in psychoanalytic theories, raises a nice philosophical point.

Those occasions (and there are many of them) on which we experience subjective feelings of fear but nevertheless display fearless approach behavior are interesting but they are not examples of what is meant by the technical term *"denial."* However, it is proper that, having discussed the recognition of other people's emotions, we should now ask ourselves how successful we are at recognizing our own.

Notes

1) C. Darwin, *The Expression of the Emotions*, 1872, p. 348.

2) Darwin, 1872, Chapter 12.

3) C. Darwin, *The Expression of the Emotions in Man and Animals*, 1913 Ed., 360.

4) Darwin, 1913 Ed., p. 307.

5) M. Seligman, *Behavior Therapy*, 1971.

6) C. Landis, *Journal of Comparative Psychology* **4**, 1924 and **2**, 1929.

7) M. Sherman, *Journal of Comparative Psychology* **7**, 1927.

8) P. Ekman, W. Friesen, and P. Ellsworth, *Emotion in the Human Face*, 1972; C. Izard, *The Face of Emotion*, 1971.

9) W. Goodenough, *Child Development*, 1931.

10) See Ekman et al., 1972, for a full account.

Chapter 6

Reading Our Own Emotions

The psychological approach to the question of reading our own emotions has centered predominantly
on the recognition and interpretation of internal bodily states. We are easily able to distinguish between
approach and avoidance behavior and this gross distinction is of little interest. Facial and other external
manifestations of expressive behavior are less readily
accessible and even those which are, such as trembling and perspiring, have been given little empahsis
in this type of investigation. However, the recognition
and interpretation of internal bodily changes has
been a subject of major concern since the emergence
of modern psychology, In 1890, William James proposed a revolutionary theory of emotion, which
stated that our recognition of these bodily changes is
the emotion itself. An oversimplified but nevertheless
revealing example of the application of the theory is

that "we feel frightened because we are running away." According to James, "common sense says we lose our fortune, are sorry and weep; we meet a bear, are frightened and run; we are insulted by a rival, are angry and strike ... but the more rational statement is that we feel sorry because we cry."[1]

In support of his theory, James argued that actors, when playing emotional scenes, experience the relevant feeling. He also said that it is impossible to have an emotional reaction without the accompanying bodily sensations such as palpitations, dryness of the mouth, and so on.

This highly original theory is contradicted by several types of evidence and argument, and has few supporters. The most pertinent objections for our purposes are these. Despite many intensive and sophisticated attempts to link specific bodily states and reactions with subjective emotional report, the results have been almost entirely unsuccessful. With some slight exceptions, it has proved impossible either to detect or deduce a person's emotional state from a study of his bodily or physiological reactions. Instead, one finds only a broad division between differing levels of arousal or activation of the system— certainly far too crude a division to lend credibility to James's theory that we experience the emotion by recognizing internal bodily changes. Closely related to this objection is the fact that the organs and systems that mediate the bodily changes James was discussing are insensitive and slow to react—again, an inadequate source for the rapid and complex range of subjective emotional feelings. Finally, it was discovered that the direct and artificial stimulation (e.g., by drugs) of the organs and systems reponsible for mediating those bodily changes did not produce the expected emotional reactions. The drug used in most of these experiments, adrenaline, is capable of producing widespread and intense activation of the sympathetic nervous system, and the subjects who were given administrations of the drug did in fact display the expected physiological reactions, such as increased heart rate, sweating, increased respiration, and so on. What they did not experience, however, was a normal and genuine emotional reaction. Instead they described what finally became called the "as if" reaction. Subjects would characteristically describe an unusual experience in which they felt "as if" something were about to happen, but only rarely did they recount experiences that corresponded with their idea of previous emotional experiences, and the majority of them were able to distinguish between the drug-induced reactions and a genuine emotional state. In this theory at least, uncommon sense did not succeed.

A theory that more closely approaches the common-sense view was proposed by W. Cannon, who recognized that the experience of emotion and the associated bodily feelings may occur together or independently.[2] Cannon's theory placed undue reliance on one particular structure of the brain, the hypothalamus, but the emphasis on cognitive factors in emotional experience, and acknowledgement that emotional (internal) reactions and subjective feelings may run independent courses, were both useful advances. A modern version of this theory, which places even greater emphasis on the person's cognitive appraisal of the situation, was proposed by S. Schachter and J. Singer. Starting from the fact that the range and subtlety of subjective emotional feelings greatly exceeds the restricted number of bodily (visceral) reactions, they argued that the way in which we view the situation "exerts a steering function." When bodily feelings are aroused, it is our appreciation of the situation in which we find ourself that determines "whether the state of physiological arousal will be labelled as 'anger,' 'joy,' 'fear,' or whatever." Contrary to the view put forward by James, they argue that the state of physiological arousal alone is not sufficient to induce an emotion.[3]

Schachter put forward some novel propositions and illustrated them in a number of interesting experiments. He argued that, even if the person finds himself in a situation of great danger but remains without accompanying bodily sensations (such as trembling), he will not experience fear. But if, in that same situation of danger, he does have bodily reactions, he will then experience fear. Last, if the same bodily reactions are experienced in a pleasant and festive situation, they may be labeled by the person as "happiness" or "joy." Evidence in support of this view of emotional behavior was obtained in a number of experiments during which subjects were given injections of adrenaline or an inert substance and then placed in a specially contrived situation with an experimental stooge who displayed either euphoric or angry behavior. Schachter and Singer interpreted their results as showing that, given the bodily reactions produced by the drug, their experimental subjects reported that they felt either euphoric or angry depending on which type of behavior the provoking stooge had displayed. In those subjects among whom no bodily reactions were stimulated (because an inert substance was used), there was little evidence of their having experienced either of these two emotional states, anger or euphoria. Taken at face value, the interpretation of the experiments supports the hypothesis that emotional feelings are far less likely to be experienced in the absence of aroused bodily states, but that once bodily states *are* aroused, we tend to interpret the ensuing emotion in terms of the situation in which we find ourselves.

If it is possible to distinguish between high and low levels of these bodily states (or levels of arousal), as it seems to be, then our cognitive appraisal of the situation may indeed "exert a steering function." Unfortunately the ingenuity of much of Schachter's work is not always matched by the experimental rigor one would like to see, and it might be best to regard the findings as tentative. Some of the technical difficulties in the interpretation of these studies include the failure to ascertain their subjects' understanding of the situation in which they found themselves; determinations of the bodily states appear to have been taken before and after rather than during the subject's exposure to the stooge situation; also in both experiments, some of the subjects behaved contrary to theoretical predictions. These reservations notwithstanding, the notion that when in a state of physiological arousal, people can quite readily be manipulated into feeling either euphoric or angry or, presumably, fearful, is an intriguing one.

One of Schachter's main propositions, that an emotional experience will not occur in the absence of physiological arousal, appears to be contradicted by some of the facts discussed in this book. It will be recalled that discordances between subjective emotional feeling and bodily reaction have been repeatedly observed. For example, veteran parachutists report little subjective fear despite the presence of quite marked physiological reactivity. In another context, phobic subjects will sometimes report high levels of fear but display no physiological disturbance. These observations imply a need to revise Schachter's proposals and the resulting modifications may simplify matters.

A Poorly Developed Skill

Returning to the specific question of whether or not we are capable of recognizing or "reading" our internal emotional reactions, and particularly those associated with fear, it must be admitted that we do not seem to be talented. Subjects whose internal reactions are being electronically monitored can give accurate reports of these inner reactions at extreme levels of high or low arousal, but their estimates made in the extensive middle ground between the two extremes are poor. For example, most people can assess the state of tension in their major muscle groups when these are in a flaccid or tight condition. However, it is commonly observed that they will report feeling relaxed even when these major muscles are in a state of tension.[4] Yet they often describe localized muscle tension despite an absence of recorded flexion. Heart rate can be estimated best when it sharply accelerated but under other conditions our guesses are poor. Another useful index of internal arousal, the electrical resistance of the skin, is of course unknown to most people and even instruction in its meaning and significance would not make its fluctuations accessible (see the Appendix).

The signs on which we rely in attempting to gauge our own reactions consist mainly of heart palpitations, tremor, muscle tension, stomach discomfort, respiratory disturbance, sweating, and dryness of the mouth. Like heart rate, these signs seem to reach recognition threshold only at extreme levels. We are not able to pick up the smaller changes in muscle tension, or sweating, or even in tremor. In sum, we can read only the headlines.

It is probable that individuals vary widely in ability to read their own reactions, but the range of variation and its relation to other individual attributes is unknown. An even more interesting question is whether or not we can learn to improve our internal reading ability. It seems certain that we can.

Apart from the intrinsic pleasure which improved reading would provide ("know thyself" in modern dress?), certain practical benefits might ensue, the most obvious being improved self-regulation of emotional reactions and expression. Early and accurate recognition of the premonitory signs of fear—or anger—may enable one to engage in more effective alternate and adaptive behavior.

The major reason for expecting that improved internal reading is possible rests on recent advances in the learned control of our internal processes and reactions. Although Russian psychologists have for some years claimed that they are able to condition some surprising changes in internal processes (e.g., kidney functions), the immediate impetus for Western research came from B. F. Skinner's work on operant conditioning[5] and Neal Miller's research on the conditioning of autonomic nervous system functions in small animals.[6] The considerable theoretical problems of Skinner's general system aside, the practical and technological advances it helped to produce have now been applied to the control of heart rate, to skin resistance, and even to changes in the electrical activity of the brain.

The principal method used in regulating these functions is feedback control. It has been shown repeatedly that if you provide people with clear information about the particular function in question (e.g., heart rate) and instruct them to increase or decrease the rate, they can usually manage to do so within a few practice sessions.[7] There are of course limits to the degree of control it is possible to achieve and it has been found that continuous monitoring and rewards are desirable for good results. To date, most of these reports claim short-term increases in the control of inner functions; enduring control may be far more difficult to obtain. Nonetheless the major step has now been taken, and this achievement of conscious control of inner functions pertinent to emotion encourages the hope that we can now learn to improve our reading.

Notes

1) W. James, *Principles of Psychology*, 1890.

2) W. Cannon, *Wisdom of the Body*, 1932.

3) S. Schachter and J. Singer, *Psychological Review*, **69**, 1962, p. 380.

4) S. Rachman, *Behaviour Research and Therapy* **6**, 1968.

5) e.g., B. F. Skinner, *Science and Human Behavior*, 1953.

6) N. Miller, *Science* **163**, 1969.

7) See S. Rachman and C. Philips, *Psychology and Medicine*, 1978, for further information.

Chapter 7

Learning and Biology: Innate and Early Fears

Dissatisfaction with introspectionist psychology led to the development of Behaviorism early in this century. Although it was primarily a revolution in methodology, Behaviorism also introduced new borders for psychology. The early growth of this new psychology was shaped by an understandable but unnecessary fusion of Behaviorism with Environmentalism—the view that most or all important aspects of human behavior are explicable in terms of nurture rather than nature. There is no necessary connection between these ideas, and experimentalists with a special interest in the psychology of learning have successfully separated environmentalism from a behavioristic methodology. As a result, the interesting relations between nature and nurture can be considered as problems in their own right.

Deciding whether some form of behavior is innate or not is no easy matter, especially where people are concerned. As in the consideration of human fears, we are for the most part forced to resort to argument by exclusion. If we encounter a fear that is difficult to explain in terms of the person's past experiences, the possibility of innate determination needs to be considered. The absence of appropriate learning experiences is still the main basis for deciding whether fears are innate or acquired. Regrettably, this criterion was identified with a number of unnecessary assumptions, and as a result discussions of innate fears have become confused. Three of the major assumptions are worth noting in order that we can discard them.

It was assumed that innate fears are (or should be) immutable, common to all members of a species and present at all times and all ages. It is now obvious how these three assumptions precluded any possibility of recognizing innate fears. For one thing, we are aware that fears fluctuate and that they are age-related. These facts tell us nothing about how the fears are generated; they could as easily be innate or learned. Moreover, possibly innate fears arise in childhood in a fashion that resembles maturational growth (see below).

Our considerably improved ability to reduce fears for therapeutic reasons (see Chapter 9), confirms the mutability of fears but is of little assistance in deciding whether the fears themselves were innate or learned. It is true, however, that the fears displayed by animals, where in certain instances there is a greater presumption of innate determination, are as easily or even more easily modified. The major point remains: the mutability or immutability of a fear has no bearing on how it arose in the first place.

After a long period, in which agreement about the learned origin of human fears seemed so conclusive that no alternative views were entertained, the possibility of innate origins is now under reconsideration. In recent years several writers have postulated the existence of some innate fears in people (e.g., fear of the dark, snakes, strangers) but it is difficult to confirm or deny these claims. Despite some suggestive evidence, such as the sharply skewed frequency distribution (unusually common occurrence) of certain fears such as that of snakes, it remains an open question.

There are fewer grounds for hesitation about acknowledging the existence of innate fears in animals. Some of the examples set forward by J. A. Gray include "mobbing" in chaffinches and a fear of snakes in many chimpanzees.[1] I. M. Marks has also drawn attention to the evidence of innate fears among monkeys.[2] Most impressive are the observations on isolated monkeys who were exposed to selected slides of other monkeys in threatening, fearful, playful, and other poses. G. Sackett found that pictures illustrating threatening monkeys elicited fearful behavior in the isolates, and thereby concluded that he was tapping an "innate releasing mechanism." Furthermore, the fearful reactions emerged in the third month of life and therefore provide an excellent example of the maturation of an innate fear. The reactions were observed to wane by the sixth month—possibly an illustration of the process of habituation of fear.[3]

Although one cannot be certain that it is an innate pattern, many human infants begin to evidence fear of strangers between six and eight months of age (a phenomenon sometimes called "eight-month anxiety") after showing indiscriminate smiling responses in the earlier months. Marks has also raised the possibility that a fear of being stared at may be innate, quoting evidence of such a fear among monkeys. While the presence of this fear is manifested (by gaze avoidance) in many socially anxious people, the animal evidence cannot provide grounds for considering it to be innate in humans. Marks also proposes other examples of innate fears, such as the fear of a visual cliff and other perceptual stimuli.

Sudden, Novel or Intense

However, as human infants exhibit fear in response to a wide range of sudden, novel, or intense stimuli, it may be preferable to determine which stimulus attributes are innately capable of evoking fear. A related question that will be discussed later is whether we can identify individual differences in susceptibility to acquire fears; and, if so, is this susceptibility innate?

J. A. Gray has formulated a useful and simple guide: "... it would appear to be possible to subsume all fear stimuli under one of four general principles; intensity, novelty, 'special evolutionary dangers' ... and stimuli arising from social interaction."[4] Although it might be possible to collapse the attribute of *suddenness* into a combination of intensity and novelty, there are reasons for adding it to Gray's list of four principles. He also discusses another type of fear-eliciting situation, described as a "lack of stimulation," and quotes as an example the failure of a stimulus to occur "at a point in time or space where it usually occurs." This may act like a novel stimulus. Proceeding to a more complex level of analysis, one wonders whether this absence of expected and familiar stimulation may play a part in the commonly seen clinical condition known as separation anxiety. It may also provide the basis for an explanation of the common fear of darkness.

Gray points out that stimuli classed under the principles of intensity or novelty (e.g., noise, strange objects, pain) tend to diminish readily with age. In other words, they are subject to habituation. He contrasts these types of stimuli with the special fears of "predators and conspecifics," which take time to mature. This group of fears—in humans they would be classified under the heading of "social interactions"—shows a gradual increase with age. As we shall see, there is evidence that a crossover in the sources of most of our fears occurs roughly at the end of childhood and beginning of adolescence.

The gradual decline in those fears aroused by intense and novel stimulation suggests habituation, whereas the increase in social fears suggests a process of increasing sensitization. Although there are exceptions, the fear of strangers generally emerges at about six months and starts to wane at the end of the first year. Presumably, social fears are also subject to habituation, and their gradual erosion is interpreted as an increase in social confidence. Returning to those fears which appear to be based on sudden, intense, or novel stimulation, Gray states, "It seems that we come into the world ready to be frightened by any intense or novel stimuli, but readily become used to such stimuli, provided that they are not followed by any more disastrous consequences . . . what happens when they are followed by such consequences takes us into the field of learning ..."[5] The acquisition and maintenance of fears is discussed in later chapters.

During infancy, fearful reactions can be evoked by the range of stimuli described above: intense, sudden, or novel stimuli, and—for a time— unfamiliar people. With increasing age, the child's range of fears widens. He can recall past events and anticipate dangers; he can also respond to imaginative impulses and images, such as monsters or ghosts. As the child graduates to more complex fears however, he also learns to cope with the earlier sources of fear and is less likely to fear sudden noises, for example. Typical fear responses of children at different ages were described by A. Jersild and F. Holmes.[6] They observed an overall change from immediate, tangible fears to anticipatory, less tangible ones as the child matured. For instance, most two-year-old children were found to respond fearfully to loud noises and to events associated with noise, whereas only a minority of six-year-old children were fearful. These older children were more inclined to fear imaginary situations. A fear of animals was present in nearly half of the children up to the age of six years, but these animal fears begin to decline in middle childhood; in a group of 15-year-olds, less than 10 percent were found to have retained this fear. The fears of new situations and of noises show a marked decline during the third and fourth years of life and are present in only a minority of six-year-olds (see Figure 2). It is assumed that most noises cease to elicit fear because the child becomes habituated to them, and similarly the fear of new situations is gradually eroded in the course of the child's day-to-day experiences. Frequent exposures to new situations will be followed either by positive

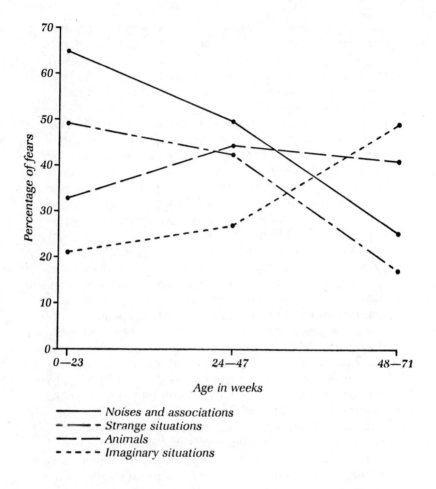

Figure 2 *The growth and decline of some fears of childhood.*
[Adapted from A. Jersild and F. Holmes, Child Development
Monograph *No. 20, 1935.]*

consequences or, more simply, by the absence of unpleasant stimulation. Consequently they will tend to disappear.

The general decline of fears with increasing age has been confirmed in a number of surveys. The findings can be summarized as follows: the fears of young children are extensive; the majority of these fears undergo a steady natural decline; the quality of the fears changes from tangible to intangible with increasing age.[7] There are some exceptions to these general trends, and the fear of meeting new people, as well as general shyness, shows little decline during early and middle childhood. M. Shepherd, B. Oppenheim, and S. Mitchell found that slightly more than half of their sample of over 6000 children were described by their parents as continuing to demonstrate some fear of meeting new people and some shyness right into middle adolescence. In the same study however, they were able to confirm that fears of darkness and of animals, present in nearly half of their five year olds, had markedly diminished in the older age groups.[8] In an experimental investigation of the fluctuations of fears with increasing age, F. Holmes exposed more than 50 children between ages of two and six years to several experimental situations of a potentially frightening character.[9] The percentage of children in whom fear responses were elicited by the presence of a strange person decreased from 31 percent in the four-year-olds to 0 percent in the five-year-old group. Other examples include the fear of being in a dark room, which declined from 47 percent of two-year-olds to 0 percent of five-year-olds, and the fear of being left alone, which dropped from 12 to 0 percent between the ages of two and five years. A microscopic examination of the decline of fear responses in young children was reported by E. Slater.[10] Forty two-year-old children were closely observed during their first four weeks of attendance at a nursery school. During the first week the majority displayed signs of uneasiness and apprehension, but by the end of the fourth week all but three of them had adapted successfully (see Figure 3).

Despite their widespread occurrence, children's fears rarely constitute a problem. In an intensive survey of more than 2000 10 and 11-year-old schoolchildren, M. Rutter and his colleagues found that 126 (5.7 percent) had some psychiatric disorder.[11] Of these children, only 16 were found to have a clinically significant fear. The most common fears were of spiders (five cases) and of the dark (six cases). These children are part of that small minority who do not lose their fears of the dark and of insects or animals.

Persistence

The persistence of some fears throughout and beyond childhood is of interest, in view of the findings of I. M. Marks and M. Gelder on the subject of neurotic phobic conditions in adults.[12] They found that adult patients who complained of circumscribed fears, especially of animals, reported having had the

Figure 3 *The decline of signs of fear in nursery school children during the first four weeks of attendance. [Adapted from E. Slater,* Society for Research in Child Development Monograph, *No. 4, 1939.]*

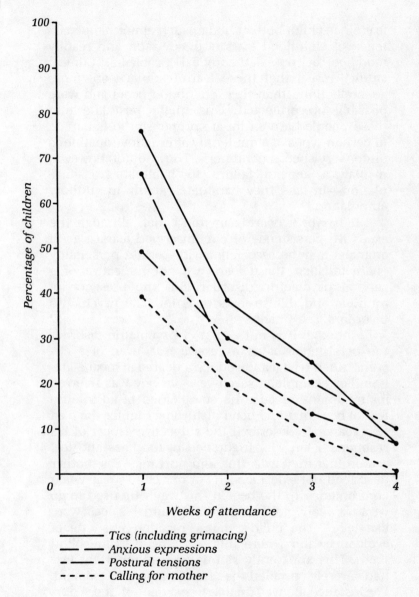

Weeks of attendance

——————— Tics (including grimacing)
— — — — Anxious expressions
— · — · — Postural tensions
- - - - - Calling for mother

fear since childhood. Although such abnormal persistence of childhood fears is uncommon and readily
modified, it poses theoretical problems. Clinical
studies reveal that these fearful adults were more
generally timid than their childhood peers and were
possibly overprotected. One might postulate that
these people have an innate propensity to habituate
to certain types of stimuli only after many repetitions
under very special conditions. They do not, however,
display a general failure to habituate to stimulation—in fact, they habituate rapidly to auditory
stimulation.[13]

It is worth bearing in mind that, although the
excessive persistence of circumscribed fears (e.g., of
animals) may be associated with certain personality
characteristics, these fears are not indicative of a
general psychiatric disorder. But the presence of
multiple and diffuse fears does indicate psychiatric
disorders (see Chapter 8).

Although it is not a sign of psychiatric disorder
the persistence of an excessive fear, even of a circumscribed type, can produce a degree of incapacitation. For example, a seven-year-old boy was referred
for treatment because he complained of an intense
fear of bees that had been disturbing him for the past
two years. He described the subjective aspect of his
reaction: "I am very frightened of the bees and feel
scared that they will sting and hurt me." His mother
described the external signs of her child's fear when
confronted with the bee, in this way: "He used to go
white, sweaty, cold and trembly and his legs were
like jelly." The child's motor reaction was one of
avoidance, and where this was unsuccessful, blind
flight. This apparently simple and unimportant fear
had severely curtailed the child's range of movement.
For instance, he was unable to play out of doors dur-

ing the summer and had to be driven to and from
school during spring and summer terms. On a
number of occasions he had been unable to avoid
coming into contact with bees and these experiences
had produced intense fear reactions. The child's attempts to escape from bees had led to a number of
disturbing experiences, which had finally prompted
him and his parents to seek assistance. On at least
two occasions he had run across busy streets when
confronted by a bee and his parents were concerned
lest he come to harm because of his intense, blind-
escape reactions.

It appears then, that we are born with a propensity to develop fears of intense, sudden, or novel
stimuli and certain types of social stimulation. During early childhood we display extensive fears that
then undergo a slow natural decline. As age increases, the quality of fears changes from tangible to
intangible.

The Biological Significance of Fear

As we have seen, Gray included "special evolutionary
dangers" as one of the four general principles sub-
suming fear stimuli.[14] In fact many writers from
Darwin to Freud, and the modern ethologists, have
been intrigued by the biological significance of fear.
Like Darwin, Freud speculated that human fears retain some of their prehistorical features. "Others, like
the fear of small animals, thunderstorms, etc., might
perhaps be accounted for as vestigial traces of the
congenital preparedness to meet real dangers which
is so strongly developed in other animals." Consistent with the rest of his theory, he went on to specify

that it is "only that part of this archaic heritage is appropriate which has reference to the loss of the object."[15]

Martin Seligman's theory of preparedness shares a similar biological orientation. "The great majority of phobias are about objects of natural importance to the survival of the species ... it does not deny that other phobias are possible, it only claims that they should be less frequent, since they are less prepared."[16] He goes on to argue that human phobias "are largely restricted to objects that have threatened survival, potential predators, unfamiliar places, and the dark."[17] He postulates that certain kinds of fears are readily acquired because of an inherited biological preparedness. These phobias "are highly prepared to be learned by humans, and like other highly prepared relationships they are selective and resistant to extinction, and probably are non-cognitive."[18] The main features of prepared fears (for our purposes, phobias can be regarded as intense fears) are as follows: they are readily acquired, extremely stable, selective, of biological significance, and probably noncognitive.

Having noted the historical context of Seligman's theory, in order to appreciate its contemporary significance it is necessary first to say something about earlier attempts to explain the acquisition of fear and similar types of response. In common with most learning theories, the conditioning theory of fears and phobias rests in part on the so-called equipotentiality premise. As Seligman and J. Hager observed, it was believed by most learning theorists that "what an organism learned about is a matter of relative indifference. In classical conditioning, the choice of conditioned stimulus, unconditioned stimulus, and response matters little; that is, all conditioned stimuli and unconditioned stimuli can be associated more or less equally well, and general laws exist which describe the acquisition, extinction, inhibition, delay of reinforcement, and spontaneous recovery of all conditioned and unconditioned stimuli."[19] Seligman quotes Pavlov's famous claim that "any natural phenomenon chosen at will may be converted into a conditioned stimulus ... any visual stimulus, any desired sound, any odor and the stimulation of any part of the skin."[20] Learning theorists shared this view. For example, M. May wrote, "The general rule is that *any stimulus may become a danger signal provided it is immediately and repeatedly followed with any unpleasant, injurious, or painful experience.*"[21]

Seligman convincingly argued that this premise is untenable and proposed that it be replaced by the concept of preparedness.[22] In 1972 he developed this alternative idea with particular reference to phobias.[23]

In keeping with the views of Pavlov, the conditioning theory of fear acquisition (Chapter 10) carried the implicit assumption that any stimulus can be transformed into a fear signal. In addition it was assumed that, given comparable exposures, all stimuli have roughly an equal chance of being transformed into fear signals. Some reservations, however, were noted. For example H. J. Eysenck and S. Rachman argued that "neutral stimuli which are of relevance in the fear-producing situation and/or make an impact on the person in the situation, are more likely to develop phobic qualities than weak or irrelevant stimuli."[24] Even when reservations of this sort were noted, little attempt was made to specify their nature or implications.

Lock and Key

In retrospect we can now see that the equipotentiality premise began posing difficulties years ago. For example it has been pointed out that H. English[25] was only partly successful in his attempt to replicate J. B. Watson's demonstration[26] of the acquisition of the fear of white rats (see Chapter 9). English found that fear reactions could be conditioned only to selected stimuli. Along similar lines, E. Bregman failed in her thorough attempt to condition a group of infants to fear a range of simple and biologically insignificant objects. The repeated presentation of geometrically shaped wooden objects and of cloth curtains, in conjunction with a disagreeably loud and startling sound of an electric bell, did not produce conditioned fear reactions to the stimuli (which were biologically insignificant. She concluded that changes in emotional behavior are difficult to engender by joint stimulation in early life, and therefore conditioning cannot provide a comprehensive explanation of the acquisition of emotional responses in infancy.[27] An engaging account of some weaknesses of the equipotentiality premise can be found in the writings of C. W. Valentine. In his analysis of Watson's demonstration, Valentine wondered whether the fear of the rat "was readily established partly because there was an existing innate tendency, though as yet unawakened, to fear the rat." He then went on to describe some of his own tests in which he had tried to condition fear to an unfamiliar object which "could not be supposed to have any innate fear attached to it, namely, an old pair of opera glasses." Overcoming his resistance, he performed some tests on his own child despite causing "momentary discomfort to one's little ones." But the child was "an exceptionally healthy, strong and jovial youngster, and I hardened my heart sufficiently to try one or two simple tests with her."[28]

His demonstration followed the same lines as that of Watson, and when Valentine's child, aged one year, stretched out to touch the opera glasses, he loudly blew a wooden whistle behind her. The child "quietly turned around as if to see where the noise came from." This procedure was repeated several times but not once did the child show any fear of the opera glasses. Later in the afternoon the same experiment was repeated with a caterpillar. At the first loud noise, the child gave a loud scream and turned away from the caterpillar. This procedure was repeated four times, and the effect was the same each time. The tests were continued for the next few days and the child showed evidence of an unstable fear of the caterpillar. Although the fear showed signs of spontaneous fading, it was readily restored after only slight provocation. In summarizing the result, Valentine used a telling description: "Here we have again the *rousing of the lurking fear* by the added disturbance of the whistle" [italics added].[29] Using the analogy of a *lock and key*, Valentine stressed that the noise itself became aversive when associated with the caterpillar, not with the opera glasses.

Valentine's case for the selective quality of fear acquisition was supported by observations on other young children. He quoted, for example, a two-year-old child who readily acquired a fear of dogs at slight provocation, and this behavior was contrasted "with the absence of fear even when real pain was suffered under circumstances in which no object stimulating an innate tendency to fear is present."[30]

Demonstrations of this type and the impressive experimental information assembled by Seligman and Hager are a serious challenge to the equipotentiality premise, and to other theories that rely on the premise.[31] The corollary for fears, that all stimuli have an equal chance of being transformed into fear signals, is not verified by surveys of the distribution of fears either in a general population or in psychiatric samples.[32] Subject only to their prominence in the environment, many objects and situations should have an equal probability of becoming fear-provoking. What we find instead, however, is that some fears are exceedingly common—far too common for the conditioning theory. Other fears are far too rare. Fear of the dark is common among children, but a fear of pyjamas is unheard of. For animal phobias, one might expect that within a city population the fear of lambs would be about as prevalent as the fear of snakes. In actuality, however, the fear of snakes is common and that of lambs rare. Moreover, a genuine fear of snakes often is reported by people who have had no contact with them. This means that a fear of snakes can be acquired in the absence of direct contact—a conclusion that opens three possibilities. Either the fear of snakes is innate or it can be transmitted indirectly, or the fear of snakes is "lurking" and will appear with only slight provocation. The last two of these possibilities are of course compatible.

As opposed to prepared associations, *unprepared* connections should be more difficult to acquire and more transient. The following three cases[33] of patients who developed unprepared phobias are presented because of their inherent interest and because they led to some surprising conclusions.

The first patient, Mrs. V., was admitted to hospital with a chronic and severe neurotic disorder in which the main features were compulsive rituals centered on a powerful fear of chocolate—scarcely the basis for a prepared fear of biological significance. She complained of and demonstrated extreme fear when confronted with chocolate or any object or place associated with chocolate. She avoided most brown objects and as a result would never agree to sit on any furniture that had brown in it. On one occasion she walked up eight flights of stairs rather than push the elevator button because she saw a brown stain close to the button. She took great care to avoid any shops that might stock chocolate or any public places where chocolate might be eaten. In the course of several years the fear grew until she was forced to cease working and became increasingly confined. Before admission to the hospital, she was practically housebound. There was no denying the authenticity of her distress when she was presented with chocolate, nor was there any doubt about the vigor of the avoidance behavior evoked by such confrontation. Because of the rarity of this complaint, and because a fear of chocolate has no biological significance and is unrelated to natural dangers, it meets the defining characteristics of an unprepared connection.

According to the patient and the independent account given by her husband, her psychiatric complaints began shortly after the death of her mother to whom she was inordinately attached. After the death she was depressed for a prolonged period and became conscious of a strong aversion towards—and probably fear of—cemeteries and funeral parlors. She first became aware of a slight distaste for chocolate several months after the death of her mother; but it was nearly four years after this event that she realized she was actively avoiding chocolate and had indeed become extremely frightened of it. Prior to her mother's death she had eaten chocolate with enjoyment but this pleasure apparently waned gradually in the period after her mother's death. (In the course of her otherwise largely unsuccessful treatment, the patient regained the ability to touch and even to eat small pieces of chocolate, but the pleasurable taste did not return.)

The most relevant characteristics of this patient's intense fear of chocolate were: its rarity, its gradual onset, its intensity and the accompanying avoidance behavior, the widespread generalization from chocolate to a wide variety of brown objects, and its resistance to modification. The rarity, gradual acquisition, and biological insignificance render it different from the common, recognized *prepared* phobias—it is an *unprepared* fear.

The second illustration[34] was provided by a psychiatric patient who complained of an intense and disabling fear of fiery colors, particularly oranges and reds. Like Mrs. V., she experienced considerable distress when confronted with any of these colors and as a result had developed extensive and persistent patterns of avoidance. She too had become virtually housebound because of her fear. Given its rarity, gradual onset, intensity, widespread generalization, associated avoidance behavior and resistance to treatment, this too can be classed as an unprepared fear. Apart from the association of red and orange with the idea of fire, a fear of these colors cannot be said to have any biological significance. In fact, as it turned out, this fear was more closely associated with subjective feelings of distress, particularly symptoms of feeling hot and flushed, than it was with fires or fire hazards.

The third unusual phobia was that of a young woman who was virtually blind from early infancy and complained of an excessive fear of vegetables and plants, particularly their leaves. The phobia had its origin in early childhood, and, like the other two patients, this person expressed and displayed intense fear of the objects and engaged in extensive and active avoidance. She attributed the genesis of the fear to a series of extremely unpleasant experiences she had undergone as a child, claiming that some of the other children had taunted and teased her by rubbing vegetables and plants on her face in order to irritate her. In her view this had produced an intense dislike of vegetables and plants that later turned into fear. Her phobia handicapped her in a number of ways and prevented her from engaging in ordinary social activities. For example, she was unable to eat in public places or in unfamiliar homes in which vegetables or salads might be served. She took care to avoid certain areas where she knew there might be shops that stocked vegetables or plants. Each week this patient had two or more vivid and terrifying dreams in which vegetables or plants featured prominently. These dreams seemed to increase the severity of the phobia. Like the other two patients, she made little progress in therapy despite receiving concentrated help.[35]

These extraordinary examples present us with an apparent conflict of evidence. On the one hand, the fears can be regarded as unprepared because they are rare, of no apparent biological significance, and unrelated to natural dangers. On the other, Seligman hypothesizes that prepared learning—*not* unprepared learning—is unusually resistant to extinction, is noncognitive, and generalizes widely. So these phobias have the defining features of unpreparedness (lack of biological significance, rarity, and gradual acquisition), but the empirical properties that are hypothesized to cohere with preparedness—

resistance to extinction, irrationality, and wide generalization.

Among the possible resolutions considered by Rachman and Seligman, it was suggested that the analysis of preparedness in phobias may retain its value but that some of the hypothesized consequences of having an unprepared phobia may need revision. "In particular, it need not follow that comparatively unprepared phobias will necessarily show easy extinction and narrow generalization."[36] They also considered the symbolic element in each of these three cases and the further possibility that these rare instances may reflect a peculiar sampling problem.

These possibilities were taken up in a retrospective survey carried out by P. de Silva, Rachman, and Seligman. Sixty-nine phobic and 82 obsessional patients treated at the Maudsley Hospital in London were rated for the preparedness of their fears, that is, for the evolutionary significance of the content and behavior of the disorder. Although a satisfactory and reliable rating system was finally developed, it was found that the degree of preparedness was not correlated with any significant feature of the fear or of the patients' clinical condition and progress. Although they were unable to find support for the clinical predictions that flow from the theory of preparedness, the authors were careful to point out that their study did not disprove the theory. "It is entirely possible for the essentials of the theory to be in order even if the clinical implications drawn from it are found to be incorrect. So for example, the argument that the distribution of human fears is non-random and therefore indicative of evolutionary pressure on learning to be afraid of specific objects or situations is not weakened. And it is this non-randomness that forms the core of the preparedness concept."[37]

In this clinical sample they found that the great majority of phobias and obsessions were prepared. Unprepared phobias were rare, but unprepared obsessions were not uncommon. Only three of the 69 phobic patients had unprepared phobias, but, as has been pointed out, these clinically observed unprepared phobias do not conform to the pattern predicted by the original theory. It is of course possible that the apparent conflict between theory and clinical material arises precisely from the fact that the material is clinical; in other words, those rare occasions when unprepared fears persist, and lead the person to seek professional help, may be quite distinctive. A more appropriate test of the preparedness theory of fears will have to be based on an examination of the fears of a large random sample of people.

The theory poses other problems. For example, the major emphasis on *rapid acquisition* as a primary criterion of a prepared phobia, influenced by the literature on taste aversions, restricts the applicability of the theory. Clinical evidence (e.g. I. M. Marks[38]) shows that some of the common, resistant phobias such as agoraphobia and social phobias are acquired slowly and gradually. As the valuable, methodical research of Professor A. Öhman[39] and his colleagues at Uppsala University has demonstrated, the most striking feature of "prepared" fears is their resistance to modification. A definition of biologically relevant fears that is based on resistance to modification (perhaps supplemented by reference to the ease of acquisition) may be preferable.[40] Furthermore, the inclusion of a "belongingness" factor, such as that observed in the acquisition of taste aversions, would also strengthen the argument. Even "prepared" fears need the correct key before they are unlocked.[41]

Despite the difficulties inherent in attempting to evaluate any biological-evolutionary arguments applied to human behavior, the major sections of Seligman's theory are open to examination. Among its other merits, the theory emphasizes the biological nature of fear, has a broad sweep, and helps to impose some degree of order on the disparate information on human fears. Even if the theory fails to attract adequate support in the future, it has uncovered the untenable equipotentiality premise and opened the way to a coherent set of positive alternatives.

Notes

1) J. Gray, *The Psychology of Fear and Stress*, 1971.

2) I. Marks, *Fears and Phobias*, 1969.

3) G. Sackett, *Science* **154**, 1966.

4) Gray, 1971, p. 20.

5) Gray, 1971, p. 22.

6) A. Jersild and F. Holmes, *Children's Fears*, 1935.

7) See, for example, S. Agras et al., *Comprehensive Psychiatry*, 1969: S. Rachman, *Phobias: Their Nature and Control*, 1968.

8) M. Shepherd, B. Oppenheim, and S. Mitchell, *Childhood Behavior and Mental Health*, 1971.

9) F. Holmes, *Child Development Monographs*, No. 20, 1935.

10) E. Slater, *Society for Research in Child Development Monograph*, No. 4, 1939.

11) M. Rutter et al., *Education, Health and Behavior*, 1970.

12) I. M. Marks and M. Gelder, *British Journal of Psychiatry* **1**, 1967.

13) M. Lader and A. Mathews, *Behavior Research and Therapy* **6**, 1968.

14) Gray, 1971, p. 20.

15) Freud, 1926, in *Collected Papers of Sigmund Freud*, Vol. III, 1950, p. 168.

16) M. Seligman, in M. Seligman and J. Hager, Eds., *The Biological Boundaries of Learning*, 1972, p. 460.

17) Seligman and Hager, 1972, p. 465.

18) Seligman, 1972, p. 455.

19) Seligman and Hager, 1972, p. 2.

20) Seligman, 1972, p. 455.

21) M. May, *A Social Psychology of War and Peace*, 1944, p. 72.

22) M. Seligman, *Psychological Review* **77**, 1970.

23) M. Seligman, *Behavior Therapy* **2**, 1971.

24) H. J. Eysenck and S. Rachman, *The Causes and Cures of Neurosis*, 1965, p. 81.

25) H. English, *Journal of Abnormal and Social Psychology* **34**, 1929.

26) J. Watson and R. Rayner, *Journal of Experimental Psychology* **3**, 1920.

27) E. Bregman, *Journal of Genetic Psychology* **45**, 1934.

28) C. W. Valentine, *The Psychology of Early Childhood*, 1946, p. 216.

29) Valentine, 1946, p. 218.

30) Valentine, 1946, p. 214.

31) Seligman and Hager, 1972.

32) e.g., Agras et al., 1969; S. Rachman, *The Meanings of Fear*, 1974.

33) The first and third of these cases of unprepared phobias were originally described by S. Rachman and M. Seligman, *Behavior Research and Therapy* 14, 1976. My thanks to Professor Seligman and P. de Silva for permission to quote extensively from the two papers concerned. (The second paper is

by P. de Silva, S. Rachman, and M. Seligman, *Behavior Research and Therapy* **15**, 1977.)

34) A large part of this information was gathered by S. Grey.

35) See Rachman and Seligman, 1976; Rachman and Hodgson, *Obsessions and Compulsions*, 1979.

36) Rachman and Seligman, 1976, p. 338.

37) de Silva, Rachman, and Seligman, 1977, p. 76.

38) I. Marks, *Fears and Phobias*, 1969.

39) A. Öhman et al., *Behavioural Analysis and Modification* **2**, 1978.

40) S. Rachman, *Behavioural Analysis and Modification* **2**, 1978.

41) For examples, see J. Garcia and D. Koelling, *Psychonomic Science* **4**, 1966; for examples in children, see Valentine, 1946.

Chapter 8

Types and Degrees of Fear

Research into ways of modifying fear has led to a demand (not satisfactorily fulfilled[1]) for methods and instruments capable of describing and measuring the range and intensity of fears. To this end, Joseph Wolpe and Peter Lang[2] among others, constructed fear inventories. The early version of Wolpe and Lang's scale was developed and refined by other workers and applied to substantial numbers of university students and selected groups of psychiatric patients. These inventories contain between 30 and 150 items, each referring to a range of objects and situations that are presumed to evoke a measure of fear in at least a proportion of the population. The subject is required to rate each item for the degree of fear it usually arouses in him, and for this purpose a five-point scale is generally employed—ranging from one, meaning no fear at all, to three indicating moderate fear, and five indicating extreme fear.

The resulting pattern of fears can then be

examined for clinical purposes. For research, the item scores of a large sample of subjects are intercorrelated and subjected to factorial analysis in order to determine whether or not there are "clusters" of fears. Typical items used in inventories of this kind include the following: sharp objects, germs, blood, feeling rejected by others, public speaking, snakes, deformed people, examinations, and so on. As with all inventories, the results can reflect only the questions that are fed in. Unfortunately, the chronic and diffuse types of fears are poorly represented, and the more episodic, acute, and stimulus-provoked fears are overrepresented.

Nevertheless, the results of investigations carried out predominantly on groups of American students have revealed some interesting findings. In all the factor analytic studies, a fear of certain kinds of social situations or events emerges as a clear and strong factor. Similarly a fear of animals and/or insects is always present, as is a fear of harm, injury, or loss. In addition, some other variations have been described, such as a factor denoting a fear of water, or a specific fear of death. The fears and factors observed in psychiatric samples bear similarities to those revealed in nonpsychiatric groups, but tend to be more widespread and intense in the disturbed groups. Overall, psychiatric groups endorse a greater number of fear items and also rate their fears as being more intense than do subjects in nonpsychiatric samples. It has also been found that the fear inventory scores show moderately high correlations with standard tests of general anxiety such as the Taylor Manifest Anxiety Scale. In addition to the general surveys of fear, some inventories have been constructed to tap specific types of fear such as public-speaking fears, test-taking fears, and so on. Again, the total scores on these subscales tend to show a moderately high correlation with fear and anxiety scales of a general character.

In all the major investigations it has been observed that women express fears of more objects and situations than men and that they also indicate higher degrees of fear. It has been suggested, however, that this sex difference, indicating excessive timidity in women, may reflect the greater willingness of women to admit their fears rather than an accurate portrayal of the differences between men and women. Although there is sound evidence to support the argument that women will more readily admit to fears, the data on behavioral avoidance tests and physiological indices support the view that the reported sexual differences in timidity are authentic. It appears that female fearfulness is genuine and male fearfulness, although present and admitted, is partly disguised.

In a psychiatric sample studied by G. F. Lawlis it was found that the major fear factor comprised social situations.[3] The patients endorsed fears relating to the loss of approval, feelings of rejection by others, loss of status, humiliation, and so on. In the same study, a second major factor was composed of items relating to fear of small animals and insects, such as snakes, spiders, and rats. This factor is interesting because of its comparability to similar factors detected in populations of students, and because much of the research on the experimental and clinical reduction of fears has relied on subjects with circumscribed fears of animals and insects.

Abnormal Fears

In an attempt to discover the types and degrees of fear that exist in a normal population, S. Agras, D.

Sylvester, and D. Oliveau[4] interviewed 325 randomly chosen residents of Burlington, Vermont. Although one can quibble with the classificatory system which they adopted, their findings are useful. Depending on the estimated intensity of the fear, Agras and his colleagues classed the replies into four categories: common fears (mild), intense fears, phobias, clinical phobias (most severe).

A fear of snakes was the most commonly reported, with no less than 39 percent of the respondents reporting at least mild fear of this reptile. Twenty-five percent of them expressed an intense fear of snakes. The second most common fear was heights. Among the most severe fears, those classified as clinical phobias, agoraphobia (fear of public places, transport, being alone, and so on) was the most common, with fears of injury and illness a close second.

Broadly speaking, two patterns of prevalence emerged from the data. The majority of fears reached their peak in early adulthood and then declined in the succeeding years. The second and less common pattern was for a more gradual development of fear reaching a peak in middle or late adulthood. Examples of the first pattern were seen in fears of animals, darkness, strangers, doctors, heights, and so on. The second pattern was characteristic of fears of death, injury, illness, separation, and crowds. The fears that showed the greatest incidence in early childhood were strangers, darkness, injections, and doctors. Those with the latest age of onset were to do with injury, illness, and crowds.

Agras and his colleagues cautioned that theories based on psychiatric experience with a few phobic patients "cannot be generalized to all phobias" because psychiatrists see only a small, and presumably nonrandom, sample of self-selected patients. In their study only a quarter of the people with phobias rated as clinically disabling were receiving psychiatric care. They were able to conclude, "psychiatrists do not see the milder cases of phobia nor do they see a representative sample of the different types of phobia."

They are certainly correct in drawing attention to the dangers of overgeneralizing about the nature of fear on the basis of a grossly unrepresentative, self-selected sample of the potential population (a serious drawback to all *clinical theories*, such as psychoanalysis). Fortunately, the intensive and extensive research into the processes of fear reduction that was initiated by Wolpe's pioneering research[5] has gone a long way to providing us with a better balanced body of information concerning fear.

The importance of their finding that in psychiatric clinics one sees a grossly *unrepresentative* sample of the fearful people in the community cannot be exaggerated. If certain key features, such as the intensity of the fear are held constant, research carried out on *nonpsychiatric samples* will be superior to that conducted on clinical samples. The nonclinical samples are far more likely to provide a sound, balanced representation of the phenomenon of fear. For this reason—and because of the unwarranted assumption that intense fears are by definition pathological—criticisms of laboratory research on the grounds that they are mere analogies are misguided. To the contrary, an undue reliance on research findings obtained from samples of people who have been diagnosed by a psychiatrist (usually as "phobic"), is far more likely to lead to mistaken conclusions, than placing most weight on well conducted "analogue" research.

It need hardly be said that the fears expressed by

psychiatric patients are not *ipso facto* pathological; the great majority are normal fears. The distinction between the so-called pathological fears (phobias) and normal fears does not rest on the clinical status of the fearful person. It is a distinction that is easy to draw when comparing the extreme examples of pathology and of fear, but which usually depends on shades of intensity. If, as seems unavoidable, the intensity of a fear is graded on a continuum, it comes as no surprise to find that a cut-off point between normal and "pathological" is difficult to determine. The difficulty does not suffocate the attempt, and "pathological" fears, or phobias, are generally defined as excessive fear reactions that are both persistent and unadaptive. All three of the key adjectives are of course relative terms and the definition happily assumes a unitary type of fear reaction. Despite these drawbacks clinicians find some utility in the definition even if purists grimace.

All of the three components of fear described in Chapter 1 are observed in moderate to intense degree among people with phobias. The subjective aspect of a phobia is experienced by the person as an alarming feeling of intense fear or panic and may be expressed in a variety of ways. Some patients for example report they feel as if they are dying; others feel they are suffocating, and still others that they are going to faint or collapse. The bodily reactions include a combination of these feelings or responses: rapid respiration, sweating, trembling, palpitations, muscular tension or weakness, involuntary excretions, "butterflies in the stomach," nausea, dryness of the mouth. In the grip of a phobic reaction, the patient may flee blindly, or may wish to do so, or he may become inert and feel incapable of movement. The facial and other manifestations of fear evident to other people include evidence of tension, staring, trembling, pallor, and so on. These various manifestations can be illustrated by reference to phobic cases, the most common of which are agoraphobia, animal phobias, social phobias, sexual phobias and phobias of being trapped.

Severe chronic agoraphobia is illustrated by the case of a 45-year-old man whose symptoms had persisted for 10 years without much change. He complained primarily of an inability to walk about in public and of a strong fear of being alone at any time. When he attempted to leave his home unaccompanied he experienced a severe fear reaction, which he described as a feeling that "something dreadful was about to happen" to him. He had in fact experienced a number of panic attacks during which he felt that he was going to die (of a heart attack). The bodily reactions that accompanied these subjective feelings of apprehension included breathlessness, palpitations, and feelings of weakness that forced him to support himself against the nearest wall. He avoided a large number of situations and, when he was induced by pressing demand to leave his home, he restricted his walking to those routes he knew contained walls on which he could support himself if necessary. In practice, it meant that whenever he walked outside his home for any distance he was obliged to creep alongside a wall, touching it as he proceeded.

A medical student, who complained of an intense fear of figures in authority and of examination situations, described his feelings as bordering on panic whenever he was unable to avoid the presence of his teachers, senior colleagues, and so on. He was quite unable to cope with these people, felt extremely frightened, and trembled and sweated in a way that was clearly visible. The bodily reactions in his case were sweating, muscular tension, blushing and flushing, and palpitations. In addition, the muscular tension often centered on the muscles of the throat region and this prevented him from speaking normally in the presence of authority figures. Whenever and wherever possible, he avoided coming into contact with his teachers. This unadaptive behavior was interfering with his education, apart from the heavy burden it imposed on him in day-to-day matters affecting his social life.

A third example, of a sexual phobia, was that of a young woman who was frightened of pain and discomfort that might be induced by penetration of her vagina, either by the use of tampons or during intercourse. In both of these circumstances she experienced powerful anticipatory fears marked by gross trembling, sweating, and pallor, and sometimes her general feelings of bodily weakness were translated into fainting spells of short duration.

In his lucid guide to the clinical phenomena of phobias, I. M. Marks attempted a clinical classification of phobic complaints.[6] The major categories are social phobias, specific animal and insect phobias, illness phobias, and agoraphobic disorders. In a survey carried out in a major psychiatric teaching hospital, he found that 60 percent of the phobic cases were in the category of agoraphobia. The social phobias were surprisingly low—constituting only 8 percent of the total—but this figure may be a reflection of diagnostic practice rather than the actual occurrence of this phobia in the patients at that hospital. Various types of illness phobias accounted for 15 percent of the sample; animal phobias, 3 percent; and miscellaneous specific phobias, 14 percent.

The animal phobias were confined almost entirely to women, had their origins in early childhood, and showed a reasonably unchanging course over many years. The agoraphobic group also had a preponderance of women (75 percent of the sample), with the age of onset being later—generally after puberty. The patients' fears tended to be accompanied by high levels of anxiety, depression, and other symptoms. Although the disorder was found to persist for longer than a year in most cases, it did show fluctuations from time to time with periods of comparative freedom from fear. What is described as agoraphobia in clinical practice generally comprises a number of interrelated fears, such as a fear of being alone, difficulty in leaving the home, and fears of closed spaces, transport vehicles, social situations, and so on. The social phobias are more evenly distributed between men and women and constitute fears of contact with other people—fears of social conversation, eating or drinking in public, speaking in front of strangers or a group of people. Like the agoraphobic disorders, social phobias tend to emerge after puberty, usually between the ages of 15 and 30. In many people they are associated with depression, and in a few with high levels of background anxiety. These phobias show little fluctuation over the years. The intense fears of illness, which center on specific diseases or disorders like cancer, venereal disease, cardiac disorders and so on, resemble certain other psychiatric disorders and can be difficult to distinguish from them (e.g. obsessions[7]). These illness phobias occur with equal frequency in both sexes and tend to make their appearance in early adulthood.

The agoraphobic disorders, which feature prominently in most clinics, have been the subject of considerable research and a number of surveys. One of the most interesting of these was carried out by Marks and Herst on 900 female members of a voluntary association for agoraphobics called "The Open Door."[8] The information was gathered by questionnaires, and supplemented by interviews with a small number of subjects. In this group the most common and intense fears were: speaking to audiences, riding in underground trains, crowds of people, traveling in buses or trains, heights, going to the hairdresser, streets, and open spaces. Other problems reported by this group of patients were exhaustion, tension, obsessions, depression, and loneliness. A quarter of them also complained of moderate to severe fears of disease, dying, and fainting. Forty percent of them complained of some sexual difficulty, and a significant minority were so handicapped that they were unable to obtain or maintain employment. It is not clear whether agoraphobic disorders are precipitated by environmental stresses in a direct manner, if at all. Estimates of the importance that should be attached to the precipitating factors present at the onset of the disorder range widely. In the survey carried out by Marks, a substantial number of agoraphobics reported that their major difficulties started after a significant change had occurred in their life: "serious illness in patient or relative, acute danger or discomfort, leaving home, bereavement, engagement, marriage, pregnancy, miscarriage, childbirth ..."[9]

Agoraphobias, like social phobias, occasionally have a specific focus, but more commonly the manifestations are diffuse. The fears of animals or insects are, with few exceptions, confined to the phobic object and variations on that theme. People with such phobias hardly ever complain of chronically high levels of anxiety or of incapacitation or inconvenience outside of those situations in which the animal or insect does or may feature. The fear has a confined focus. It is a curious fact that, despite their onset in early childhood and their unvarying persistence, these focal fears are more easily reduced or eliminated than the diffuse fears acquired in early adulthood.

Fear of Death

In contrast to the considerable attention psychologists have devoted to the study of tangible fears, little systematic research has been applied to the nature of what are sometimes called existentialist fears. The shortage of information is illustrated by the literature on the fear of death. Research into this profound problem has been characterized by what D. Lester describes as a lack of ingenuity. He also points out that our understanding of this fear has increased very little compared to the progress in other areas of psychology.[10] The studies have relied on interviews or on simple questionnaire techniques, and most of the resulting information is negative. For example, the many attempts that have been made to relate fear of death to demographic variables such as age, occupation, income, urban or rural location, and so forth have failed to produce correlations of any great interest. The potentially rewarding analysis of the relation between religious convictions and attitudes towards death, has so far not proceeded beyond superficial approaches. Two isolated findings worth noting are that women express more preoccupation with death and fears of death, and that people who have completed a university education are better able and willing to discuss their conceptions and fears of death than are people who have not completed any form of higher education.

Lester has suggested that the unsatisfactory quality of presently available information about the fear of death is partly the result of a failure to distinguish between different aspects of the fear. He points out that earlier workers had argued successfully for a distinction to be made between a fear of one's own death, a fear of the death of others, and a fear of the effects of death.

In his monograph on dying, J. Hinton distinguished between the fear of one's own death, other people's death and a fear of the dead or their spirits.[11] Some support for these distinctions was later provided in a small study carried out by L. Collett and Lester.[12] They found that in a group of students the fear of one's own death and the fear of other people's death were uncorrelated (the correlation was only 0.03). An important aspect of the fear of death is the expectation of pain and suffering, and Hinton quotes a survey in which 90 percent of the respondents expressed a desire for a rapid end, presumably in the hope of avoiding pain.

It should be remembered that a fear of death is not always recognizable as such. When closely analyzed, many intensely frightening experiences, particularly those of a pathological type, are resolved into a fear of death. For example, numbers of patients who suffer from chronic and severe fears of being alone or of leaving the safety of their dens (agoraphobia) are most acutely aware of cardiac discomfort. These fears sometimes reflect a fear of death by heart failure. In cases of disease phobia, the connection with a fear of death is plain. In a group of psychiatric patients, G. Bianchi found excessive and irrational fears of cancer to be the most common disease-phobia (47 percent), closely followed by the fear of heart disease (30 percent).[13] He reported that patients who suffered from these morbid fears were more anxious, moody, and self-pitying than a comparable group of patients who had no phobias of disease.

A fear of death is of course neither universal nor unchanging. Numbers of people anticipate their own death with composure (longing for easeful death), and others seek a premature end by suicide. In some circumstances, one's death might be socially approved and feared less or not at all. The most obvious examples are seen in times of war, one of the most spectacular being that of the Kamikazes who eagerly volunteered for an honorable death.

In wartime, the social and personal pressures directed at the suppression of displays of fear provide an instructive example of the discrepancy between the various components of fear. Despite the presence of autonomic and other bodily feelings recognized as those of fear, the necessity to inhibit avoidance behavior obliges combat soldiers to maintain themselves in contact with intensely frightening circumstances. The accounts given by R. Grinker and J. Spiegel of the experiences of air crews during World War II show how the enormous social pressures maintained the men in intensely frightening missions even though the subjective and physiological components of their fears reached extraordinarily high levels.[14]

Chronic and Acute Fears

It is easy to distinguish between fears of short duration and chronic fears—those which sometimes last for several years, despite some fluctuations. Although relatively little scientific information about the nature of these chronic fears has been collected, it is not too difficult to describe some of their qualities, at least as they appear in clinical practice. Although they should not be taken as defining characteristics of chronic fears, the following three features often appear to be associated with chronicity: moderate or low level of fear, the content often is interpersonal, the eliciting stimuli tend to be multiple and difficult to specify. By contrast, acute fears tend to be more specific, specifiable, and circumscribed. Some people understandably prefer to distinguish between acute and chronic fears on the grounds that the acute are responses to easily identifiable, danger signals. Whereas this distinction undoubtedly has some value, it fails to explain acute fears that arise for no detectable reason. A description of such unprovoked panic attacks is provided by Malcolm Lader and Andrew Mathews.[15]

Although the chronicity of fears should not be confused with a stable predisposition to react fearfully, there is probably a significant overlap between the two phenomena. The possibility of a stable predisposition to react fearfully has been the subject of methodical study by C. Spielberger and other workers. This predisposition is commonly called *trait anxiety*, and is contrasted with *state anxiety*, which is regarded as a transitory emotional state of the kind treated in the greater part of this book—that is, acute feelings of apprehension, heightened psychophysiological reactivity, avoidance behavior. It should be noted however that Spielberger uses the subjective component of fear as the defining characteristic of this emotion: "... trait anxiety refers to relatively stable individual differences in anxiety proneness, that is, to differences in this disposition to perceive a wide range of stimulus situation as dangerous or threatening, and in the tendency to respond to such threats with anxiety state reactions. Anxiety trait may also be regarded as reflecting individual differences in the frequency and intensity with which anxiety states have been manifested in the past, and in the probability that such states will be experienced in future."[16]

The division of anxiety into these two categories is supported by a considerable amount of psychometric data, supplemented by some experimental demonstrations. For example, Spielberger and colleagues showed that, although the anxiety state scores of patients waiting to undergo surgery were significantly increased, their anxiety *trait* scores remained unaffected by this acute stress.[17] Experimental separations of the two concepts, as in this study, carry more weight than the overly enthusiastic collection of questionnaire responses from widely differing groups of arbitrarily chosen samples of subjects. Moreover, the scales developed by Spielberger, like others of comparable construction, have internal problems. Furthermore, some workers have failed to confirm the postulated independence of the two concepts of anxiety state and anxiety as a trait. For example, N. Endler and D. Magnusson found a correlation of 0.68 between the two scales.[18] In addition, they obtained data indicating that the two measures, the state and trait scales, are themselves heterogeneous.

Despite these difficulties, the distinction between state and trait anxiety is worth maintaining for the present time. Progress will probably be facilitated by redirecting more of the research efforts towards experimental rather than psychometric analyses of these concepts and their attributes. It is also to be hoped that further studies will be undertaken on the nature of chronic fears, and eventually on the relationship between this somewhat neglected type of fear and the concept of trait anxiety.

Individual Differences in Fear

The inadequacy of Spielberger's concept of trait anxiety aside, there are well founded reasons for believing in the existence of substantial individual differences in the ease with which people acquire new fears and the persistence with which fears endure. Although the acquisition and endurance of fears are probably related characteristics, it is not certain. The possibility that persistence of old fears may be a reflection of a slow rate of habituation to certain types of stimuli is a strong one, and it does not necessarily follow that slow habituators are the same people who readily acquire new and excessive fear reactions.

Individual differences in the acquisition of fears have received more attention than differences in habituation rate, and attempts have been made to link fearfulness with other attributes of personality. One such major attempt has been made by H. J. Eysenck[19] who proposed that neurotic disorders can be incorporated within his two-dimensional model of personality.[20] According to this scheme, two major dimensions along which personality can be viewed are extroversion-introversion on the one scale and neuroticism on the other scale, at right angles to the first (see Figure 4). This two-dimensional scheme has been the subject of a great deal of research and the evidence in support of it is considerable. The "typical extrovert" is outgoing, sociable, impulsive, optimistic,

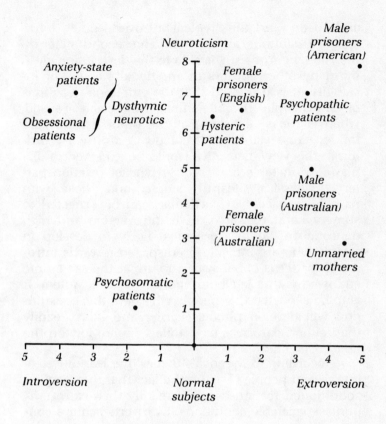

Figure 4 *The dimensions of personality. This pictorial summary of several surveys, in which introversion and neuroticism scales were used, shows the results obtained from various groups of subjects. Neurotic anxiety states, characterized by excessive fearfulness, are seen as a combination of high neuroticism and high introversion—upper left quadrant of the scheme. [From H. J. Eysenck,* Fact and Fiction in Psychology. *London: Penguin, 1965.]*

and so on, and the "typical introvert" quiet, introspective, cautious, and serious. The second major dimension, neuroticism, is akin to the description given by many other authors of emotional stability or instability. It is proposed that the emotional reactions of some people are labile, intense, and easily aroused, whereas those of people at the other extreme are milder, more stable, and difficult to arouse. According to this view, neurotics would be expected to display the unstable and intense type of reaction pattern. Excessively fearful people, and those with pathological fears in particular, can be expected to show a combination of high introversion and high neuroticism. Phobias are most likely to develop in people who are innately predisposed towards introverted patterns of behavior and are at the same time endowed with a labile autonomic nervous system. It is to be expected that people who have this constitution will develop phobias earlier and more readily than either extroverts or people who are low on the neuroticism scale.

According to Eysenck's theory, the fearfulness of introverted people rests on the fact that they acquire conditioned responses more readily than extroverts, under specifiable conditions. Extroverts acquire conditioned responses with difficulty, except under specific training conditions. In his book on fear, J. A. Gray attempted an important reinterpretation of parts of the Eysenckian theory: "Eysenck's suggestion is that [the extrovert] is bad at conditioning; my alternative suggestion is that he is bad at fear. That is, the extrovert is relatively insensitive to punishment and the threat of punishment." Gray's sophisticated revision comprises two principal hypotheses. In the first place, he postulates that neurotic tendencies are correlated with high sensitivity to environmental events. The second postulate is that, "increasing degrees of introversion represent increasing sensitivity to punishment rather than to reward." Although his proposals undoubtedly simplify some complex phenomena and notions, the wider utility of Gray's theory will not become apparent until further research on the principal hypotheses has been completed. The lucid presentation of the theory ensures that experimental tests can be designed and conducted without difficulty.[21]

Notes

1) T. Borkovec, et al., in A. Ciminero, Ed., *Handbook of Behavioral Assessment*, 1976.

2) J. Wolpe and P. Lang, *Behaviour Research and Therapy* **2**, 1964.

3) G. F. Lawlis, *Behaviour Research and Therapy* **9**, 1971.

4) S. Agras, D. Sylvester, and D. Oliveau, *Comprehensive Psychiatry* **10**, 1969.

5) J. Wolpe, *Psychotherapy by Reciprocal Inhibition*, 1958.

6) I. M. Marks, *Fears and Phobias*, 1969.

7) S. Rachman and R. Hodgson, *Obsessions and Compulsions*, 1979.

8) I. M. Marks and E. R. Herst, *Social Psychiatry* **5**, 1970.

9) Marks and Herst, 1970, p. 128.

10) D. Lester, *Psychological Bulletin* **67**, 1967.

11) J. Hinton, *Dying*, 1967.

12) L. Collett and D. Lester, *Journal of Psychology* **72**, 1969.

13) G. Bianchi, *Australian Journal of Psychiatry* **5**, 1971.

14) R. Grinker and J. Spiegel, *Men under Stress*, 1945.

15) M. Lader and A. Mathews, *Behaviour Research and Therapy* **6**, 1968.

16) C. Spielberger, *Anxiety: Current Trends*, 1972, p. 39.

17) C. Spielberger et al., *Journal of Consulting and Clinical Psychology* **40**, 1973.

18) N. Endler and D. Magnusson, in C. Spielberger, Ed., *Cross-Cultural Anxiety*, 1976.

19) H. J. Eysenck, *The Biological Basis of Personality*, 1967.

20) The recent addition of a third major dimension, psychoticism, has no immediate relevance to the question of individual differences in fear-propensity.

21) J. A. Gray, *The Psychology of Fear and Stress* 1971, pp. 230, 233.

Chapter 9
The Reduction
of Fear

Advances in the techniques for reducing fear have been impressive, as mentioned at the beginning of this book. In fact the techniques for *changing* fear have preceded a full study of the phenomenon itself.

The advances have been part of a wider scientific movement culminating in new forms of psychological treatment, collectively described as behavior therapy.[1] The term *behavior therapy* refers both to a group of techniques for treating a variety of psychological disorders and deficits and also to a theory of psychological problems and their modification. Many of the underlying ideas and some of the methods of behavior therapy are exemplified in the approach to the problem of reducing fear.

One of the most interesting antecedents of the current approach to fear reduction is found in the work of J. B. Watson, the father of behavioristic psychology, and of Mary Cover Jones. Watson and R. Rayner gave details of their important demonstration of how a fear can be acquired. They taught a young boy, known as little Albert, to fear a white rat and similar stimuli, by repeatedly associating the appearance of the rat with a frightening loud noise.[2] With this work in mind, Jones in 1924 applied a conditioning method in order to overcome the fears of a three-year-old boy, Peter. The child displayed a fear of white rats, rabbits, fur, cotton wool and other stimuli of this type. Because the fear of the rabbits appeared to be a focus of Peter's general fears, it was decided to reduce this one first. He was gradually introduced to contacts with a rabbit during his daily play period. He was placed in a play group with three fearless children, and the rabbit was brought into the room for short periods each day. Peter's tolerance of the rabbit gradually improved. The progressive steps used in the process included placing the rabbit in a cage twelve feet away, then four feet away, then close by but still in the cage; then the rabbit was set free in the room; eventually Peter was fondling the rabbit. Another method involved the use of feeding responses. The boy was given desired food whenever the rabbit was shown, and as a result the fear was eliminated gradually in favor of a positive response. Using these techniques, Jones overcame Peter's fear of rabbits and related fears. The follow-up study of this child showed no resurgence of the fear of rabbits or related stimuli.[3]

The similarities between Jones's method and more recent variations can be illustrated by reference to a case described by Eysenck and Rachman. The seven-year-old boy with a phobia of bees described on page 120 in Chapter 7 was referred for treatment. The phobia, which was intense and interfered with many of his activities (e.g., playing in the garden), had been present for three years. Although the boy could not remember having received a bee sting, he knew of several people who had been stung and/or had displayed excessive fear of bees. After a full investigation had elicited the nature of his fear, a list of fear-producing situations was compiled. The techniques chosen to help him overcome the fear were feeding responses, social approval, and exposure to visual stimuli that were progressively more realistic. At first the boy was shown small photographs of bees and then he was assisted through the following stages: large photographs, colored photographs, dead bees in a bottle at the far end of the room, dead bee in bottle brought gradually closer, dead bee out of the bottle, dead bee on coat, gradually increasing manipulation of the dead bee, introduction of several dead bees, playing imaginative games with the dead bees. The boy made gradual and systematic progress, and after eight sessions he and his mother both reported a considerable improvement. His mother stated that he was "Very much improved ... he no longer has the physical reaction. He used to go white, sweaty, cold and trembling, and his legs were like jelly. He can now play alone in the garden quite comfortably." A long-term follow-up study showed no recurrence of the phobia.[4]

Mary Cover Jones's prescience is shown by the fact that all five of her recommended methods for overcoming fear are used, in modern dress, in present-day clinics and schools. Pointing out that neither verbal reassurance nor disapproval is a satisfactory means of reducing fear, she recommended the following five methods: social imitation, feeding responses, systematic distraction, affectionate responses, or direct conditioning.

Systematic Desensitization

In recent times a major advance was recorded by a medical psychologist, Professor Joseph Wolpe, who carried out pioneering studies on the induction and treatment of experimental neurotic conditions in animals and then translated his findings into clinical practice.[5] The fear-reduction technique he developed for clinical purposes, *systematic desensitization*, has also had many applications in nonclinical settings. The technique comprises two main elements: First the subject is given systematic training in muscle relaxation, and second he is asked to imagine increasingly fearful scenes while in a state of calm relaxation. In practice, the technique is one of gradual and graduated imaginal presentation of fear-producing scenes, the nature and grading of the scenes having been decided upon by subject and therapist in discussion. With repeated practice of the imaginal experience of the fearful scenes, the subject or patient gradually acquires the ability to tolerate the fearful ideas or scenes in his imagination and this improvement generally transfers to the real situation. The clinical value of desensitization aside, let us examine the contribution it has made towards our increased understanding of fear and its modification.

Much of our knowledge about fear has been obtained from the study of subjects who show an excessive fear of spiders, snakes, worms, and the like.[6] Prompted by Wolpe's experimental reports and clinical accounts, P. Lang and D. Lazovik carried out an experiment which became the model for a flood of similar studies on modification of fear.[7] Their pioneer experiment, carefully designed and executed, was carried out on 24 snake-phobic students at Pittsburgh University. Each subject was chosen from a larger pool of fearful students, who in turn had been chosen from a still larger group of randomly selected students. The 24 experimental subjects were chosen not only on the grounds of their subjective estimates of their own fear, but also on the basis of their overtly observed fear in a behavioral avoidance test during which they were exposed to a live but harmless snake. Having verified that their subjects were indeed intensely fearful, Lang and Lazovik divided them into two groups, one of which received desensitization while the other acted as a no-treatment control group. Each subject in the experimental group was given up to 11 sessions of systematic desensitization during which they were asked to imagine increasingly fearful situations involving snakes, while they remained in a deeply relaxed state. The control subjects were given relaxation training and participated, like the experimental subjects, in the construction of a graded list of fear-provoking situations involving snakes. At the termination of the experimental treatment period both groups of subjects were reassessed and the results showed that the subjects who had received desensitization were significantly less fearful of snakes than their control group counterparts. These reductions in fear were observed in both subjective and psychometric ratings as well as in the overt behavioral avoidance tests. Moreover, these changes were found to be maintained for at least six months when the follow-up investigation was carried out. In a subsequent study by Lang, Lazovik, and Reynolds it was demonstrated that desensitization produces a *specific change* over and above any modification that might result from the general therapeutic preliminaries or atmosphere.[8]

In this second experiment, control subjects, who were given a cleverly designed form of pseudotherapy, showed little change. It was also shown to be unnecessary for the experimental therapists to delve into the presumed basic causes of the subjects' fear of snakes. The development of a sympathetic relationship between the therapist and his subject was not sufficient to bring about changes in the fear of snakes. Last, their experimental results demonstrated that desensitization of a specific fear generalizes in a positive fashion to other fears and that modest all-round reductions in fear might be expected.

Virtually all of the conclusions reached by Lang and his colleagues have now been confirmed by other experimenters, using the same and different techniques, the same and different subjects, the same and different assessment procedures. The extent of the investivations and the surprising degree of agreement in their outcome has never been matched in any similar undertaking in abnormal psychology or its clinical applications.[9]

The rehearsal of fearful scenes in imagination while the subject is in a state of relaxation—desensitization—has proved to be a robust technique for reducing fear. Numerous variations have been attempted in experimental studies—shortening the imaginal rehearsal time, abbreviating the number of training sessions, not graduating the fearful scenes, and so on—and in virtually all studies at least a moderate degree of fear reduction has been obtained. In addition to providing general support for Wolpe's claims, workers have also explored the nature of the desensitization process itself. For example, several attempts have been made to isolate the effective elements in the procedure. Thus far the evidence suggests that the fear-reducing effects of desensitization are potentiated by the combined action of relaxation instructions and graduated presentations of fearful images. However, the role and action of muscle-relaxation training has been the subject of critical reexamination.[10] Although muscle-relaxation training facilitates desensitization, it is not a prerequisite for the reduction of fear.

The experimental evidence on reduction of fear by desensitization can be summarized in this way. The imaginal rehearsal of graded fearful scenes effectively reduces fear; this process can be facilitated by relaxation. The power of desensitization is greatly enhanced by *in vivo* exposures. The reductions in fear are reflected in subjective reactions as well as by increases in overt approach behavior—but less clearly or reliably by psychophysiological indexes, such as skin-resistance changes. The subjective and behavioral measures of fear correlate moderately well with each other, but slightly or not at all with psychophysiological indexes of change. The measures of fear reduction do not change at the same speed.

It is unnecessary to ascertain the origin or putative symbolic significance of a fear in order to eliminate it. Neither is it necessary to change the subject's basic attitudes or to attempt to modify aspects of his personality in order to reduce his fears. The elimination of a fear, or a clinical phobia, is rarely followed by the appearance of new fears or substitute problems. The extent of the response to desensitization, that is, the degree of fear reduction, is not related to the subject's suggestibility. Relaxation, alone or accompanied by pseudotherapeutic interviews, does not reduce fears of phobias. The establishment of a sympathetic relationship with the subject does not itself reduce the fear although it might facilitate the process. Interpretive methods combined with relaxation reduce fear slightly or not at all.

Although presentations of imaginary fear-evoking scenes confer numerous practical advantages, evidence suggests that real-life exposures are usually more effective, particularly if they are graduated. We also have evidence that the reduction of fear by desensitization can be carried out as an automated procedure and, although the practical consequences of automation should not be underestimated, their theoretical significance is greater. While we need not discount the possible contribution a sympathetic therapist or experimenter might make to reducing someone's fears, a wholly satisfactory explanation of desensitization effects must take into account the expendability of a therapist. Certainly any attempt to account for the fear-reducing effects of desensitization which relies wholly or largely on the personality or presence of a therapist is unlikely to succeed.

Although this book is not concerned with the clinical application of fear-reducing techniques, it is worth mentioning that desensitization, among other techniques of behavior therapy, has been applied to clinical populations with some degree of success.[11]

Flooding

Since the early 1970s a new fear-reducing technique called *flooding* has been introduced into both experimental investigations and clinical practice. Although there are one or two variations on the main technique, the essence of flooding is the prolonged exposure of a fearful subject to intense stimulation. The impetus for the development of this technique came largely from experimental investigations on small animals: fears were artificially engendered and then reduced in the animals by exposing them to the intense fear-evoking stimuli and preventing their escape. It was found that in many circumstances this exposure to high-intensity stimulation led to rapid reductions in fear. The introduction of flooding was also stimulated by the clinical work of T. Stampfl who developed a treatment technique called *implosive therapy*, in which patients were deliberately required to imagine scenes of great unpleasantness that were derived from the psychodynamic explorations carried out by the therapist.[12] The material derived in this way was introduced into treatment and the person was asked to relive in his imagination distressing experiences of his past, particularly his childhood. Although the theoretical explanations proposed by Stampfl are unconvincing, some of the clinical effects he reported generated considerable interest and contributed to the development of the flooding technique. Flooding is usually carried out in real life, although it can of course be presented to the subject in imagination only. After the subject and therapist or experimenter have determined the nature of the subject's most intense fears, he is exposed to them either in actuality or in imagination, for prolonged periods. This technique can reduce the fear substantially and, when it does, it is usually within a surprisingly brief period. The clinical effects of flooding are still under active investigation but the indications are encouraging.[13]

Therapeutic Modeling

In view of the extensive and convincing evidence that desensitization is capable of reducing fear, any method that is claimed to produce results superior to those of desensitization bears close inspection. The first claim of this type was made by A. Bandura, E. Blanchard, and B. Ritter.[14] They reported that the technique of live imitation (modeling) followed by the fearful subject participating in approach behavior, produced a significantly larger reduction in fear of snakes than did desensitization (see Figure 5). This experimental report was remarkable for the magnitude of the change obtained by imitation (modeling) plus participation—in 92 percent of the subjects the excessive fear of snakes was virtually eliminated. The practical application of imitation learning, usually called *modeling* nowadays, is also interesting for two other reasons. It was one of the two principal methods recommended by Mary Cover Jones in her 1924 paper: "social imitation (in which) we allowed subjects to share, under controlled conditions, the social activity of a group of children especially chosen with a view to prestige effect."[15] Moreover, in addition to its therapeutic value, imitation learning is important in attempting to construct a satisfactory explanation of the genesis and course of fear.

A good deal of the recent work is the product of Bandura and his colleagues who argue that modeling has three important psychological functions: the models transmit new patterns of coping behavior, prevent or interrupt unnecessary responses (includ-

Figure 5 *The results of an experiment on the reduction of a fear of snakes, showing mean improvements from pretest to post-treatment test. Increases in approach responses are indicative of fear reduction. Both desensitization and modeling treatments were superior to the control condition, and participant modeling was most effective of all. [From A. Bandura, E. Blanchard, and B. Ritter,* Journal of Personality and Social Psychology **13**. *Copyright © 1969 by the American Psychological Association. Reprinted by permission.]*

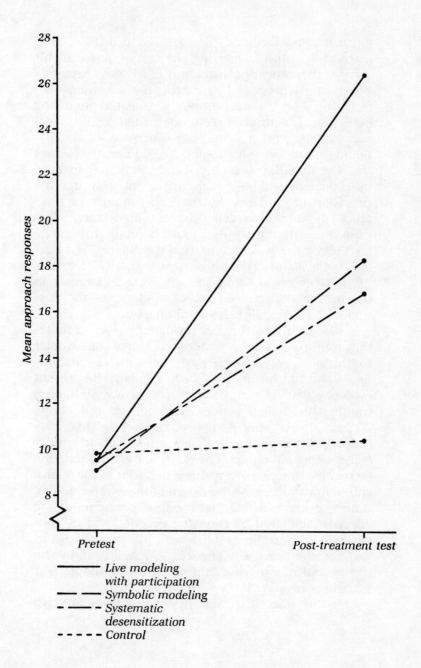

Mean approach responses

28
26
24
22
20
18
16
14
12
10
8

Pretest   Post-treatment test

——— Live modeling
      with participation
— — Symbolic modeling
— · — Systematic
      desensitization
- - - - Control

ing fear), and facilitate the expression of previously learned adaptive behavior.[16] In consequence of his general theoretical position and of his own research, Bandura has proposed a new therapeutic strategy for reducing fear. He recommends repeated modeling experiences, with multiple models the fearful subject can imitate, and a progressive increase in the demands made on the subject. In addition, he argues that the imitation learning should be supplemented by repeated, real-life practice that incorporates the provision of guidance by the experimenter or therapist. By way of a general recommendation, Bandura urges that attempts should be made to arrange for the regular reinforcement of newly acquired fearless behavior in order to ensure that it will endure. All these efforts are aimed at achieving an increase in the person's "perceived self-competence"—the postulated basis for all behavioral change.

Research into the fear-reducing power of imitation training has been conducted along lines similar to those of research carried out with desensitization—and the results have been similar. The present evidence can be summarized in this way. Imitation training (modeling) produces significant reductions of fear under specified circumstances. This fear-reduction is enduring and also generalizes to similar fear-evoking situations. The continuation of modeling by real-life practice of approach behavior to the fearful situation will increase the extent of the fear reduction. It also seems probable that the therapeutic modeling effect is facilitated by repeated practice and by prolonged exposure times, both within a session and in real life situations. The effect is also facilitated by the use of multiple models and the use of multiple fear situations or stimuli.[17]

At this stage it would appear that there are two

major determinants of the fear-reducing effects of modeling training. These appear to be the number of successful exposures to the model and the total time of successful exposures to the model. Of course it is not argued that modeling is a necessary condition for the reduction of fear, but rather that it can facilitate such reductions.

Naturally the introduction of this other powerful method for reducing fear has been welcome. However, modeling does raise some problems that require explanation. For example, if it is so successful in reducing fear, why do not timid people automatically model fearless conduct in their natural environments? Why is it that the exposure to a model within an experimental or clinical context appears to achieve what has not been achieved elsewhere, despite the presence of other fearless models? The possible replies to these questions are several, and all of them may contribute to a final answer. First, large numbers of people do in fact lose many of their fears in the natural environment. As we have seen in the section on children's fears, the great majority of these decline in middle to late childhood and certainly by the time of adolescence. Presumably, a significant part of the explanation for this natural disappearance of fear can be attributed to the spontaneous occurrence of repeated exposures to fearless models in the environment. An explanation for some failures of spontaneous fear reduction might rest with the fact that some people are repeatedly exposed to *fearful* models and, as we have already seen, children probably learn some fears by modeling their parents. If a person has been repeatedly exposed to a fearful mother or other person, it is possible that he will continue to experience and manifest fear in a wider variety of situations than will his peers. Finally, some intense fears are not easily reduced—by modeling or any other deliberate systematic procedure. Although it is too early to be sure, it seems probable that those people and those fears which are resistant to change will respond readily to neither desensitization, flooding, nor modeling.

Although significant advances have been made, we must not exaggerate what can be achieved. In some studies modeling made little impact.[18] In research into the treatment of patients with severe obsessional problems, we have also had some clinical failures; for example, some of them were unable to approach their dreaded situations despite intensive modeling treatment.[19] This type of failure is largely the result of extraordinarily high levels of fear.

Three obstacles to the successful use of therapeutic modeling can be discerned, but they are not insuperable. First, as mentioned earlier, some people simply do not experience fear-reduction. Second, some learn the necessary skill or bravery during the sessions of modeling, but fail to translate the learning into performance. Third, some people acquire skills or bravery through modeling and even transfer their new skills to the natural environment for a short period, but they then experience a failure of maintenance—this is not a new clinical problem, of course, but one for which therapeutic modeling confers no immunity.

The advantageous features of therapeutic modeling include the following. It is capable of acting rapidly. It can transmit large and complex units of behavior. It is readily accepted by most people—the problems of noncooperation are ones of skepticism rather than reluctance or distaste. It is simple to explain and easily understood. Last, it is easy to provide advice, practical advice at that, about how to reduce and prevent fears.

A Comparison of the Three Methods

In summary, what are the findings on fear reduction? Except for those disabling fears which require the assistance of a professional therapist, what are the simplest and most effective methods for overcoming or reducing fears?

The fearful person should be exposed repeatedly to demonstrations of increasingly fearless coping behavior exhibited by an appropriate model. After several repetitions of this passive form of modeling, he should be gradually integrated into the modeling exercises. That is, he should imitate the coping behavior of the model in gradual and graduated steps until he is able to approximate the fearless behavior himself. The model should provide feedback and encouragement in the course of his attempts at guided participation. In children, the process can be facilitated by the use of feeding and affectionate responses at critical stages in the learning process, particularly when hesitations occur. Another important technique for overcoming fears is the rehearsal of increasingly fearless coping behavior, either in imagination or actuality, preferably while the subject is in a calm state.

The reduction of disabling fears may require the assistance of a professional therapist, although it is as well to bear in mind that roughly two-thirds of all neurotic conditions in which fear is prominent improve spontaneously within a two-year period.[20] Where professional assistance is obtained, it may take one of three forms, alone or in combination. Most frequently, tranquilizing drugs will be prescribed. Depending on the history and severity of the pathological fear and the general state of the person, either psychotherapy or behavior therapy might be recommended. The effects of psychotherapy con-

The three major fear-reduction methods

Method	Description
Systematic desensitization	Gradual and graduated
	Facilitated by relaxation
	Enhanced by in vivo practice
Flooding	Rapid exposure to the avoided stimuli
	In vivo most effective
	Anxiety evocation unnecessary
	When effective, results obtained quickly
Modeling	Usually graduated
	Well suited to group administration and to prevention
	Enhanced by in vivo participation

tinue to be a controversial issue and in intensive treatment such as psychoanalysis, the person is more likely to experience general changes of a diffuse kind rather than a remission of the specific fears for which he initially sought assistance.[21]

Of the three major behavioral methods, desensitization and flooding are the most widely practiced at present, and their success rate is high, particularly when the fears are circumscribed (but not only then). The newly developed method of flooding is not fully understood, but the indications are that it provides a rapid alternative to desensitization—without a loss of effectiveness. In practice the major problem may be one of obtaining the active cooperation of patients, although early experience with this technique has been surprisingly free of problems. Given a choice between the slow, steady method of desensitization and the fast, uncomfortable method of flooding, the majority of patients appear to prefer the quick method. The therapeutic value of modeling has not yet been fully exploited, but present evidence suggests it is likely to become an exceptionally useful procedure for reducing existing fears and for preventing the emergence of new ones.[22] Methods of preventing fear are discussed in Chapter 14.

Notes

1) There is an impressively large literature on behavior therapy, including no less than seven journals devoted exclusively to the subject. A full reading list is unwarranted and the selection given here should provide an adequate opening and an historical perspective. Wolpe (1958) is a seminal work by one of the leading contributors to the growth of behavior therapy. Bandura (1969) is a scholarly text that covers most aspects of the subject with critical understanding, combined with fresh and constructive ideas. Several texts that are well worth consulting include Rimm and Masters, 1975, O'Leary and Wilson, 1975, Eysenck, 1976, Feldman and Broadhurst, 1976.

2) J. Watson and R. Rayner, *Journal of Experimental Psychology* **3**, 1920.

3) M. C. Jones, *Pedagogical Seminars* **31**, 1924.

4) H. J. Eysenck and S. Rachman, *The Causes and Cures of Neurosis*, 1965, p. 210.

5) J. Wolpe, *Psychotherapy by Reciprocal Inhibition*, 1958, and *The Practice of Behavior Therapy*, 1973.

6) See H. J. Eysenck, *Case Studies in Behaviour Therapy*, 1976; D. Rimm and J. Masters, *Behavior Therapy: Techniques and Empirical Findings*, 1974; G. Paul, *Insight versus Desensitization*, 1966; S. Rachman, *Psychological Bulletin* **67**, 1967, and *The Effects of Psychotherapy*, 1971.

7) P. Lang and D. Lazowik, *Journal of Abnormal and Social Psychology* **66**, 1963.

8) P. Lang, D. Lazowik, and C. Reynolds, *Journal of Abnormal and Social Psychology* **70**, 1966.

9) Rachman, 1967, 1971.

10) S. Rachman, *Behaviour Research and Therapy* **6**, 1968.

11) Reviews are provided in Eysenck, 1976; Marks, 1969; Meyer and Chesser, 1970; Beech, 1968; Bandura, 1969; O'Leary and Wilson, 1975; Rachman, 1971; Rimm and Masters, 1975; and many others.

12) T. Stampfl, in D. Levis, Ed., *Learning Approaches to Therapeutic Behavior Change*, 1970.

13) Rachman, 1971; Rachman and G. T. Wilson, *The Effects of Psychotherapy*, 2d Ed., in preparation.

14) A. Bandura, E. Blanchard, and B. Ritter, *Journal of Personality and Social Psychology* **13**, 1969.

15) Jones, 1924, p. 390.

16) A. Bandura, *The Principles of Behavior Modification*, 1969; Bandura, *Social Learning Theory*, 1976; T. Rosenthal and Bandura, in A. Bergin and S. Garfield, Eds., *Handbook of Psychotherapy and Behavior Change*, 2d Ed., 1971.

17) S. Rachman, *Behavior Therapy* 3, 1972; Rachman, in M. Feldman and A. Broadhurst, Eds., *Theoretical Bases of Behavior Therapy*, 1976.

18) G. Roper, S. Rachman, and I. Marks, *Behavior Research and Therapy*, 1975.

19) S. Rachman, R. Hodgson, and I. Marks, *Behaviour Research and Therapy* **11**, 1973.

20) S. Rachman, *The Effects of Psychotherapy*, 1971; Rachman and G. T. Wilson, in preparation.

21) D. Hamburg, Ed., *Report of an ad hoc Committee on Central Fact-gathering Data*, 1967.

22) Bandura, 1969; Rachman, 1976; Rosenthal and Bandura, 1978.

Chapter 10

The Conditioning Theory of Fear Acquisition

It has been shown in countless experiments that animals readily acquire fears.[1] The evidence accumulated in these experiments (particularly those on the induction of neuroses), supplemented by naturalistic and clinical observations, led to the formulation of a theory that was intended to explain the genesis and spread of fears. It is assumed that fears are acquired and that the process of acquisition is one of conditioning.

Although the conditioning theory of fear acquisition, in one or another version, appears to be influential there has not been much debate about its merits. The theory is interesting in its own right and also because it is incorporated into other theories, especially those on avoidance behavior. From a practical point of view, it underlies much of the thinking incorporated into those forms of behavior therapy directed at fear reduction (such as desensitization and flooding, discussed in Chapter 9). One version of the theory originated in the important work of O. H. Mowrer, who stated, "the position here taken is that anxiety is a learned response, occurring to signals (conditioned stimuli) that are premonitory of (i.e. have in the past been followed by) situations of injury or pain (unconditioned stimuli)." He went on to argue that fear "may effectively motivate human beings" and that the reduction of fear "may serve powerfully to reinforce behaviour that brings about such a state of relief or security."[2] Mowrer's theory owed most to the writings of Pavlov, Freud, James, and Watson and the developments from Mowrer's position follow in the same tradition, amply encouraged by the fruitful research on the experimental induction of fears in animals. As it provides a clear illustration of the main features and flaws of conditioning theories, I will take as my main example a version with which I have been associated.

Basing their theory on a combination of research findings—drawn from the field of experimental neuroses (including the original experiments of Wolpe[3]), their own clinical observations, and the influential writings of Mowrer, and of J. Watson and R. Rayner[4]—J. Wolpe and S. Rachman proposed, "Any neutral stimulus, simple or complex, that happens to make an impact on an individual at about the time that a fear reaction is evoked, acquires the ability to evoke fear subsequently ... there will be generalization of fear reactions to stimuli resembling the conditioned stimulus."[5] This conception was elaborated by Rachman and C. Costello who summarized the essentials of the theory in six statements. After restating the elements of the original proposition, they added three new features. It was argued that neutral stimuli which are of relevance in the particular situation are more likely to become fear signals, that the repetition of the association between fear and the new phobic stimuli will strengthen the fear, and that associations of high-intensity fear situations and neutral stimuli are more likely to produce conditioned fear reactions.[6] In 1965, three more elements were added and further consideration was given to the determinants of the strength of the fear. H. J. Eysenck and Rachman proposed that fear reactions are more likely to occur under conditions of excessive confinement.[7] They also incorporated the motivating qualities of the fear reaction in a manner originally proposed by Mowrer. Shortly after this extension was published, some of the difficulties now acknowledged began to appear. This led to a revision that for the first time incorporated the possibility, indeed the certainty, that emotional reactions, including fear, can be acquired vicariously. This revision, which allowed that fears may be acquired directly *or* vicariously,[8] led to a critical scrutiny of the whole theory.

Before we embark on an analysis of the limitations of the conditioning theory, it might be well to give a concise account of some of the arguments and evidence in favor of the theory.

Acquisition of Fears by Conditioning

The major features of the theory are as follows. It is assumed that fears are acquired and that the process of acquisition is a form of conditioning. Neutral stimuli that are associated with a fear or pain-producing state of affairs, develop fearful qualities, that is, they become fear conditioned stimuli. The strength of the fear is determined by the number of repetitions of the association between the pain/fear experience and the stimuli, and also by the intensity of the fear or pain experienced in the presence of the stimuli. Stimuli resembling the fear-evoking ones also acquire fearful properties, that is, they become secondary conditioned stimuli. The likelihood of fear developing is increased by confinement, by exposure to high-intensity pain and/or fear situations and by frequent repetition of the association between the new conditioned stimulus and the pain/fear. It was proposed further that once objects or situations acquire fear-provoking qualities, they develop motivating properties—that is, a secondary fear-drive emerges. Behavior patterns such as avoidance actions, which successfully reduce fear, increase in strength.

Supporting evidence was drawn from six sources: research on the induction of fear in animals, the development of anxiety states in combat soldiers, experiments on the induction of fear in a small number of children, clinical observations (e.g., dental phobias), incidental findings from the use of aversion therapy, and a few experiments on the effects of traumatic stimulation.

The strongest and most systematic evidence was drawn from a multitude of experiments on laboratory animals. Evidently it is easy to generate fear reactions in animals by exposing them to a conjunction of neutral and aversive stimulation, usually electric shock. These acquired fear reactions (usually inferred from the emergence of avoidance behavior, physiological disturbances and disruptive behavior, or by some combination of these three indexes) can be produced readily by employing conventional conditioning procedures. There is little room for doubt about the facility with which fear reactions can be conditioned—at least in animals tested under laboratory constraints. As we shall see, however, there are grounds for doubting whether the laboratory process of fear acquisition provides an adequate foundation for theorizing about fear acquisition in nonlaboratory conditions, and in human subjects in or out of the laboratory. The demonstration that fears can be generated by conditioning does not mean that is how they are ordinarily acquired.

Observations and analysis of people under combat conditions clearly show that intense fear can result from traumatic stimulation (Chapters 3 and 4). J. Flanagan reported that the overwhelming majority of combat air crew experienced fear during their missions and although these reactions were relatively transient, they often presaged the development of (reversible) combat fatigue. A minority of combat crew-members developed significant, lasting fears.[9] The form of these fears and the conditions under which they arose are consistent with conditioning theory.

In clinical practice it is not uncommon for patients to give an account of the development of their fears that can be construed in conditioning terms (e.g., they might date from a specific experience). Similarly, from a study conducted on 34 cases of dental phobia we learn that every subject reported having had a traumatic dental experience (such as fearing suffocation from an anaesthetic mask) on at least one occasion in childhood.[10] However, these 34 people were found to be generally neurotic while another 10 comparison subjects who had experienced comparable traumatic incidents with dentists during their childhood, showed little sign of dental fears. Then, as mentioned in Chapter 9, Watson and Rayner provided a classical demonstration of the genesis of a fear in a young child, little Albert—a finding that was tested by a number of research workers, with varying degrees of success and failure (see page 124).

Incidental observations arising out of the use of aversion therapy, a technique explicitly based on classical conditioning theory, provide some support for the theory.[11] After undergoing repeated associations between alcohol and chemically-induced nausea, many patients experience nausea when they taste or even smell alcohol. In a famous case reported by D. Hammersley, a successfully treated patient subsequently changed his mind and decided that abstinence was not the lesser of two evils.[12] He then embarked on a "de-conditioning" program and repeatedly drank himself through many episodes of intense nausea until this conditioned reaction to alcohol subsided and finally disappeared.

R. Hallam and S. Rachman described yet another reaction: "Another alcoholic patient who had been given whisky to drink during (electrical) aversion treatment accused the therapist of adding a chemical to the whisky to give it a bad taste." (This is a common report even when no chemicals are used). The same patient "went into a bar against advice during treatment, but on trying to raise a glass of whisky to his mouth he had a panic attack and returned to hospital in an anxious state."[13]

Bancroft observed the development of intense anxiety reactions among some of his patients, but he was careful to point out that the large majority showed no signs of conditioned fear reactions, regardless of the success or failure of the treatment program.[14] These incidental clinical findings indicate that what appear to be conditioned fear responses can develop during aversion treatment; it does not necessarily follow that they are causally relevant to the outcome of therapy. Moreover, there is a serious difficulty in all this. In contrast to evidence of the kind referred to here, other results from research on aversion therapy have failed to confirm predictions drawn from the theory (see below).

A final source of support for a conditioning theory of fear acquisition comes from experiments in which subjects were given injections of scoline, which produces a temporary suspension of breathing.[15] Not surprisingly, most of the subjects who were subjected to this harrowing experience developed intense fears of the stimuli encountered in, or connected with, the experimental situation. In fact the intensity of their fears tended to increase, even in the absence of further unpleasant experiences.

The conditioning theory of fear acquisition does not require single trial or traumatic onset, but fears that arise in an acute manner are more readily accommodated than those of uncertain onset. Even though acute onset fears are more easily accommodated (partly I suspect because our conception of conditioned fear is based on laboratory experiments in which the aversive stimulus often is traumatic), we also have to account for fears that are produced by experiences of a subtraumatic or even of a non-traumatic nature.

Fears that emerge in the absence of any identifiable learning experience present difficulties for the theory. Hence, fears that develop gradually (e.g. social fears) and cannot be traced to specific occurrences are a potential embarrassment.

Although the importance of the phenomenon of acquired taste aversions was not made evident until

1966, it may provide buttressing for the conditioning theory. J. Garcia and his colleagues were the first to demonstrate that strong and lasting aversive reactions can be acquired with ease when the appropriate taste stimulus is associated with illness.[16] The phenomenon was given the catch name of "sauce Bearnaise" by M. Seligman and J. Hager who elucidated the theoretical significance of the research.[17] If we allow that the genesis of these taste aversions is a form of conditioning, and if we also agree to an equation between the acquisition of a taste aversion and the acquisition of a fear, this recent literature may yet provide the best evidence for a conditioning theory of fear acquisition. In Seligman's use of these findings, phobias are seen as instances of highly "prepared" learning—and as, we have seen, this prepared learning is "selective, highly resistant to extinction, probably noncognitive and can be acquired in one trial."[18]

Although the issue is far from settled, the preliminary results from a current investigation of the similarities between fear and taste aversions suggest that people may show comparable psychophysiological reactions to, and avoidance of, nasty tastes and frightening objects.[19] We also have some evidence that taste aversions can be modified by graded practice in much the same way as fears are reduced. It is still unclear whether the subjective reactions differ in any significant respects.

The idea that taste aversions and fear are related, also receives some indirect support from findings such as the elevated incidence of food aversions among neurotic subjects. In an interesting study reported in 1945, R. Wallen compared 214 normal adults with 95 subjects of comparable age who had been rejected from the U.S. Navy on the grounds of neurosis.[20] The neurotic subjects reported four times as many food aversions as the normal subjects. As neurotics have more fears than nonneurotic subjects, it seems possible that they have a sensitivity of some type that predisposes them to acquire fears and aversions more easily than other people. If the acquisition of taste aversions is used as a basis for supporting or expanding the conditioning theory of fear, it will have to take into account the unexpected temporal stretch of the taste aversion phenomenon (the delay that supervenes between tasting the food and the onset of nausea). Classical conditioning is of course expedited by temporal proximity between stimuli; although there are convincing examples of conditioned responses being established even when delays are prolonged, these tend to be exceptions. But experimentally induced taste aversions are easily, powerfully, and rapidly established, even when long delays occur between the two stimulus events. It is plain therefore that if the taste aversion phenomenon is to provide the basis for a new or revised conditioning theory of fear, the temporal qualities of classical conditioning processes must be deemphasized.

Certainly the evidence provides strong support for the notion that fears can be acquired by a conditioning process. This conclusion is justified even though some of the evidence is subject to contrary interpretations, or is inherently weak. The strongest evidence, both in the sense of its replicability and completeness, comes from the genesis of fear in laboratory animals. This voluminous and hard evidence is supported by some limited findings on the induction of fear reactions in adult humans (but it should be noted that the stimuli employed were of a traumatic nature). The work on the induction of fear in children is not consistent, is based on a very small sampling, and all of the experiments can be criticized for errors of confounding, experimenter contamination, and other flaws. Psychiatric reports and other clinical observations provide interesting supporting evidence but unfortunately the quality of information is unsatisfactory, comprising as it almost always does a selected set of observations rarely supported by external confirmatory evidence. It also suffers from the serious weakness that the subject or the patient's account of the genesis of his fear relies on an accurate memory and powers of recall. Most people will agree that this is an unsatisfactory basis for theory building. Because it has greater immediacy and the possibility of at least some external confirmation, the evidence on combat fears and combat neuroses, has something to recommend it. Regrettably, almost none of this valuable information was collected in a systematic manner; it therefore suffers from incompleteness, selection bias, and the interpretive gloss placed on the accounts by the reporting psychiatrist or psychologist. Nevertheless it is material rich in interest and authentic in quality. Fortunately military combat is an exceptional experience and, for purposes of psychological theorizing, it would be unwise to overemphasize the significance of fears acquired in these unnatural circumstances. Also, the intriguing research on taste aversions may well have opened the door for the development of an adequate theory of non-rational fears. In outlining the types and sources of evidence in support of the conditioning theory of fear acquisition, an attempt has been made to convey the impression that there is a good deal to be said in its favor. Why then is it necessary to revise it? Although it has merits, and some experimental and clinical support, its applicability is limited. Whatever its value, the theory is not a satisfactory *comprehensive* account of the genesis and maintenance of fears.

Notes

1) See P. Broadhurst, in H. J. Eysenck, Ed., *Handbook of Abnormal Psychology*, 2d Ed., 1972. Also see J. Wolpe, *Psychotherapy by Reciprocal Inhibition*, 1958.

2) O. H. Mowrer, *Psychological Review* **46**, 1939, p. 565.

3) J. Wolpe, *Psychotherapy by Reciprocal Inhibition*, 1958.

4) J. Watson and R. Rayner, *Journal of Experimental Psychology* **3**, 1920.

5) J. Wolpe and S. Rachman, *Journal of Nervous and Mental Disease* **131**, 1960, p. 145.

6) S. Rachman and C. Costello, *American Journal of Psychiatry* **118**, 1961.

7) H. J. Eysenck and S. Rachman, *The Causes and Cures of Neurosis*, 1965.

8) S. Rachman, *Phobias: Their Nature and Control*, 1968.

9) J. Flanagan, Ed., *USAAF Aviation Psychology Research Program Report No. 1*, 1948.

10) H. Lautch, *British Journal of Psychiatry* **119**, 1971.

11) S. Rachman and J. Teasdale, *Aversion Therapy and Behaviour Disorders*, 1969.

12) D. Hammersley, in R. Wallerstein, *Hospital Treatment of Alcoholism*, 1957.

13) R. S. Hallam and S. Rachman, in M. Hersen et al., Eds., *Progress in Behavior Modification*, Vol. II, 1976.

14) J. Bancroft, *British Journal of Psychiatry* **115**, 1966.

15) R. Sanderson, S. Laverty, and D. Campbell, *Nature* **196**, 1963.

16) See J. Garcia and R. Koelling, *Psychonomic Science* **4**, 1966; J. Garcia, F. Ervin, and R. Koelling, *Psychonomic Science* **5**, 1966.

17) M. Seligman and J. Hager, Eds., *Biological Boundaries of Learning*, 1972.

18) M. Seligman, in Seligman and Hager, 1972, p. 451.

19) S. Rachman, H. Shackleton, and P. de Silva, in preparation.

20) R. Wallen, *Journal of Abnormal and Social Psychology* **40**, 1945.

Chapter 11
... And
Why It Failed

There are six arguments against acceptance of the conditioning theory of fear acquisition. (1) The failure of people to acquire fears in theoretically fear-evoking situations (such as air raids). (2) It is difficult to produce conditioned fear reactions in human subjects, even under controlled laboratory conditions. (3) The conditioning theory rests on the untenable equipotentiality premise. (4) The distribution of fears in normal and neurotic populations is difficult to reconcile with the conditioning theory. (5) A significant number of phobic people recount histories that cannot be accommodated by the conditioning theory. (6) Fears can be reduced by vicarious processes and it seems highly likely that they can be acquired by similar processes.

The Arguments

1) Failure to acquire fear It would seem that few experiences could be more frightening than undergoing an air raid. However, as we have seen, during World War II, the great majority of people endured air raids extraordinarily well, contrary to the universal expectation of mass panic. Exposure to repeated bombing did not produce significant increases in psychiatric disorders. Although short-lived fear reactions were common, surprisingly few persistent phobic reactions emerged.

The observations of comparative fearlessness enduring despite repeated exposures to intense trauma, uncontrollability, and uncertainty are contrary to the conditioning theory of fear acquisition. People subjected to repeated air raids should acquire multiple conditioned fear reactions and these should be strengthened with repeated exposure.

2) Conditioning human fears A thorough attempt (by E. Bregman) to condition fear in 15 normal infants was a failure.[1] Evidence from a different source and of a different nature is consistent with this failure, and with wartime observations, in showing that people fail to acquire fears in situations where the theory predicts that they should occur. R. S. Hallam and S. Rachman point out that many writers on the subject of electrical aversion therapy, "appeared to assume that the successful administration of treatment would result in the development of a miniphobia—repeated associations of the conditioned stimulus with an unpleasant electrical shock would result in a situation in which the presentation of the stimulus produces fear reactions."[2]

To the contrary, I. Marks and M. Gelder found that most of their patients reported indifference to the conditioned stimuli employed in electrical aversion therapy; it was rare to find someone who complained of fear after undergoing the course of treatment. The same observation was reported by J. Bancroft and by Hallam, Rachman and W. Falkowski.[3]

Because the expected conditioned fear reactions did not emerge, and for some related reasons, Hallam and Rachman carried out two studies that were intended to provide a laboratory analogue of electrical aversion therapy. The results failed to confirm the prediction that conditioned fear reactions would develop. "The 'conditioned response' did not resemble, in either magnitude or direction, the cardiac responses of phobic patients who are presented with their phobic stimulus, nor did subjects report anxiety or discomfort in the presence of the conditioned stimulus." We were similarly unsuccessful in our search for evidence of conditioned fear reactions developing in alcoholic patients who undertook aversion therapy. "In effect, the results show that when alcoholics who have undergone aversion therapy are compared with alcoholics treated in other ways, there is no difference in their subjective anxiety responses to alcoholic stimuli or in the peripheral autonomic responses that usually accompany states of fear or anxiety. Subjective distaste for alcohol seems to be the only specific consequence of aversion therapy."[4]

3) *The equipotentiality premise* The conditioning theory of fear acquisition assumes that any stimulus can be transformed into a fear signal; the choice of stimulus is a matter of indifference. As pointed out in

Chapter 7, Seligman has convincingly argued that this premise is untenable, and hence its incorporation in conditioning theory is a flaw.

4) The distribution of fears   Given the equipotentiality premise, the corollary for fear acquisition would be that all stimuli have an equal chance of being transformed into fear signals. However, as we know, this is not borne out by surveys of the distribution of fears, either in a general population or in psychiatric samples. For example, the epidemiological study of common fears carried out in a Vermont city by S. Agras, D. Sylvester and D. Oliveau showed that the prevalence of a fear of snakes was 390 per 1000 people, while fear of the dentist was only 198 per 1000—despite the fact that contact with the dentist was almost certainly much more frequent, and indeed much more likely to be painful. To take another example from their survey, the prevalence of snake fears among the 30-year-old respondents was more than five times as great as their fear of injections.[5]

Anthropological observations of an isolated Indian community in Canada are consistent with the view that the distribution of fears is nonrandom. A. I. Hallowell pointed out that the Indians were fearless of certain dangerous animals such as wolves and bears, but were considerably frightened by some harmless creatures—notably frogs and toads.[6]

Subject only to their prominence in the environment, many subjects and situations should have an equal probability of becoming fear provoking. What we find instead, however, is that some fears are exceedingly common—much too common for the conditioning theory. Other fears are much too rare. The fear of snakes is common and the fear of lambs is rare; moreover, a genuine fear of snakes often is reported by people who have had no contact with the reptiles. Consequently one is forced to conclude that a fear of snakes can be acquired even in the absence of direct contact—and this significant concession opens three possibilities. Either the fear of snakes is innate or it can be transmitted indirectly, or the fear of snakes is "lurking" and will appear with only slight provocation. The last two of these three possibilities are of course compatible.

5) *Patients' reports of fear onset* Whatever its value, the conditioning theory is not a satisfactorily comprehensive account of the genesis of fears. It had become apparent that clinically it is often difficult to determine the origin of a patient's phobia. In similar vein, I. M. Marks described "many phobias where there was no apparent trauma to initiate the phobia."[7] Indeed, it can be extremely difficult to find a convincing precipitant of a phobia.[8] A. B. Goorney and P. J. O'Connor encountered this problem in their analysis of the excessive fears of British peacetime air crews. In a study of 97 cases of excessive anxiety encountered in R.A.F. crews, they were able to attribute the fears of a quarter of all their cases to specific precipitants such as accidents or frightening incidents. In one-third of the cases there was no discernible cause, and in the remainder the precipitants—such as a return to flying after a long abstention—were not of a traumatic or conditioning type.[9]

6) *The vicarious transmissions of fear* The significant advances made in our understanding of the processes of observational learning and modeling made it plain that we acquire much of our behavior, including emotional responses, by vicarious experiences.[10] It is probable that fears can be acquired either directly or vicariously and that stimuli are likely to develop fearful qualities if they are associated, directly or vicariously, with painful or frightening experiences. It must be conceded however that, at this stage, the evidence in support of vicarious acquisition of fear in humans is indirect and largely anecdotal—this is entirely understandable owing to the ethical objections to experiments in which one sets out to induce lasting fears in subjects. As pointed out in Chapter 2, it was observed during the war that the fears or lack of fears displayed by mothers in the course of air raids, was an important determinant of whether or not their children developed similar fears. It was found that if children observed adults exhibiting overt signs of fear or other emotional upset, this increased the likelihood of the children becoming frightened. Along the same lines, E. John commented on the social facilitation and inhibition of children's fears during air raids. She obtained a correlation of 0.59 between the fears of mother and child.[11] In normal conditions also, there is a good deal of correspondence between the fears of children within the same family, correlations ranging between 0.65 and 0.74.[12] Similarly, C. Hagman found a correlation of 0.67 between the total number of fears exhibited by children and their mothers.[13] R. Grinker and J. Spiegel provided clear examples of combat airmen who acquired fears after observing a crew mate expressing intense fear.[14] In their survey of 1700 infantry troops in the Italian theater during World War II, S. Stouffer and his colleagues found that 70 percent of the respondents had a negative reaction to seeing a comrade "crack up." Half of the total sample said that it made them feel anxious and/or like cracking up themselves.[15]

So far demonstrations of the direct transmission of fear have been confined to animal subjects. For example R. Miller, J. Murphy, and I. Mirsky reported three experiments on monkeys, which showed that fear can be transmitted from a fearful model to an observer monkey. It was also found that fear can be transmitted by pictorial representations of fearful monkeys. In all the experiments the observers, although calm during the modeling session, had themselves been subjected to the fearful situation at some time in the past. Moreover, the transmission of *fear* was deduced from the occurrence of avoidance behavior. The authors also noted that their monkeys appeared not to respond fearfully when exposed to fearful models of other species.[16] However it should be pointed out that exposure to fearful models will not necessarily produce fear in the observers, be they monkeys or humans.

It can of course be argued that, in most of the examples of fear transmission cited above, a conditioning explanation can suffice. This defense is persuasive insofar as the examples are ones in which neutral and frightening stimuli have been presented in temporal and spatial contiguity. However, the *social* transmission of fear introduces the possibility of the indirect acquisition of fears. That possibility, indeed likelihood, poses serious difficulties for a conditioning theory. If it is confirmed that fear reactions can be acquired even to stimuli the person has never encountered, then the conditioning theory cannot be adequate. And as argued earlier, there are grounds for believing that fears *can* be acquired by indirect transmission—not necessarily by vicarious social learning only. Also, since studies on the distribution of fears have revealed that people report fears of objects or situations they have never actually encountered (see point 4 in this discussion), a conclusion that indirect transmission *does* occur seems inevitable.

In sum, these six arguments oblige us to conclude that the conditioning theory of fear acquisition, is neither comprehensive nor adequate.

Integration

Although they are serious, the weaknesses of the conditioning theory are not necessarily fatal. One can either search for an entirely new theory to replace it, or take the reformist view and seek modifications and extensions of the theory. At its best the conditioning theory can provide a partial explanation for the genesis of some fears. However, it cannot explain the observed distribution of fears, the uncertain point of onset of phobias, the indirect transmission of fears, the ready acquisition of prepared phobias, and the failure of fears to arise in situations demanded by the theory.

The research on taste aversions indicates how intense and lasting reactions can be acquired very rapidly, and the conditioning theory may receive an unexpected boost from these findings—if we are willing to assume that they are analogous to acquired fears.

In addition to providing an account of the conditions in which fear is acquired, an adequate theory of the genesis of fears needs to accommodate the following information as well. Fears can emerge suddenly or gradually. Individual differences in susceptibility to the acquisition of fears appear to be substantial. Fears can be acquired indirectly—and that includes the acquisition of fears of objects or situations the person has never encountered. All things considered, people acquire comparatively few fears. The distribution of fears in the population is nonrandom.

Pathways to Fear

In my opinion, we have to acknowledge at least three major processes of fear acquisition. Conditioning may be an important fear-induction process, but two other—indirect—processes can be identified. Of these two, one—vicarious acquisition—has already been described and it was pointed out that the evidence to support this notion is still sparse. The conviction that fears can be acquired vicariously is drawn indirectly from the successful demonstration of vicarious *fear reduction* and, to a lesser degree, from the incidental and anecdotal evidence referred to in Chapters 2 through 4. Strangely enough, the third process of acquisition by transmission of information and/or instruction, has been overlooked—despite the fact that it is obvious, or perhaps because it is too obvious. Although I am unaware of any conventionally acceptable evidence that fear can be acquired through the transmission of information (and particularly by instruction), it seems to be undeniable. Information giving is an inherent part of child rearing and is carried on almost continuously by parents and peers, particularly in the child's earliest years. It is probable that informational and instructional processes provide the basis for most of the commonly encountered fears of everyday life. Indeed, if we draw on the controllability theory, informing a person that an organism or situation is uncontrollable and potentially aversive may be sufficient to induce a fear. Fears acquired informationally are more likely to be mild than severe. Like the acquisition of fear by vicarious experience, informational and instructional processes are compatible with the fact that people display fears of situations and objects they have never encountered. Acceptance of the notion that fears can be acquired by informational processes also enables us to explain some, but by no means all, of the *failures* to acquire fear in situations in which, on the basis of the conditioning theory, such fear might be expected to arise. We learn by information and instruction which situations to fear, and we also learn to distinguish them from those situations and objects that are not dangerous and are therefore not to be feared. Moreover we are taught to cope with dangers and to endure the accompanying discomfort of pain.

Persuasive evidence, if persuasion is needed, should not be difficult to collect. In theory it is a simple matter of demonstrating that people who begin with no fear of object X display signs of such a fear shortly after being informed that X is dangerous. The following two examples are chosen from a host of possibilities in the hope that they are both clear and convincing. In the first of our hypothetical experiments, a group of trainee laboratory workers are introduced to specimens and animals in a pathology laboratory. After confirming the absence of significant fear, half of the trainees are informed (correctly) that direct contact with specific contaminated animals and specimens is dangerous and may cause them to acquire lethal diseases. At least a degree of fear will be transmitted in this way—even in the absence of contact with the specimens (other than during the pretest of course) or of exposure to a fearful model. The exposure-free transmission of information is a sufficient cause of fear.

In our second hypothetical experiment, the same general procedure is used to transmit appropriate fear to soldiers who are being trained to defuse bombs. This time they are warned that certain noises and/or sights indicate that the bomb is about to explode. This information, unaccompanied by direct or indirect exposures, should be sufficient to induce significant and lasting fear.

Hallam has pointed out that we may have an asymmetrical phenomenon;[17] information is an effective inducer of fear but, as Mary Cover Jones found out many years ago, it is a weak *reducer* of fear.[18]

The considerable individual differences in the range and intensity of fears need to be encompassed by any theory for which comprehensiveness is claimed. Just as the conditioning theory of fear acquisition rests on the assumption that most fears are acquired, so the three-process hypothesis outlined here is based on a similar assumption (but see page 198 below). This is not to deny that there are biological differences in the propensity to develop fears. Study of the biological basis of personality[19] supports the likelihood of a genetic contribution to the general level of human fearfulness. Of greater interest is the question whether or not the propensity to fearfulness is related to other important aspects of personality neuroticism. If the concept of three processes of fear acquisition has any validity, it may turn out that some people are particularly prone to develop fears one way (say, by a process of conditioning) whereas others are more susceptible to fears that are socially transmitted by vicarious learning or by information processes. Whether this speculation is eventually confirmed or not, it seems possible that we will un-cover a connection between prepared fearful stimuli and acquisition of fears by a conditioning process. We can expect that those fears which are transmitted by informational and instructional processes are likely to comprise a large number of nonprepared stimuli—what is not prepared, has to be provided.

It can be seen that we are moving towards a po-sition in which it is postulated that an ease of connec-tion prevails between certain people and certain stimuli, and—on the contrary—some people are rel-atively invulnerable to certain fear stimuli. In addition to postulating an appropriate fit between person and stimulus, we also have to take into account the oc-currence of "critical moments." In attempting to ex-plain those fears that have an acute onset, one needs to know why the fear emerges at the particular time it does. Clinical experience makes it plain that certain patients experience critical incidents in which the fear has its onset. What is particularly interesting is the fact that quite frequently these same people have been exposed to the same stimulus repeatedly in the past without acquiring the fear. It seems that, for acute onset fears, there are certain psychological states in which the person is vulnerable to the acqui-sition of fear. To take a clinical example, in those agoraphobic patients who report an acute onset of fear—of public transport, crowded spaces, open spaces, or other—one needs to know why the fear arose on the day that it did, at the time that it did. And why do they acquire it when on hundreds or thousands of previous exposures to the same set of stimuli, they remained unaffected?

Thus, in framing an explanation for fears of acute onset, we must try to match the person with the stimulus and the critical moment of onset. (For agoraphobias, it seems likely that the critical incident occurs when the person is already in an emotionally upset or apprehensive state. Another predisposing factor seems to be physical illness accompanied by feelings of weakness, nausea, dizziness, and so on.) Similarly, soldiers were found to be more vulnerable when they were tired and hungry.[20]

In summary, the classical conditioning theory of fear acquisition can account for only part of the available information. It is suggested that fears can be acquired by indirect processes. The two most important of these are the vicarious acquisition of fear, and the informational and instructional transmission of fear. It is speculated that intense fears of biological significance (what Seligman calls "prepared phobias") are more likely to be acquired by a conditioning process. The common everyday fears are probably acquired by the indirect and socially transmitted processes (information-giving and vicarious exposure).

Any of these three processes, alone or in combination, can lead to the acquisition of fear. By drawing on one or more of them, we should be able to explain most of the common features of human fear, including the observed distribution of fears in normal and clinical populations, the nonrandom incidence of fear, sudden or gradual acquisition of fears, the indirect transmission of fears, and failures of fears to arise under stress conditions. The interesting question of what happens when one or more of the pathways conflict (e.g., information versus conditioning) remains to be answered.

Until this point, fear acquisition has been considered largely in terms of the "lump theory." If a Langian analysis, emphasizing the different components of fear, is applied to the three-process approach to fear acquisition, we can speculate that in fears acquired by a conditioning process (which for present purposes, includes the taste aversion phenomenon), the components that will be most prominent are the psychophysiological and behavioral, and the subjective component will be minor by comparison. Where fears have been transmitted indirectly (vicariously or informationally) we might expect the subjective aspect to be predominant and the psychophysiological changes and behavioral effects to be the minor ones. This line of reasoning appears to be compatible with Seligman's concept of prepared phobias—which, it will be remembered, he described as being noncognitive and resistant to extinction. By contrast, nonprepared fears might be expected to have a larger cognitive element—that is they can be more readily acquired, and indeed reduced, by cognitive manipulations. It has to be admitted, however, that so far the attempts to relate prepared phobias to therapeutic outcome have yielded unexpected or unrewarding results.[21]

Notes

1) E. Bregman, *Journal of Genetic Psychology* **45**, 1934.

2) R. S. Hallam and S. Rachman, in M. Hersen et al., *Progress in Behavior Modification*, Vol. II, 1976, p. 183.

3) I. Marks and M. Gelder, *British Journal of Psychiatry* **117**, 1967; J. Bancroft, *British Journal of Psychiatry* **115**, 1971; R. S. Hallam, S. Rachman, and W. Falkowski, *Behaviour Research and Therapy* **10**, 1972.

4) Hallam and Rachman, 1976, p. 194.

5) S. Agras, D. Sylvester, and D. Oliveau, *Comprehensive Psychiatry*, 1969.

6) A. J. Hallowell, *Journal of Social Psychology* **9**, 1938.

7) I. Marks, *Fears and Phobias*, 1969, p. 92.

8) P. de Silva, S. Rachman, and M. Seligman, *Behaviour Research and Therapy* **15**, 1977.

9) A. B. Goorney and P. J. O'Connor, *British Journal of Psychiatry* **119**, 1971.

10) A. Bandura, *Principles of Behavior Modification*, 1969; *Psychological Review* **84**, 1977.

11) E. John, *British Journal of Educational Psychology* **11**, 1941.

12) R. May, *The Meaning of Anxiety*, 1950.

13) C. Hagman, *Journal of Experimental Psychology* **1**, 1932.

14) R. Grinker and J. Spiegel, *Men Under Stress*, 1945.

15) S. Stouffer et al., *The American Soldier*, 1949; see also J. Dollard, *Fear in Battle*, 1942. If we allow that taste aversions and fears share some common attributes (see page 180), then the steep increase in the occurrence of discrete episodes of specific aversions during pregnancy strengthens the view that acute onset fears may well arise during periods of increased psychological vulnerability, e. g., fatigue, stress, etc.

16) R. Miller, J. Murphy, and I. Mirsky, *Journal of Clinical Psychology* **15**, 1959.

17) R. Hallam, personal communication, 1977.

18) M. C. Jones, *Pedagogical Seminars* **31**, 1924.

19) For example, H. J. Eysenck, *The Biological Basis of Personality*, 1967; J.A. Gray, *The Psychology of Fear and Stress*, 1971.

20) Stouffer et al., 1949.

21) de Silva et al., 1977.

Chapter 12

Habituation and Sensitization

At various points in this book, reference has been made to fears that habituate—that is, the fearful reactions decline after repetitive exposures to provoking stimulation. Habituation is a common and fairly rapid process. Even when extreme stimulation is involved it can occur smoothly (adaptation to air raids is one of the most telling examples of this process). Habituation can be cited as a partial explanation for the decline of childhood fears, combat fears, and parachuting fears, but exceptions are encountered. Some fears persist unaltered for long periods, and others increase in strength. Since the persistence of fears will be considered in Chapter 16, this section is confined to the habituation and sensitization of fears.

In the discussion of innate and acquired fears (Chapter 7), it was suggested that innate fears reflect an inborn tendency to respond persistently and intensely to objects or situations with certain stimulus attributes (such as novelty, intensity, suddenness). This concept assumes a heightened sensitivity to particular stimulus complexes. Such sensitivity is open to modification, and a neat fit is suggested by J. F. Mackworth's hypothesis that habituation constitutes a decrease in *sensitivity* to stimulation and a decrease in readiness to respond.[1] Viewed in habituation terms, the fading of innate fears (as in childhood) can be regarded as a decline in sensitivity observed after repetitive exposures to the stimulus. Decreasing readiness to respond is often an expression of this declining sensitivity.

The "spontaneous" decline of acquired fears can also be regarded as a function of repeated stimulus exposures, leading once again to a decreasing readiness to respond fearfully—a form of habituation. It is assumed here that these decremental processes, decreasing sensitivity and decreasing readiness to respond, are closely related but not identical.

In their interesting exposition, P. Groves and R. Thompson have argued that habituation comprises two independent processes. The first is the commonly recognized one of habituation resulting from repetitive stimulation and the second is what they describe as an incremental or sensitizing process. Sensitization refers to increases in responsiveness as a result of stimulation. They assume that habituation and sensitization develop independently but interact to yield "a final behavioral outcome." During habituation training, sensitization occurs early and then decays. Habituation is assumed to be determined largely by stimulus repetition, and sensitization by stimulus intensity.[2] The fate of this theory will be watched with interest and it would be premature to extract its significance for our understanding of fear until it has been adequately tested.

The occurrence of habituation, and indeed in the Groves and Thompson theory of sensitization as well, is determined by an interaction between the subject's level of activity and the occurrence of repeated stimulation. The complexities of this interaction and the general characteristics of habituation are admirably described and explained by Mackworth. Her account and that of Groves and Thompson suggest that there is a great deal of common ground between habituation processes and fear-reduction processes.

The factors which facilitate habituation strongly resemble those which facilitate the reduction of fear. The repetition of stimulation facilitates both habituation and fear reduction. The use of depressant drugs facilitates habituation and fear reduction, as does a lowering of the subject's level of psychophysiological activity. Other factors that facilitate habituation, and probably fear reduction as well, include an increase in the rate of stimulation, attenuation of the stimuli, regularity of stimulus presentations, and reduced complexity of stimulation. Other factors too contribute to the development of habituation and, of course, the ones mentioned immediately above are all operative when other factors are equal. If we attempted to develop a technique for reducing fear which was based on present knowledge of the habituation processes, what would it look like?

First, we would attempt to reduce the subject's level of psychophysiological activity. Then we would present the fearful stimuli in an attenuated form, repetitively, regularly, frequently—in simplified form—and possibly administer a suïtable depressant drug. What is surprising about this hypothetical habituation treatment is the extent to which it resembles Wolpe's desensitization treatment technique.

However, the two concepts developed independently, and it was not until 1966 that Malcolm Lader and Lorna Wing first proposed that the desensitization technique might profitably be conceived of as a form of habituation. They suggested that desensitization was a form of habituation training, since it consists of the repetitive presentation of attenuated (fearful) stimuli. They proposed further that the effect of the relaxation training was to lower the subject's level of psychophysiological activity and thereby ensure more satisfactory and quicker habituation. In their own words, desensitization can be "more simply regarded as straightforward habituation carried out when the habituation rate is maximal, i.e., with the patient at as low a level of activity as possible."[3] They arrived at this proposal as a result of their research into factors that influence habituation, and of their experience in treating patients by desensitization. Later, their argument was bolstered by experimental evidence that bore directly on the hypothesis.[4] One of the most interesting pieces of evidence was the discovery of a significant correlation between habituation rate in certain laboratory test conditions and the response to treatment of various types of phobic patients. Broadly speaking, it was found that those patients who are slow to habituate are likely to respond less well to desensitization treatment than those who habituate easily and quickly.

P. Lang, B. Melamed, and J. Hart obtained corroborative evidence from samples of nonpsychiatric subjects. People who had a fear of public speaking showed slow habituation to auditory stimulation (like Lader's patients with social fears), whereas the spider-phobic subjects resembled Lader's patients with circumscribed phobias in that they showed easy habituation. Under specified experimental conditions, high correlations between habituation to short films of snakes and to auditory tones were recorded from snake-phobic subjects.[5]

Problems

The model has an appealing simplicity and is capable of generating specific, clear predictions. It is not without difficulties, however, and they include the following. First, it has not always been possible to replicate the initial correlation that led Lader and his collaborators to postulate that desensitization and similar fear-reduction processes can satisfactorily be construed in terms of habituation. Failures to confirm a correlation between habituation rate to auditory tones and to phobic stimuli, were reported by Patricia Gillan and S. Rachman and by R. Klorman.[6] In Klorman's words, "no relationship was found between physiological adaptation to tone and fear change in this study." Another objection to the habituation interpretation of fear-reduction processes is that, although these processes generally produce enduring decrements, habituation training characteristically produces transient changes. Moreover, it has been objected, habituation describes a decremental process affecting nonlearned, rather than learned behavior.

Although it is true that the effects of habituation

training generally show less endurance than other types of decremental change, it is now known that under given conditions, habituation effects are persistent. The evidence and arguments on this point are presented by H. Kimmel who concluded that habituation is *not* "an entirely temporary state of affairs which dissipates completely when the stimulus is withheld."[7] Despite this development, it is fair to say that the durability of habituation effects has not yet been clarified, and the theoretical significance of the relative transience of habituation remains to be determined.

The Lader-Wing habituation model is based on the assumption that each person has a *general* rate of habituation, and that this can be accurately measured. This notion too has to be tested, and it is quite possible that the extent of this presumed generality has been exaggerated. In my opinion, this assumption is not essential for the successful application of a habituation model; no critical changes would be needed if the assumption failed to gather support. But the model does encounter some difficulty in explaining the persistence of certain circumscribed fears. In terms of the Lader-Wing hypothesis, patients with these circumscribed fears should have a low level of physiological activity and, consequently, habituate rapidly. It is difficult to see therefore why naturally occurring habituation does not eliminate these often longstanding fears (e.g., of birds, heights, or whatever). The technical problems of specifying in advance what is a satisfactorily low level of activity, or indeed an unsatisfactorily high level, may in the long run reduce the value of the model. Finally it seems unlikely that the habituation model would have been able to predict the successful therapeutic results of the flooding technique. As we shall presently see, however, the newly accumulated evidence on therapeutic flooding does not necessarily exclude a habituation explanation.

Sensitization

When the possibility of using the flooding method as a form of therapy was first proposed, some writers were apprehensive about the danger of inadvertently producing lasting increases of fear in some subjects. In any event, the therapeutic use of flooding has been attended by thankfully few mishaps or unwanted effects. The possibility of producing sensitization still exists however. It is not clear what factors produce exacerbations—they may be fatigue or emotional arousal, but fortunately they appear to be rather uncommon. In their analysis of the habituation process, Thompson and his colleagues reached the inevitable conclusion that although repeated presentations of stimulation often result in a decrement in responsiveness (i.e., habituation), so in other circumstances repeated stimulation can produce an increment (i.e., sensitization).[8] Further information on this incremental process was provided by Kimmel[9] and, from a different point of view, by H. J. Eysenck. He has observed that in a number of experiments, contrary to what might have been predicted from classical learning theory, repeated exposure to the fear stimulus led to an *increase* in responsiveness: "... the important thing is the build-up of neurotic and emotional potential, increasing over time ... and this is quite contrary ... to most commonly taught learning theory." Fear reactions that are quite mild become stronger and stronger "and finally there may be a sudden flare-up into a proper neurotic breakdown." Eysenck has proposed a new explanation for this process, sometimes called incubation or—after one of the first observers of these enigmatic increases in reactivity— the Napalkov effect. His explanation rests on a distinction between conditioned responses that act as drives, and other conditioned responses that do not. According to Eysenck, conditioned fear responses have to be distinguished from other types of conditioned response because they "produce drive states and consequently the ordinary laws of extinction do not apply."[10] The value of this theory will no doubt be assessed by laboratory testing and the outcome of this, and other explanations, will be watched with great interest. As mentioned earlier, Groves and Thompson speculated that sensitization arises from an interaction between the intensity of the stimulation and the person's level of activity. The next step is to add substance to these broad concepts.

J. Wolpe's own explanation of the fear-reducing effects of desensitization is somewhat different.[11] It is based on the concept of reciprocal inhibition, borrowed from physiology. He argues that the therapeutic benefits of desensitization derive from the repeated evocation of small amounts of fear and their immediate suppression by relaxation, an incompatible relationship between fear and relaxation being assumed. Whenever, in the course of desensitization treatment, the therapist evokes a small amount of fear in the patient and then suppresses it by encouraging deep relaxation, a contribution is made to a long-lasting or permanent reduction of fear. Each step in treatment adds another block towards the construction of enduring fearlessness. There is a good deal of evidence to support Wolpe's theory.[12] It has been found in some studies that the desensitization method will produce substantial reductions in fear only if the repeated presentations of imaginary fearful stimuli are accompanied by deep relaxation. These findings support Wolpe's idea of a necessary interaction between fear experiences and their suppression by relaxation. It has also been found that fearful subjects who relax well and obtain clear and evocative images on instruction will show the greatest improvement after desensitization.

On the other hand, some findings are not consistent with the theory. For example, it has been found that the omission of relaxation does not necessarily prevent the reduction of fear.[13] It has been observed that, at crucial points, Wolpe's theory is not sufficently explicit, and his attempt to draw an analogy between a physiological process of inhibition and a psychological one is not entirely satisfactory. Despite the fact that fear and relaxation are known to be incompatible in many circumstances, they are not always so—for example, sheer muscle relaxation does not preclude the experience of subjective fear.

It is difficult to accommodate the recent findings on the fear-reducing effects of flooding techniques in either Wolpe's theory or the habituation model. Certainly, neither explanation could have predicted the outcome of recent research. Consequently, they will have to be modified and extended, or it might even be possible that we are dealing with processes that are so different as to require entirely separate explanations. It is too early to decide this issue, largely because of the shortage of critical information. It is also possible of course that our increased understanding of fear and its reduction, may in turn lead to modifications of the prevailing conceptions of habituation and other inhibition processes. So, for example, can one achieve rapid habituation by prolonged exposure to intense stimulation—as in the flooding treatment of fear responses? What might have seemed an outlandish suggestion five years ago now seems probable. Attention has already been drawn to the neglected evidence of rapid habituation to air raids, and in 1974 Klorman showed that fearful subjects can habituate to intensely fearful phobic stimuli.[14] In fact, when the order of presentation of stimuli went from high to low intensity, habituation to intensely and mildly fearful stimuli was equivalent. Klorman's findings have in some measure been confirmed by the research of G. Sartory, S. Rachman, and S. Grey, who also obtained clear evidence of habituation to highly feared stimuli.[15,16]

The fear-reducing effects of modeling procedures raise fewer theoretical complications than flooding.[17] There are many obvious similarities between modeling and desensitization (repeated exposures to attenuated fear stimuli) and in fact the most prominent theory to account for modeling effects has features that resemble both Lader's and Wolpe's ideas. A. Bandura's distinctive contribution has been the emphasis he places on cognitive factors and on the undoubted occurrence of fear reduction by vicarious exposures.[18] Simply watching a suitable model engaging in fearless behavior generally leads to a partial reduction in one's own fear.

Another possible candidate for a unitary explanation of all three fear-reduction methods—desensitization, flooding, and modeling—is reinforcement theory, originally introduced by Skinner.[19] Although this theory has attractive aspects, it falls short in some respects, most notably in its inability to explain symbolic modeling effects. Also it does not explain satisfactorily the fear-reducing effects of automated desensitization.[20]

If this chapter leaves one with a feeling of incompleteness, that is both understandable and desirable, since the major problems cannot be resolved at present. Progress has been made, and the habituation model in particular has become more promising lately despite the numerous remaining difficulties. It is important to bear in mind that even in its most successful form, the habituation model is still at the *descriptive* stage; but the drift of the evidence and thinking now seems to justify a larger investment of theoretical effort. In Chapter 16 some of the major obstacles are examined in more detail.

Notes

1) J. F. Mackworth, *Vigilance and Habituation*, 1969.

2) P. Groves and R. Thompson, *Psychological Review* **77**, 1970; Thompson et al., in H. Peeke and M. Herz, Eds., *Habituation*, 1973.

3) M. Lader and L. Wing, *Physiological Measures, Sedative Drugs, and Morbid Anxiety*, 1966, p. 145.

4) M. Lader and A. Mathews, *Behaviour Research and Therapy* **6**, 1968.

5) P. Lang, B. Melamed, and J. Hart, *Journal of Abnormal Psychology* **76**, 1970.

6) P. Gillan and S. Rachman, *British Journal of Psychiatry* **124**, 1974; R. Klorman, *Psychophysiology* **11**, 1974.

7) H. Kimmel, in H. Peeke and M. Herz, Eds., *Habituation*, 1973, p. 222.

8) Thompson et al., 1973.

9) Kimmel, 1973.

10) H. J. Eysenck, *You and Neurosis*, 1977, pp. 82, 83, 88.

11) J. Wolpe, *Psychotherapy by Reciprocal Inhibition*, 1958.

12) For example, P. Lang, in D. Levis, Ed., *Learning Approaches to Therapeutic Behaviour Change*, 1970; S. Rachman, *Psychological Bulletin* **67**, 1967; Rachman, *The Effects of Psychotherapy*, 1971; Rachman, in M. Feldman and A. Broadhurst, Eds., *Theoretical and Experimental Bases of Behaviour Therapy*, 1976.

13) S. Rachman, *Behaviour Research and Therapy* **6**, 1968.

14) R. Klorman, *Psychophysiology* **11**, 1974.

15) G. Sartory, S. Rachman, and S. Grey, *Behaviour Research and Therapy* **15**, 1977.

16) G. Sartory, S. Grey, and S. Rachman, *Behaviour Research and Therapy* **16**, 1978.

17) A. Bandura, *Principles of Behavior Modification*, 1969; Rachman, 1976.

18) Bandura, 1969.

19) For example, B. F. Skinner, *Science and Human Behavior*, 1953.

20) S. Rachman, *Behavior Therapy* **3**, 1972.

Chapter 13

Psychoanalytic Views

Psychoanalytic writers and academic psychologists do not merely give different accounts of fear; on critical points they are in direct conflict. A clear example of one such disagreement and its important practical consequences is the way in which they view the fear of animals and insects. As noted in Chapter 9, more than 100 experimental studies on the desensitization of fear have now been published. With very few exceptions, it has been found that desensitization successfully reduces fear. In the great majority of these experiments, the focus of study has been either a fear of spiders or a fear of snakes, and consequently a great deal of information about these fears is now available. Broadly speaking, most of the experimental psychologists who carried out these investigations would adhere to the theory that the fears have been acquired either directly or vicariously, and furthermore that the fears are subject to relearning or unlearning by means of desensitization or related learning techniques. The recently developed techniques of therapeutic modeling and flooding are if anything even more powerful fear reducers than desensitization. It is now incontestable that many fears, even intense ones, can be reduced or eliminated easily and rapidly by behavioral methods.[1]

In contrast, psychoanalytic writers regard these fears as the overt manifestations of some more profound underlying fear, usually of a sexual nature. Their reduction or elimination is assumed to require deep analysis and prolonged efforts. Reference to two contemporary contributions will illustrate the complexity of the sexual symbolism which is a central feature of psychoanalytic theorizing on the subject of fear.

Melitta Sperling, writing in the *Journal of the American Psychoanalytic Association* in 1971, pointed out that "most investigators seem to agree that the spider is a representative of the dangerous (orally devouring and anally castrating) mother, and that the main problem of these patients seems to center around their sexual identification and bi-sexuality." Developing these ideas, she writes, "it is my contention that the choice of the spider symbol indicates a fixation to the pregenital and in particular to the anal-sadistic phase in a very ambivalent and predominantly hostile relationship to the mother, with an inability to separate from the hated mother."[2]

The depth and seriousness of a fear of spiders is plain:

The spider symbolism as well as the symptoms most frequently found associated with it, such as severe sleep disturbances and phobias, are also an indication of unresolved separation conflict and a high degree of ambivalence which intensifies bisexuality and the problem of sexual identification. The mechanisms of defense employed in spider symbolism and in phobias are denial, externalization, projection, splitting and displacement. They indicate the primitive, ambivalent, narcissistic ego organization of this phase. The personalities of these patients, and in the others in cases where it was possible to study them, showed marked paranoid trends. They also used psychosomatic symptoms in stress situations, either episodically or more persistently for the immediate (somatic) discharge of threatening impulses. The spider symbolism in most cases remained latent and became manifest in traumatic life situations and in analysis when the phobic and psychosomatic defences were invalidated. In the analytic situation the spider symbolism was indicative of a specific mother transference.[3]

The only comfort that can be offered in the face of such a demoralizing array of problems—bisexuality, anally castrating mothers, primitive egos, paranoid trends, psychosomatic symptoms, and the rest—is that a fear of spiders generally can be desensitized within five sessions, or reduced by participant modeling within three sessions.

It would seem from Sperling's account that the development of a fear of spiders is to be regarded, like other fears, as a form of psychological defense against some more threatening problems or impulses. In most cases the spider symbolism is latent and becomes manifest when the phobic and psychosomatic defenses are invalidated. If, as seems reasonable, one were to consider the reduction or entire elimination of a spider fear during modeling or desensitization as "an invalidation" of a "phobic defense," then the spider symbolism should presumably be made manifest by this change. In the experiments referred to no such dramatic changes have been observed. On the contrary, the whole process of desensitizing the fear of spiders and other creatures is bland, unsurprising, and at times boring.

Sperling was greatly influenced in her approach to spider fears by the views of one of Freud's closest associates, Karl Abraham, who wrote a classic paper on the subject in 1922.[4] He maintained that the fear of spiders is symbolic of an unconscious fear of bisexual genitalia: "the penis embedded in the female genitals." The second meaning Abraham attributed to the spider is that of a phallic, wicked mother. In their contribution to the *Journal of the American Psychoanalytic Association* in 1969, L. Newman and R. Stoller supported Abraham's view and illustrated it by reference to a psychotic patient who was physically deformed and had hermaphroditic genitalia.[5]

Most of the psychoanalytic writing on the subject is speculation prompted by observation of one patient, or at most a small selection of patients with a common problem. The difficulties one faces in attempting to evaluate this work will be gone into presently. Meanwhile, even if Abraham and his successors are entirely correct in their assumption that a fear of spiders is symbolic of a fear of bisexual genitalia and/or of a phallic, wicked mother, there is room for optimism. Fears of bisexual genitalia and wicked mothers appear to be amenable to easy desensitization—spider fears are simple to deal with.

Classic Case

In 1905, Freud[6] laid the foundations for a psychoanalytic theory of fears with the publication of "The analysis of a phobia in a five-year-old boy," commonly referred to as the case of little Hans, the boy who feared horses. The importance of this contribution is attested to by Ernest Jones, E. Glover, Abraham and other writers on the subject. According to Jones, "the brilliant success of child analysis" was "indeed inaugurated by the study of this very case."[7] Glover said that it supported the concepts of castration anxiety, the Oedipus complex, repression and others.[8] One of Freud's most famous papers, it describes and discusses in great detail (over 140 pages) the events of a few months. The case material on which the analysis was based was collected by the father of little Hans, and he kept Freud informed of developments by regular written reports. In addition the father had several consultations with Freud concerning the boy's fear (both of the parents were lay adherents of psychoanalysis).

During the analysis Freud saw the little boy only once. The essence of the study is that, at the age of four, Hans began to complain of a fear of horses. Shortly afterwards he appeared to show some degree of generalization, and began to fear other large animals such as giraffes, and objects that resembled a horse's muzzle. During a two-week illness the fear waned but then returned in a slightly more intense form, only to show a gradual decline in the course of the succeeding six months. During the period when he complained of the fear, Hans was engaged by his father in repeated conversations and interrogations, and the father then communicated his interpretations to Freud. The material on which Freud's extended account is based, and which provided the raw material for a theory of fear, was almost entirely third-hand—and the reporter was himself a central figure emotionally involved in the matter.

Naturally the theory has undergone some revisions but the major propositions set out by Freud are still accepted by numbers of psychoanalytic writers. It is assumed that the observed or reported fear, the *manifest* fear, is symbolic of a deeper but more threatening or unacceptable fear; the underlying or *latent* fear is, with rare exceptions, presumed to be sexual in nature. The latent fear is so threatening or unacceptable that it is unconsciously transformed into a more acceptable fear, such as that of spiders or snakes or horses. It is a means of defending one's self against more serious psychological disturbance and the mechanisms employed are those of denial, reaction formation, displacement and repression, among others. The fear is generally precipitated by an increase in *id* impulses.

Little Hans's fear of horses was interpreted as being a symbol of a more serious latent fear—in him, as in so many others, it was a fear of his father, engendered by anticipation of punishment (probably castration) for having experienced sexual desires for his mother. It can be seen that the fear of horses was interpreted as a manifestation of the child's Oedipus complex: Hans experienced a sexual desire for his mother, followed by a fear of retribution from his father. These thoughts were unacceptable and the fear of the father was transformed into a more acceptable manifest fear, that of horses.

The full report has been discussed at length by J. Wolpe and S. Rachman who conducted a critical examination of the evidence on which Freud relied. They concluded that much of the testimony was unreliable, pointing out that the child demonstrably misled everyone on several occasions, that he gave conflicting reports, and, most important of all, that what purport to be Hans's views and feelings are simply the father speaking.[9] Freud conceded, "It is true that during the analysis Hans had to be told many things which he could not say himself, that he had to be presented with thoughts which he had so far showed no signs of possessing and that his attention had to be turned in the direction from which his father was expecting something to come. This detracts from the evidential value of the analysis, but the procedure is the same in every case."[10]

The critics quote several examples in which the child's reports were distorted, misinterpreted, and even constructed for him. Wolpe and Rachman dispute each of the six major points put forward by Freud in the construction of his theory. They regard as unsupported the following contentions: the child had a sexual desire for his mother, he hated and feared his father and wished to kill him, his sexual excitement and desire for his mother were transformed into anxiety, his fear of horses was symbolic of his fear of his father, the purpose of the illness was to keep him near his mother, and, finally, his phobia disappeared because he resolved his Oedipus complex.

Some idea of the quality of the evidence can be conveyed by the following brief extracts, but the full impact of the father's introduction and interpretations can be appreciated only by reading the entire case record. In conformity with Freud's belief in the sexual basis of all phobias, the father, encouraged by Freud himself, repeatedly told little Hans that his fear of horses was really a fear of their penises. The child pointed out that he was afraid of being bitten by a horse, and when he said, "a widdler [penis] doesn't bite," his father replied, "Perhaps it does, though."

After further interpretations along the same lines, Freud remarks, "Doctor and patient, father and son, were therefore at one in ascribing the chief share in the pathogenesis of Hans' present condition to his habit of onanism."[11] When the phobia persisted despite this insight, the father proposed to little Hans that he should sleep in a sack to prevent him from wanting to touch his penis. Later, while they were visiting the zoo, the father reminded the child that he was afraid of large animals because they "have big widdlers and you're really afraid of big widdlers." This was denied by the boy, without any effect on the father's views.

In his monograph Freud emphasizes the child's supposed hostility towards his younger sister, providing the following exchange. The father was talking to little Hans about the birth of the younger child, Hanna. Father: "What did Hanna look like?" Hans: "All white and lovely. So pretty." Those are the words reported, but in Freud's account this is how it comes out. "Hans (hypocritically): 'All white and lovely. So pretty.'"[12]

Incidentally, the little boy's explanation of the origin of his phobia was straightforward. He claimed that it started when he witnessed a street accident in which a horse collapsed, and his father added that, "all of this was confirmed by my wife as well as the fact that the anxiety broke out immediately afterwards."[13] By any standards, the monograph on little Hans is a poor product and cannot provide a suitable foundation for constructing a theory of fear.

The debate on the strengths and weaknesses of psychoanalysis has occupied armies of writers, psychologists, psychiatrists, and others. The questions are complex and, if worried through to the end, lead inevitably to considerations of a philosophical nature.[14] In particular it becomes necessary to make up one's mind about the nature of scientific methodology and evidence.

My view is that the crucial reliance placed on the verbal testimony given by nonrepresentative people (many of them psychiatric patients), gathered over a large number of sessions in the course of a treatment lasting several years, is misplaced.[15] The interpretation and selection that necessarily appear in the report finally given by the psychoanalyst should also be regarded with caution. The absence of public demonstration, repetition, and accountability undermine one's confidence in the evidence. Many of the fundamental theoretical propositions of analysis seem to be inadequately based. As a result of these reservations one becomes unwilling to accept the view that observed and reported fears are merely manifestations of a more fundamental, latent fear. Furthermore, it is hard to see why one should accept the assumption that virtually all fears are manifestations, direct or indirect, of sexual problems and conflicts.

Freud specifically asserted that phobias never occur if the person has a normal sexual adjustment. "The main point in the problem of phobias seems to me that *phobias do not occur at all when the vita sexualis is normal.*"[16] He made no attempt to substantiate this claim of a necessary connection between phobias and sexual life, and it remains unproven. It is almost certainly incorrect. Although I know of no reliable statistics on the proportions, it is probable that the large majority of people with phobias have a satisfactory sexual life. During the past 20 years my colleagues and I have assessed and treated a substantial number of phobic patients and although many of them do report multiple problems, including sexual difficulties, a large number have satisfactory sexual lives. They establish and maintain satisfying sexual relationships. Proponents of the Freudian theory may well object that a normal "vita sexualis" is something other than, or more than, satisfactory sexual relationships. If so, three steps must be taken: the nature of the normal vita sexualis must be specified, the nature of the necessary connection with phobias needs to be explained, and Freud's misleading generalization should be qualified or quietly interred.

The recently accumulated evidence on the reduction of fear among experimental subjects by desensitization and related techniques poses formidable problems for psychoanalytic theorists. Manifest or latent, fears can be readily reduced or eliminated. Following the psychoanalytic view, the elimination of what is presumably a manifest fear (of spiders, for example) should leave the latent fear unaltered. But, if it is assumed (and it is) that the appearance of a manifest fear is part of psychological defense reaction, then it is only reasonable to expect that the elimination of the defensive reaction should be followed by some other attempt at defense. The elimination of one manifest fear should be followed by the substitution of a new one or, failing that, by the occurrence of some other, perhaps worse, psychological disturbance. These two prime possibilities have in fact been explored in the experimental studies mentioned in Chapter 9.

After the successful reduction of a circumscribed fear, such as that of snakes, the appearance of a new fear is rare. Second, after the successful reduction of one of these fears the appearance of some general disturbance, perhaps diffuse anxiety or depression, is also rare. The evidence is straightforward. In the overwhelming number of cases the reduction or elimination of a circumscribed fear is not followed by untoward effects.[17]

Another important consequence of the research findings on reducing fear is the conclusion that it is possible to bring about substantial reductions in fear without first undertaking a major analysis of the fear itself or of the subject's personality, childhood, sexual life, or other topics that are so important in psychoanalytic theory. It is perfectly possible to approach the fear directly, describe and measure it directly, and modify it directly.[18] In other words, one can proceed on the assumption that the fear is manifest and need not have latent roots.

Does this mean that there are no "psychoanalytic" fears? Not necessarily: it remains entirely possible that many fears are partly or largely symbolic, and it is of course true that some fears are implicitly or explicitly sexual in content. There is no way of estimating the frequency with which "psychoanalytic" fears occur, but present evidence suggests that only a small percentage of human fears belong in this category. In my view, then, the psychoanalytic theory cannot succeed as a comprehensive account of human fears. It may help us ultimately to understand some of the more unusual fears.

It is a pity that psychoanalytic writers have not yet attempted to apply the three-systems conception of fear to aspects of their theories. Is it possible in some way to link discordances between subjective and autonomic indexes of fear to analytic ideas of *unconscious* fears? Is autonomic disturbance without subjective fear recognition an example of unconscious fear? Both of these questions raise interesting possibilities.

Although it might be agreed that psychoanalysis cannot provide a satisfactory general theory of fear, the voluminous literature on sexual fears and on symbolism contains many fascinating ideas. Unfortunately their successful exploitation is hindered by claims of exaggerated generality: all spider fears are symbolic of bisexual genitalia, all snakes are phallic symbols, and so on. The implausibility of these claims too easily prompts a total rejection of symbolism, but neither total rejection nor total acceptance are comfortable positions to defend. Fears are not always exactly as they seem, but contrary to psychoanalytic beliefs, it is unwise to assume that fears are *never* as they seem.

Notes

1) See reviews by Bandura, 1969; Rachman, 1967, 1971, 1976; O'Leary and Wilson, 1975; many others.

2) M. Sperling, *Journal of the American Psychoanalytic Association* **19**, 1971, p. 493.

3) Sperling, 1971, p. 493.

4) See K. Abraham, *Selected Papers*, 1927.

5) L. Newman and R. Stoller, *Journal of the American Psychoanalytic Association* **17**, 1969.

6) S. Freud, 1905, reprinted in *The Collected Papers*, Vol. III, 1950.

7) E. Jones, *Sigmund Freud: Life and Works*, Vol. 2, 1955, pp. 289–292.

8) E. Glover, *On the Early Development of Mind*. 1956, p. 76.

9) J. Wolpe and S. Rachman, *Journal of Nervous and Mental Disease* **131**, 1960.

10) Freud, 1905, p. 246.

11) Freud, 1905, p. 173.

12) Freud, 1905, p. 216.

13) Freud, 1905, p. 193.

14) For an incisive analysis, see A. Grünbaum, in R. Stern et al., Eds., *Science and Psychotherapy*, 1977.

15) See, for example, the data collected by the Fact-gathering Committee of the American Psychoanalytic Association and reported in 1967 (D. Hamburg, Ed.). To quote only two of the many unrepresentative features of the analytic patients, 60 percent of them were *at least* college graduates, compared to 6 percent of the general population. Every 14th analysand was a psychiatrist, and so on. See also Rachman, 1971, for a discussion of the significance of these data.

16) Freud, 1950 Ed., Vol. I, p. 120.

17) For example, see B. R. Sloane et al., *Psychotherapy versus Behavior Therapy*, 1975, p. 100: "we have no evidence whatsoever of symptom substitution ... on the contrary, assessors had the informal impression that when a patient's primary symptoms improved, he often spontaneously reported improvement of other minor difficulties." For general reviews, see O'Leary and Wilson, 1971; Rachman, 1971; Ullmann and Krasner, 1969, etc. For experimental findings see Lang et al., 1970, for example. The work of Sloane et al. and the general reviews deal with the question of whether new symptoms appear after treatment of various types of disorder, not only fear.

18) For example, S. Rachman, *Psychological Bulletin* **67**, 1967; P. Lang et al., *Journal of Abnormal and Social Psychology* **70**, 1966.

Chapter 14
Adaptive Fear

The adaptive value of fear has been emphasized by Richard Lazarus[1] among others. The most important point is that the arousal of fear stimulates a search for a means of coping with impending difficulties or dangers. It is also known, however, that excessive fear can impair psychological functioning and, in particular, lead to psychomotor and intellectual errors, and disturbances of concentration and memory.[2] At the other extreme, an absence of appropriate fear can foster dangerously careless behavior. In many circumstances, moderate levels of fear seem to be adaptively valuable in the way proposed by Lazarus and others.

Examples drawn from military combat illustrate the value of appropriate fear; so do the observations made on surgical patients. Some additional occurrences of such functional fear are the use of seat

belts, hygienic precautions, preparation for examinations, and cessation of cigarette smoking. Each of
these four examples has in fact been the subject of
research, and the adaptive behavior for each was
stimulated by the use of moderately fear-provoking
communications. It appears, however, that most
communications which evoke high levels of fear are
counterproductive. So also moderately fear-provoking
messages can be counterproductive if addressed to
people who are already highly fearful or generally
neurotic.

In an extensive study of American soldiers, M. B.
Smith reported that inexperienced troops displayed
little fear and carelessly disregarded safety measures.[3] After exposure to combat, they became more
vigilant, began to express fear, and also made fewer
careless errors. Smith's account implied that there
was a causal sequence: calm and careless → combat
→ vigilance and fear → fewer errors.

In an interesting study on patients undergoing
major surgery, I. Janis divided the patients into three
groups, based on the degree of fear they expressed
prior to the operation. The highly anxious patients
continued to display considerable fear after the operation and also suffered a great deal of pain and discomfort. The moderately fearful patients coped better
and showed little fear after operation and less pain.
The unexpected finding was that those patients who
were apparently fearless suffered an excessive
amount of postoperative discomfort and pain and
also displayed significantly more anger and resent-
ment. Janis concluded, "a moderate amount of anticipatory fear about realistic threats is necessary for
the development of effective inner defenses for coping with subsequent danger and deprivation."[4]

Supporting evidence for this view is provided by
research into the immunizing effects of warning

people to expect stress. In a series of experiments Lazarus and his coworkers have shown that giving their subjects preparatory information significantly reduced the emotional distress produced by exposure to a stressful movie. They have also demonstrated in a variety of studies that certain types of mental rehearsal can also reduce the effects of stressful experiences, including fear. L. Egbert and others tested the value of providing a large group of surgical patients with preparatory explanations about the expected type and duration of postoperative pain and related information, plus reassurance. Half of the patients were given this extra preparation and the other half were given the conventional minimum of information. The fully prepared patients recovered more quickly and with less pain and discomfort.[5]

A good deal of suggestive data have convinced both Janis and Lazarus that the mental rehearsal which often follows the arousal of fear can be valuable in helping one to cope with real dangers and difficulties. If novel and sudden stimuli are both to be included in the list of stimulus qualities that are potentially fear-provoking, then we can account for at least a part of the effect of rehearsal—it acts to reduce both novelty and surprise. More generally, the effects of rehearsal can be incorporated into the model of a balance between habituation and sensitization to fear-evoking stimulation (Chapter 12).

In general, the biological value of anticipatory fears is self-evident. It may be worth bearing in mind, however, that the relation between fear arousal and vigilance is of central interest. As we have seen, there is evidence that the arousal of anticipatory fear, by enhancing vigilance, may improve the chances of survival of combat soldiers. The biological value of fear is made most apparent by considering the likely fate of a totally fearless animal.

Prevention

Although his results have not always been confirmed, Janis's original findings[6] promoted useful research on the question of fear prevention.[7] In a systematic series of studies, Barbara Melamed consistently demonstrated the value of preparing people for surgery, admission to the hospital, and dental treatment.[8] In particular the provision of filmed modeling experiences, supplemented by information and advice, produced significant reductions in fear and discomfort. A thorough replication recently carried out in London by Lesley Parkinson[9] confirmed and expanded Melamed's main findings. Children who were given special psychological preparation for tonsilectomy experienced less fear, had an easier recovery, and cooperated better than the children who received conventional care.

The major point has been proven—fear *can* be prevented by the flexible application of our new knowledge concerning fear and its modification. Useful advances have been registered in preparing children and adults for surgery, and for dental treatment.[10] The wide application and extension of these methods of psychological preparation can be predicted with full confidence.

Who Needs It?

Despite its unpleasantness, fear is not always undesirable. We have also to consider those circumstances in which fear is thrilling and sought, or simply tolerated while working for some other goal. Examples of seeking fear range from the childhood joys of hide-

and-seek games, through the rides offered in fun fairs, up to motor racing. Although we do not have a satisfactory explanation for fear-seeking behavior, the personality theory constructed by Eysenck is of some assistance.

According to H. J. Eysenck people can be described along at least two major dimensions of personality: extroversion-introversion and neuroticism.[11] People can be plotted on these dimensions, which range from one extreme to the other. Most people are of course in between the two. At the extremes, one may talk about the typical extrovert and typical introvert.

It can be deduced from the theory that extroverts are far more likely to engage in fear-seeking behavior. In a technical sense, the extroverted person is generally in a state of understimulation and hence engages in an active search for external sources of stimulation, including those of a fearful kind. Eysenck has provided a capsule description of the extremes found at either end of his extroversion—introversion dimension:

The typical extrovert is sociable, likes parties, has many friends, needs to have people to talk to and does not like reading or studying by himself. He craves excitement, takes chances, often sticks his neck out, acts on the spur of the moment, and is generally an impulsive individual.... On the other hand the typical introvert is a quiet, retiring sort of person, introspective, fond of books rather than people; he is reserved and distant except with intimate friends ... tends to plan ahead and distrust the impulse of the moment. He does not like excitement, takes matters of everyday life with proper seriousness and likes a well-ordered mode of life...[12]

After a complex chain of reasoning, which need not be gone into here, Eysenck concludes that introverts are characteristically in a state of high inter-

nal stimulation, whereas extroverts are in a state of
low internal stimulation. He goes on to say,

we can extend this whole notion by postulating that the extrovert
would be affected by what is sometimes called "stimulus
hunger," i.e. a desire for strong sensory stimulation—a desire
which would be very much less marked in the introvert. Again,
we can make certain testable deductions. We would expect extroverts for instance, to be fond of loud noise, jazz and bright
colours; we would expect them to be keen on alcohol and other
drugs, to smoke cigarettes and to indulge in more fornication
and in other types of sexual activity. There is a good deal of evidence that this is indeed so ... the very sociability which is so
characteristic a part of the extrovert picture is possibly related to
this stimulus hunger; most of our stimulation, after all, derives
from concourse with other people and the well-known tendency
of the introvert to settle down all by himself with a good book is
certainly not conducive to providing the "arousal jag" the extrovert needs so badly.[13]

This conception of Eysenck's has considerable
appeal on the grounds of its coherence, scope, neat-
ness, and ready applicability in everyday life. Applied
to fear-seeking behavior, it would enable us to make a
large number of testable deductions of considerable
interest—such as which people will seek fear jags,
and which ones will avoid them.

Another possibility, by no means incompatible
with the first, is that deliberate self-exposure to fearful situations is prompted and repeated because of
the enormous relief and satisfaction experienced
after the event. Despite its whimsical aspects (e.g.,
wearing tight shoes in order to enjoy the relief and
pleasure of taking them off), the idea is not entirely
fanciful.

In his explanation of some puzzling experimental findings, J. A. Gray argued that behavior leading to
the avoidance of fear is strengthened by the sight of
safety signals.[14] His argument is supported by nu-

merous studies of animal behavior in which the power of safety signals is clearly demonstrated. Given suitable training, animals will work long and hard to achieve such safety signals. If we extrapolate to human behavior, can it be that people endure acute fear in order to enjoy a terminal surge of relief? Is the immense relief of completing the course a sufficient motive to attract people to roller coasters? Possibly—but the owner of this weak stomach finds this perversity difficult to comprehend.

To conclude, the apparent paradox of people seeking fearful experiences may be seen as an attempt to obtain intense external stimulation. Efforts of this type will commonly be made by highly extroverted people and assiduously avoided by prize introverts.

Notes

1) R. Lazarus, *Psychological Stress and the Coping Process*, 1966.

2) H. J. Eysenck, Ed., *Handbook of Abnormal Psychology*, 1959.

3) H. B. Smith, in S. Stouffer, Ed., *The American Soldier*, 1949.

4) I. L. Janis, *Stress and Frustration*, 1971, p. 97.

5) L. Egbert, *New England Journal of Medicine* **270**, 1964.

6) I. L. Janis, *Psychological Stress*, 1958.

7) See, for example, P. Ley in S. Rachman Ed., *Contributions to Medical Psychology*, 1977; D. Vernon et al., *Psychological Responses of Children to Hospitalization*, 1965.

8) B. Melamed, in S. Rachman, Ed., *Contributions to Medical Psychology*, 1977.

9) L. Parkinson, in preparation.

10) Melamed, 1977; A. Mathews and V. Rezin, *Behaviour Research and Therapy* **15**, 1977.

11) H. J. Eysenck, *Fact and Fiction in Psychology*, 1965; *The Biological Basis of Personality*, 1967.

12) Eysenck, 1965, pp. 59−60.

13) Eysenck, 1965, pp. 84−85.

14) J. A. Gray, *The Psychology of Fear and Stress*, 1971.

Chapter 15
Tell Me, If You Can, What Is Courage?

Socrates: Then Laches, suppose we set about determining the nature of courage, and in the second place proceed to enquire how the young men may attain this quality by the help of study and pursuits. Tell me, if you can, what is courage?

In this dialogue, Socrates and the two generals, Laches and Nikias, explore the meanings of courage. By general agreement however, it is one of the less successful pieces and ends in a disappointingly inconclusive manner. They failed even to reach the question of how best to train people to act courageously. Nevertheless, Socrates successfully expanded the soldiers' conception of courage and they conceded that civilians might also possess this "very

233

noble quality." My own acquaintance with generals is limited, but I have had the good fortune to learn some interesting facts from a professional boxer.

In a regrettably brief conversation with Henry Cooper, the former British and European heavyweight boxing champion, he told me that he could not remember ever having been frightened of anyone. Although he searched his memory and was, I am sure, quite candid, he was able to recollect only some fears of flying and fast driving, but was unable to think of anyone capable of frightening him. He had not experienced fear before or during his professional fights, despite having faced some of the hardest men in the boxing world, shielded only by his skill and two leather gloves. From a psychologist's point of view, it is remarkable that repeated exposures to the punishments of boxing failed to generate any significant fear in Cooper. Moreover, he experienced none of the usual accompaniments of fear, such as palpitations and sweating.

For most of us, fear is a familiar emotion and it is difficult to imagine a life in which it plays no part. Henry Cooper seems to be one of those rare people whom we can describe as being literally fearless. Like many writers before him, O. Hobart Mowrer, a leading theoretician on the subject of emotion, linked fearlessness with courage. "May it not be," he asked, "that courage is simply the absence of fear in situations where it might well be expected to be present?"[1] Although fearlessness often is regarded as being synonymous with courage, there is some value in distinguishing it from another view of courage. Just as fear has several meanings, so there are different types of courage. As well as fearlessness (the absence of fear), we can recognize the occurrence of perseverance despite fear. One could in fact argue that it is this latter type of conduct that is the purest form of courage. It certainly requires greater effort and determination.

It is interesting that the soldiers who were studied during World War II made a discrimination that is consistent with present-day views on the relation between fear and endurance. S. Stouffer found that they distinguished between men who were cowards and men who were ill, even though both might show the same fear symptoms. The key factor stressed by the interviewees was the effort made to overcome the withdrawal tendencies engendered by intense fear. Soldiers who were visibly upset by danger were not regarded as cowards, "unless they made no apparent effort to stick out their job." If, despite trying hard, the man could not perform adequately, he was regarded as a legitimate casualty. On the other hand, a man exhibiting the same fear symptoms might be labeled a coward if he made no apparent effort to overcome his reactions and carry out his tasks. "Thus men were not blamed for being afraid. ... but they were expected to try to put up a struggle to carry on despite their fear."[2] Soldiers whose symptoms persisted long after the objective dangers had subsided, were generally regarded as being sick.

The soldiers who displayed the most courageous behavior gained the greatest admiration from their comrades. When veteran troops were asked to characterize the best combat soldiers they had ever known, fearless behavior was rated as by far the most important characteristic on which to make a judgement. As J. L. Birley noted, the admiration of courage appears to be universal. "Courage, from whatever angle we approach it, whatever origin or purpose we assign to it, no matter what form it assumes, nor even what motives underlie it, will always be a quality beloved of man."[3] This admiration even extends to courageous acts performed by one's opponents. Furthermore, in the words of Dr. Samuel Johnson, "Courage is a quality so necessary for maintaining virtue, that it is always respected, even when it is associated with vice."[4] Without exploring the reasons for this admiration, we can turn instead to examples of fearless or courageous acts, and the factors that contribute to their occurrence.

As we have seen at various points in this book, almost all studies and surveys cite a small, sometimes tiny, proportion of people who report that they do not experience fear, even in situations that are objectively threatening and that do cause the overwhelming majority of people to experience fear. One percent of the several thousands of U.S. airmen who participated in a study of combat fears reported that they experienced no fear during combat.[5] In a comparable study reported by D. Hastings and colleagues 6 percent of the airmen made a similar report.[6] Among infantry men, comparable proportions of fearless people have been reported. Until a group of such people is studied intensively, it is impossible to know whether their fearlessness reflects a rare invulnerability, constitutional or acquired, or whether they are incapable of registering their own reactions. It is of course possible that they experience the appropriate physiological reactions but for some reason or other remain unaware of such disturbances. Whatever the reasoning, they are a fascinating group about whom it is difficult not to be curious.

The large majority of people are acquainted with fear, but naturally the differences in the success with which people cope with these feelings are considerable. The evidence accumulated during wartime conclusively demonstrates that most people are adept at coping with fears. In this sense of the term *courageous*, human beings are well endowed with the ability to carry out courageous behavior. Even within this courageous species, however, there is a subgroup of people who are outstandingly competent. Wartime observations also suggest that people engaged in the following tasks were conspicuously courageous: firemen, ambulance crews, civil defense workers, policemen, bomb-disposal experts, paratroopers, submariners, pilots,[7] and—most recently—astronauts. A measure of the resilience of submarine crews is provided in figures given by I. Duff and C. Shillin.[8] Of a grand total of 126,160 patrols carried out by these crews, there were only 62 cases of psychiatric difficulty—yielding an extraordinary 0.00044 percent of psychiatric casualties. To put it another way, of 25,000 men in the service, the psychiatric breakdown rate was a mere 2.2 per 1000. The authors attribute the excellence of this group to the fact that they were volunteers and were required to meet rigid educational and physical standards for entry. Moreover the training provided was exceptionally efficient, morale was high, confidence in the men and equipment was high, and a successful rotation scheme was used.

Recent research on the personality characteristics and performance of the Mercury astronauts is especially enlightening. S. Korchin and G. Ruff carried out a longitudinal study of the seven original astronauts who were selected from 69 candidates, all of whom were experienced jet test-pilots from the military services. They performed their tasks with exemplary skill and success. Who were these men? All of them were married men in their early 30s and came from middle-class families. They grew up in small towns or farms, were Protestant, enjoyed outdoor living and sports, had obtained university degrees in engineering, and were oriented to action rather than thought. In the phrase used by the authors, they were "core American."[9]

Although aware of the dangers involved in the project, they regarded it as similar in type and not necessarily more dangerous than tasks they had already completed in test flying. They were well motivated and felt they were making an important contribution. Although "they had no special wish to face danger, they were willing to accept the risks demanded by their work." All of the men were of superior intelligence, with a mean IQ of 135. They preferred independent action whenever possible, but were not averse to working in a team. "These are strongly independent men with deep needs to master their own fate and with faith in the ability to do so."

Korchin and Ruff provide an excellent description of the features that distinguished these men from most of their fellows. Pointing out that they are not part of what I have called the "fearless group," they assert, "emotions, both negative and positive, are strongly experienced; however, control is good. Each of them has faced situations in which fear was appropriate and found that he was able to function despite its effects." They have benefited from mastery experiences and as a result, "they have confidence that they have the skills and knowledge necessary to overcome realistic threats, and they are not given to dwelling on unrealistic ones. In describing their reactions to combat, they readily admitted fear, but pointed out that they knew they were good pilots and had the resources for coping effectively with danger." They were "men of particular psychological competence."

This conclusion was supported not only by extensive observation and interviewing, but by the astronauts' performance before, during, and after the space flights. On some psychomotor and emotional tests they showed extraordinary ability. Their scores were consistently above average and unaffected by their participation in space flights.

During their journeys into space, they experienced little fear. Nor was there evidence of severe anxiety before flights. "On the contrary, the launch of the space vehicle and the flight itself often induced a feeling of exhiliration ... anxiety levels have not been extraordinarily high ... even in the instances where a possibility of death has been encountered, emotional reactions have remained within normal limits."[11]

The possibility of a constitutional invulnerability in these people must be allowed for, but their actual and perceived psychological competence seems to be the factor of dominating importance. Ruff and Korchin sum up their findings in this way: "The capacity to control emotions seems to be gained through past experience in the mastery of stress, and through confidence in training and technical readiness." This reflects the views of the astronauts themselves who placed greatest importance on competence and confidence. It is interesting that their views foreshadowed the concept of "perceived self-efficacy" recently formulated by Professor A. Bandura in an attempt to account for behavioral changes.[10] Apparently the astronauts felt "convinced that as a result of their past experience and intensive training, they are prepared to handle any emergency."[11]

Even if competence and confidence are key factors in generating courageous behavior (and it seems probable that they are), acquiring these attributes is not an easy matter. In approaching this question it is necessary first to digress briefly and consider again why we fail to acquire lasting fears even after exposure to stressful situations. As we have seen, exposures to repeated bombing raids did not produce significant increases in psychological breakdown, even though short-lived fear reactions were common. People adapted to air raids and became increasingly courageous as they became more experienced. It was also observed that people who were given socially responsible tasks to carry out, experienced a noticeable growth of courage. Perhaps this is the opposite side of the coin that M. Seligman has labeled "learned helplessness."[12] Does "required helpfulness" breed courage? Even though most of us can, if required, quote examples to support this concept (e.g., mothers who disguise and overcome their own fears in order to protect their children), it was not until recently that we acquired substantive evidence. Recall that H. Rakos and H. Schroeder assigned people who had moderate or severe fears of snakes to work as therapists in helping other fearful people overcome their reactions (see page 44). They found that "merely participating as a helper produced behavioral benefits."[13] It seems that the benefits were produced partly by the social need to engage in increasingly courageous behavior and partly from the fear-reducing effects of modeling the appropriate behavior for the observing fearful subjects. It is to be hoped that this significant example of "virtue rewarded" will promote further study of this brand of altruistic helping behavior. As a start, people who wish to strengthen their own courageous behavior might consider helping others to become more courageous.

The wartime information shows that people not only have a remarkable capacity to persevere in the face of stress, but when fear reactions do occur, they have the capacity to recover very quickly. We also possess good powers of adaptation to repeated stresses and dangers. Parachute training has been a fertile source of information about coping with fear and acquiring courage. R. Walk asked trainee parachutists to rate their subjective fear before and after jumping from a 34-foot practice tower: the trainee jumps from an exit door and drops nearly 8 feet before his fall is arrested by the straps of his parachute harness. Although the training program, requiring more than 20 practice jumps, was difficult and potentially dangerous, the large majority of trainees passed satisfactorily.[14]

At the start of the program, most of the trainees reported at least a moderate amount of fear, but this tended to subside within five jumps. Successful execution of the required jump, despite the presence of fear (i.e., a courageous act), was usually followed by a reduction of fear. Although the successful jumpers started the training program with slightly less fear than those who failed, there were few differences between the two groups in measures of physiological disturbances, such as sweating and tremor. The successful jumpers persevered satisfactorily in the face of moderate fear and mild physiological disturbances. The main differences detected between successful jumpers and failures was that of self-confidence. The jumpers who expressed confidence in their ability to undergo the program successfully, and to perform adequately in training or in combat, persevered best and completed the program most sucessfully.

In a comparison between combat soldiers and airmen, Stouffer and others found that the airmen displayed significantly more courageous behavior.[15] They had higher morale than combat soldiers, expressed more courageous attitudes, and won many more medals than their comrades on the ground (this may in part reflect differences in policy and in opportunity—see page 80). However, Stouffer attributes the differences to motivation and confidence, pointing out that the air crews consisted of volunteers and that they benefited from the high morale engendered in the small size of the group constituting a crew. Both airborne and ground combatants reported that their desire to avoid letting down their comrades played an extremely important part in helping them to control their fear. The airmen also expressed considerable self-confidence in their flying and combat skills.

As we have seen, however, it was not all roses. Many combat airmen experienced increases in fear as a function of the number of missions they completed. This gradual *erosion of courage* was especially noticeable among bomber crews. In one study the incidence of sleep disturbances was found to increase from 13 percent at the beginning of a tour of duty to 52 percent at its conclusion. The declining courage among some air crews was independently reported by R. Grinker and J. Spiegel.[16] Although it is not possible to make direct comparisons, it is conceivable that the bombers experienced worse psychological effects than the bombed.

The important influence of self-confidence on courageous behavior is borne out by observations of combat troops in the Pacific area during World War II.[17] A moderate relationship was observed between courage in combat and the soldiers' perceived adequacy of the training which they had received. The relationship between courage and precombat ratings of self-confidence was clear. Fifty-six percent of the soldiers who expressed high self-confidence before combat reported little or no fear during battle.

However, 62 percent of the soldiers who expressed little self-confidence prior to combat experienced a high degree of battle fear. Other factors also foster courageous behavior. One is possession of the appropriate skill required for dealing with a threatening situation (Chapters 3 and 4). Another is motivation. For example, it has been shown that students who are frightened of snakes can be induced to touch them if the financial incentive is large enough.

A set of conditions conveniently summarized under the term "situational demand" is also important in determining courageous behavior. These demands include the person's sense of responsibility to himself and to others, the powerful effect of group membership and group morale, and the need to avoid disapproval or ridicule. So, for example, young men will persevere in carrying out a frightening task in front of a female audience, despite the arousal of subjective fear. Modeling can be an extremely important influence in generating and maintaining courageous behavior. The research on combat fears provided ample support for this proposition; for many soldiers a courageous leader was the most critical determinant of their own perseverance and ability to cope under fire.[18] Wartime observations also showed that children exposed to air raids modeled the courageous or fearful behavior of their parents, and this finding is echoed in recent experiments in which modeling has been used with notable success as a form of therapy for phobic patients. The pendulum can swing; we are also open to the *acquisition* of fears by a process of modeling—Stouffer and colleagues found that 49 percent of the troops interviewed experienced significantly increased fear after observing a fellow soldier panic during battle. Fortunately, courage too is contagious.

"The contagiousness of courage—it is 'caught as men take diseases one of another'—may rapidly infect a whole army."[19]

In the course of carrying out some of the newer forms of treatment, clinical psychologists have encountered many examples of courage—perseverance in the face of fear. Among the new fear-reduction techniques tested by clinicians, flooding has presented specially good opportunities for observing how people overcome high levels of fear. The essence of flooding, it will be remembered (see Chapter 9), is that the person is exposed to intense stimulation of a kind that ordinarily produces fear and/or avoidance behavior. Although the method does not require the person to experience intense fear (rather, elicitation of high fear should be avoided if possible), more often than not they do have intense reactions. From our point of view the key feature of this procedure is that the fearful person is encouraged to persevere in approaching the fearful stimulus *despite* his fear reactions.

The technique and its effects can be illustrated by the case of a middle-aged woman who had intense irrational fears of disease, germs, and dirt. She suffered from her fears for many years and they had gradually distorted most aspects of her life. She had become frightened of touching "unsafe" objects, eating "dangerous" foods, touching "diseased" people, and so on. Physical contact with other people, including members of her family, was avoided. She lived almost exclusively in one room of her house and spent most of the day sitting in the only safe chair left to her. Even her safe chair had to be scrubbed down with antiseptic several times a day.

The treatment options, including flooding, were explained to her in a reassuring but frank manner and she was given a week to consider whether she wished to try the rapid uncomfortable method of flooding or whether she would prefer to try one of the slower but less uncomfortable methods, such as desensitization. After a difficult internal struggle, during which her anticipatory fear was considerable, she bravely opted for flooding. During the 15 treatment sessions she made good progress but the first three sessions were exceedingly difficult for her. She felt extremely frightened, sweated profusely, and had palpitations and other adverse reactions. Nevertheless she insisted in carrying out the program of increasing contact with dangerous and dirty objects and situations. After completing each of these early sessions she felt exhausted and limp for a couple of hours. Even so, she persevered with the program, displaying commendable courage in doing so. In her own way she was exhibiting a degree of courage that, in my terms, bears comparison with that shown by professional boxers, firemen, combat troops, and so on. After two months of treatment she was greatly improved, her fear had subsided and she was able to touch all the people and objects she had avoided previously. Unfortunately her courage diminished when she returned home and she refused further help.

Moral and Religious Courage

Naturally, courage is not confined to perseverance in carrying out some task despite the experience of the more easily recognizable forms of fear. By convention, people who persist in carrying out some action despite their fears of intense social disapproval as

opposed to physical dangers, are said to be displaying moral courage. Examples of this kind of courage
form the substance of John F. Kennedy's book *Pro-
files in Courage*. The actors in these political and social dramas persisted in their course of action despite fears, threats of disapproval, unpopularity, and
loss of office. In his interesting analysis of the basis of
moral courage, Compton Mackenzie traces the
motivating source of moral courage to the social abstractions of a pursuit of justice and truth, to feelings of compassion, and finally, to self-respect.[20]

There are of course innumerable examples of
people who were prepared to undergo great discomfort and even death in pursuit of their beliefs or the
expression of these beliefs. This is not the place for a
catalog of these admirable acts, but the example of
John Bunyan is a moving one and exemplifies the
conflict between pursuing a moral course of behavior
and the consequent risks to one's well-being. Undoubtedly the torment is increased when the person
is given a clear choice: that is, you can have your
freedom if you remain silent. Bunyan was given such
a choice. He was told that he could avoid imprison-
ment and possible death by agreeing to refrain from
preaching nonconformist religious beliefs.

To this ultimatum, Bunyan replied: "Sir, I shall
not force or compel any man to hear me; but yet, if I
come into any place where there is a people met together, I should, according to the best of my skill and
wisdom, exhort and counsel them to seek out after
the Lord Jesus Christ, for the salvation of their
souls."[21] Rather than "wound his conscience", he
endured several periods in prison, amounting to
more than 12 years. Quite apart from the danger and
physical discomfort involved, he was tortured by the

fact that a failure to bend meant abandoning his family for a considerable period of time and perhaps
forever.

But notwithstanding these helps, I found myself a man encompassed with infirmities. The parting with my wife and poor children has oft been to me in this place as pulling the flesh from my
bones, and that not only because I am somewhat too fond of
those great mercies, but also because I should have often brought
to my mind the many hardships, miseries, and wants that my
poor family was like to meet with, should I be taken from them,
especially my poor blind child, who lay near my heart and all I
had besides. Oh, the thoughts of the hardships my blind one
might go under, would break my heart to pieces!
    "Poor child," thought I, "What sorrow art thou like to have
for thy portion in this world! Thou must be beaten, must beg,
suffer hunger, cold, nakedness, and a thousand calamities,
though I cannot now endure the wind should blow upon thee." I
saw in this condition I was as a man who is pulling down his
house upon the head of his wife and children. Yet, thought I, "I
must do it—I must do it."[22]

Courage and a Three-System Analysis

If we pursue the view of fear as a complex of imperfectly related components, some fresh ideas on the
nature of courage begin to emerge. A person may be
willing to approach a frightening object or situation
but experience a high degree of subjective fear and
even some unpleasant bodily reactions. Persistence
in the face of these subjective and physical signs of
fear is the sort of courage exhibited by the patient
referred to earlier. We can describe this type of
courageous behavior as an example of the uncoupling of the three major components of fear, in which
the person's overt behavior has advanced beyond his

subjective discomfort. People who continue to approach a fearful situation without experiencing subjective fear or unpleasant bodily reactions are showing the type of courage manifested by boxer Henry Cooper. Strictly speaking, someone who displays this pattern is more accurately described as being fearless rather than courageous.

We must also consider how to regard those people who feel subjectively calm when approaching a fearful situation, but on measurement show clear signs of physiological disturbance. One suggestion is that these people should be called "autonomic cowards" because it is the autonomic branch of the nervous system that is most responsive in these situations. But a person who manifests no physiological disturbance while experiencing subjective fear can be said to possess a brave autonomic system.

Training for courage plays an important part in preparing people to undertake dangerous jobs such as fire fighting or parachuting. One element of such training, the gradual and graduated practice of the dangerous tasks likely to be encountered, seems to be of particular importance. This aspect of courage training is similar to the best established clinical method of reducing fear—desensitization. In both the clinical and social contexts, successful practice should contribute to a growing sense of self-efficacy. As we have seen, courageous behavior is determined predominantly by a combination of competence and confidence, and both of these qualities are strengthened by repeated and successful practice. It is also worth noting that in the early stages of courage training, success is far more likely if the person's motivation is raised appropriately. This should assist perseverance even in the face of subjective apprehension. It follows from this analysis that courageous behavior, which is subject to motivational and situational influences, is likely to be less consistent than fearless behavior.

Successful practice of courageous behavior should lead to a decrease in subjective fear (habituation) and finally to a state of fearlessness, as that state is defined here. Courage turns into fearlessness. Novice parachute jumpers display courage when they persevere with their jumps despite subjective fear. Veteran jumpers, having successfully habituated to the situation, no longer experience fear when jumping; they have moved from courage to fearlessness.

Notes

1) O. H. Mowrer, *Learning Theory and Behavior*, 1960, p. 435.

2) S. Stouffer et al., *The American Soldier*, 1949, Vol. 2, p. 200.

3) J. L. Birley, *The Lancet* **1**, 1923, p. 779.

4) Boswell's *Life of Johnson*.

5) J. Flanagan, *Aviation Psychology Program Research Report No. 1*, 1948.

6) D. Hastings et al., *Psychiatric Experiences of the Eighth Air Force*, 1944.

7) For example, see A. Lewis, *Lancet* **2**, 1942; Flanagan, 1948.

8) I. Duff and C. Shillin, *American Journal of Psychiatry* **103**, 1947; see also A. Behnke, *American Journal of Psychiatry* **101**, 1945.

9) S. Korchin and G. Ruff, and Ruff and Korchin, both in G. Grosser et al., *The Threat of Impending Disaster*, 1964.

10) A. Bandura, *Psychological Review* **84**, 1977.

11) Ruff and Korchin, 1964, p. 216.

12) M. Seligman, *Helplessness*, 1975.

13) R. Rakos and H. Schroeder, *Journal of Counseling Psychology* **23**, 1976.

14) R. Walk, *Journal of Abnormal and Social Psychology* **52**, 1956.

15) S. Stouffer et al., *The American Soldier*, 1949.

16) R. Grinker and J. Spiegel, *Men Under Stress*, 1945.

17) Stouffer et al., 1949.

18) Stouffer et al., 1949; Flanagan et al., 1948.

19) Birley, 1923.

20) C. Mackenzie, *Certain Aspects of Moral Courage*, 1962.

21) J. Bunyan, "Autobiography of a Soul," 1912, p. 144.

22) Bunyan, p. 137.

Chapter 16
Paradoxes and Problems

In this concluding section, attention is given to some paradoxes and a few of the problems that remain to tease psychologists in the future. It is a mixture of commentary and speculation, and it will, I hope, help to clarify some misconceptions about fear, emphasize the significance of selected theoretical developments, and provoke fresh thinking on some of the outstanding problems. The various topics fall into one of four categories: the nature of fear, its genesis, the conditions that maintain fears, and the explanation of fear-reduction processes.

The Three-Systems Analysis of Fear

Even if we believe that the three-systems analysis is superior to the unitary (or lump) theory of fear, this does not obscure the weaknesses of the new construal, nor the fact that the unitary theory retains some champions. Several important contributors continue to utilize the unitary conception, and regard the cognitive component as the major or sole indicant of fear. This approach has the merit of simplicity and there can be no argument about the skilful manner in which such writers as A. Bandura and C. Spielberger have exploited this conception.[1]

There is however much to be gained by expanding our view of fear to incorporate the three main components, and the important fact that they are loosely related. Even critics of this construction are bound to agree that it has helped to introduce fresh perspectives on the subjects of fear and courage. It has given rise to novel predictions and helped to clarify phenomena such as the desynchronous changes that often occur during treatment. But the conception is not free of problems.

To begin with, why settle for three components? Are the three sufficient and, if so, are they correctly chosen? One might question, for example, whether there is an adequate reason for including a psychophysiological component but not a bodily expression component. There is no denying the prominence of psychophysiological changes associated with the subjective report of fear but the nonspecific nature of these changes continues to produce uneasiness. Moreover, it is painfully true that we still have little understanding of the relations between various indexes of psychophysiological change, and inevitably, therefore, of the relations between the psychophysiological indexes, subjective fear and avoidance behavior. The terms "psychophysiological change" and "psychophysiological indexes" are of course convenient abstractions, but are ultimately unsatisfactory because they skirt the complexities inherent in these phenomena.

Given these unresolved difficulties, it is reassuring to turn to the less complex phenomenon of avoidance behavior. But even here we strike problems because of the elusiveness of the so-called "mental component." Only a minority of psychologists are likely to disagree with the claim that people can and do engage in an internal, cognitive equivalent of overt avoidance behavior—and *none* would disagree that establishing and maintaining an adequate scientific approach to this and related phenomena are major headaches. So far, most attention has been given to the easily manageable and observable avoidance component, and the introduction of standardized behavioral avoidance tests was a useful development. Even these tests, however, pose measurement problems, quite apart from the distortions introduced by the influence of social factors. We still do not have a scaling method that satisfactorily takes into account the fact that when one is confronted with a fearful object such as a python, moving forward from a position 20 feet away from the snake to one that is 19 feet away is by no means equivalent to taking that last step to direct contact with the snake. Psychologically, the two are not equal intervals.

The subjective component is essential to any conception of fear but, once again, we confront the old problems of meaning, definition, and measurement. Shifting from a unitary conception of fear to a three-systems analysis does not remove these traditional obstacles. This catalogue of difficulties is offered not in a spirit of despair but rather as a cautionary note. The numerous advantages of the three-systems approach outweigh the inherited difficulties.

Within the second category of topics, the genesis of fear, we must consider several questions: the importance of learning, confinement, and controllability.

Learning to Fear and Learning Not to Fear

The nonrandom distribution of fears requires an explanation. We need to explain why some fears are unduly common and why other fears are unduly uncommon. Two related possibilities are immediately evident. First, it is possible that common fears are those that are particularly stable. Second, it seems reasonable (but not necessary) to make the further assumption that the common fears are easily acquired. On the other side, we can suppose that uncommon fears are unstable and/or difficult to acquire.

If we work along these lines, the inquiry is directed towards the identification of those properties of common fears that promote stability and, secondarily, the identification of those properties that facilitate the easy acquisition of these fears. Seligman's attempt to provide an explanation of how biologically relevant fears are acquired merges these two lines of inquiry. He proposed that prepared fears are both easy to acquire and unusually stable. Having already considered this promising theory in an earlier chapter, we can turn to a less obvious possibility that arises from an idea introduced by D. Bolton.[2]

There will be little dispute over the claim that fears can be acquired and some of the evidence supporting this view is described in Chapters 10 and 11. However, recognition that fears can be acquired through learning processes does not imply that all fears arise in this way. The possibility remains that people are *predisposed* to develop some fears, perhaps the most common ones. Rather than assume that a significant proportion of the population *acquires identical fears*, we can entertain the view that the predisposition to develop the most common fears is innate and universal, or nearly so, and that what we learn is how to overcome our existing predispositions. In large part, we learn to stop responding fearfully to predisposed or prepared stimuli. Our remaining fears are those that are resistant to extinction or habituation (plus of course any additional uncommon fears that have been acquired by the conventional learning processes).

An example of learning to stop responding is the fact that most people overcome their early childhood fears (of darkness, strangers, and so on). It is less a matter of acquiring fears of the dark and of strangers than of developing the necessary competence and courage to deal effectively with existing predispositions or actual fears. Over a period of years, our fearful predispositions are weakened and shaped by habituation experiences—metaphorically resembling the shaping of sandstone by the action of the wind. To recall the quotation from Gray given on page 00, "it seems that we come into the world ready to be frightened ... but readily become used to such stimuli provided that they are not followed by any more disastrous consequences."[3]

If there is some validity in this proposition, it should follow that people who have many opportunities to come into (harmless) contact with a fearful stimulus X, are less likely to fear X than are people who never or rarely meet X. Urban children are more likely to fear snakes than rural children. Recall that, during World War II, rural populations had more fear of air raids than the repeatedly bombed urban-dwellers. Thus, paradoxically and in direct contradiction to conditioning and related theories of fear acquisition, people who seldom or never encounter one of these supposedly prepared or predisposed fearful objects are *more* likely to fear them than people who come into contact with them frequently. If one's opportunities for habituating to stimulus X are restricted, the fear will persist. The correlation between the incidence of a particular fear and the frequency with which the feared object is encountered should be *negative*.

It must be acknowledged, however, that at present we have little direct support for this notion. It rests heavily on the presumption that habituation is extremely influential in shaping fears and courageous behavior, and it seems to fit some otherwise puzzling data, such as the widespread occurrence of fears among people who have had little or no contact with the object in question (e.g., some children who live on a snake-free island fear snakes). Naturally the fears manifested by people who have never encountered the feared object or situation may have been acquired by observational learning or by the direct transmission of fear-provoking information. It is extremely likely that a great deal of indirect learning does in fact take place, but this explanation would at most account for the occurrence of fears of objects or situations not yet encountered. It would not explain, for example, why the islanders should have *more* fears than children who have been in contact with snakes—if indeed they do. Accurate information on this and related examples, would of course be of great interest.

The likelihood that many children *vicariously* acquire fears of snakes and of other commonly feared objects is high. The prominence of these objects in mythology is consistent with such a possibility. Snakes feature in the folklore of many societies and in most legends they are presented as frightening or evil creatures. However, proponents of the various theories of preparedness can use the same cultural material to argue that such objects have been incorporated into the lore and mythology because of the widespread, perhaps universal, human predisposition to fear them.

All the alternative explanations for the nonrandom distribution of fears rely on the intrinsically fearful or dangerous qualities of the commonly feared stimuli: for example, we fear intense, novel, sudden stimuli. This explanation is bound to be a part of any comprehensive account, but we must be careful to avoid entering a circular argument. Some alternative explanations also assume that the distribution of fears *reflects* the fear-provoking experience of the sample concerned. Insofar as fears are acquired by learning experiences, the distribution will indeed reflect, in part at least, the type and frequency of these experiences. But the influence of other factors, especially those which do not involve direct experience, is so large as to reshape the entire distribution curve.

Before leaving this topic, we should note that most psychological theories—social learning theory, conditioning theory, two-stage theory—assume that all our fears are acquired. They are in effect *tabula rasa* or blank slate, theories: they maintain that fears are gradually picked up by the blankly fearless infant, and then developed and added to by the child and adult. Each collection of fears should be singular and particular, but the distribution and incidence of common fears indicate a fair degree of generality.

It is highly probable that the profile of a person's fears reflects a combination of his particular experiences and those fears we are prepared or predisposed to acquire.

Confinement

Research into the artificial induction of neurotic behavior in laboratory animals confirmed that under conditions of confinement, animals are more vulnerable to the acquisition of fear. We also have some clinical descriptions that are in keeping with this observation. For example, W. Erwin provided illustrations of the effect of confinement on the genesis and persistence of neurotic fears among some of his psychiatric patients.[4] What he calls the "barber chair syndrome" can be illustrated by the following case excerpt:

At this time the patient was in a barber shop waiting to obtain a haircut and noticed himself very gradually becoming tense and anxious. Halfway through the haircut his anxiety reached maximum intensity and he left the barber's chair and took a tranquilizer which had been prescribed for him. He stated that he had gone for his haircut on a Saturday afternoon with the shop quite crowded with people, two of whom he knew. Prior to this time he had never had anxiety in association with getting a haircut. From that time until the present the patient was exceedingly anxious whenever he went for a haircut. He had even considered arranging for the barber to come to his home to cut his hair. At the present time he fortifies himself with a tranquilizing drug in order to allay his anxiety prior to entering the barber's chair. Other stimulus settings which appear to elicit anxiety responses include standing in line at the cafeteria where he works, having someone watch him sign papers or a cheque and driving an automobile without an adult present.

In addition to the minor contribution that results from the sheer physical effects of undue confinement (e.g., muscular aches), confinement during the exposure to potentially aversive conditions restricts the likelihood of the person achieving or maintaining control of the impending threat. The possibilities for developing coping strategies are restricted. It is not surprising, therefore, that the tail-gunners in heavy bomber crews had the highest fear ratings and the largest breakdown rate. For prolonged periods they were exposed to intense danger while virtually immobilized as they sat cramped in their tiny turrets. Also compatible with this observation is the dislike of serving below deck that was expressed by both U.S. and British sailors during World War II; the most unpopular duty was working in the engine room. This was attributed in part to the sheer unpleasantness of the work, but in addition it was felt to be a frightening assignment. However, it would be unwise to make too much of these incidental findings and anecdotes, particularly since, during the same combat period, the U.S. submarine crews performed extremely well, had an exeedingly small number of psychiatric breakdowns, and seemed to have few problems with fear. Despite their prolonged confinement under water, these crews were able to perform satisfactorily and with little fear.

Controllability

The concept of controllability enables us to integrate some seemingly disconnected data, but there are two difficulties. The concept needs further specification and explication, and yet—somewhat paradoxically—it is too narrow. We need to know precisely what is intended by the definition of controllability and we need to determine its central features. The unsatisfactory narrowness of the concept derives from the implicit acceptance of the view that fear is best conceived of as a unitary phenomenon. Instead, the constructive use of the concept of controllability would be facilitated by adoption of the three-systems approach.

Contrary to the implications of the original view of controllability, it appears that fear is not a binary and composite event—an acute episode that either occurs or does not occur. Rather, fear appears to take several forms. This means that the prevailing definition of controllability is too simple. Rather, we need to encompass all three components—cognitive, psychophysiological and behavioral. The narrow definition of controllability applies mainly to the cognitive element of fear—when we perceive that our actions are unable to reduce the probability of an aversive outcome, we experience apprehension. This may or may not cause, or be accompanied by, avoidance behavior and/or autonomic disturbances. But let us take some awkward cases. A person experiences subjective fear because he estimates that the aversive event is unavoidable, but he neither avoids the stimulus, nor experiences autonomic disturbances. This example, though not invalidating the definition, does illustrate its insufficiency. Our next awkward case is a person who experiences some of the components of fear, such as avoidance and autonomic signs, *despite* his perceived power of control. He knows that he can control the harmless snake as it lies in its box in the laboratory. No uncontrollable aversive event is expected. But he nevertheless experiences palpitations and sweating, and refrains from approaching the box. This example, if accepted, poses problems for the definition of controllability.

We can take the objection one step further. What if the same person, facing the same harmless snake, knows that he can control the probability of an aversive outcome, but nevertheless experiences all three fear components, including subjective fear? This would suggest that the definition is not sufficient. If this example, based on incidental observations made during numerous experiments on fear-reduction processes and in the course of therapy, is not convincing, we can turn to other information (bearing in mind, of course, that the example quoted is subject to experimental test).

In one of the surveys carried out on U.S. combat veterans of an infantry division in the Southwest Pacific theater during World War II, it was found that despite their growing sense of self-confidence in their military ability, 17 percent of the respondents continued to experience intense fear reactions during combat.[5] This information, although admittedly indirect, nevertheless points to an exceptional reversal of the expected relationship between perceived competence and fear.

The utility of the concept can be increased by incorporating a three-systems approach, and by extending the concept to include not only the capacity to reduce the probability of an aversive outcome, but also the ability to reduce the *effects* of an aversive event. It seems plausible that fear will be reduced or even avoided if the person perceives that he can control the effects of a potential aversive event; by analogy with pain, even if we cannot avoid injuries the capacity to reduce the intensity and/or the duration of the pain, is a powerful means of reducing or avoiding the associated distress. The perceived ability to deal with the effects of a fearful stimulus is useful in itself and may well confer a degree of immunity on the anticipatory phase of a fear reaction. Consider the psychological consequences that would flow from the discovery of a reliable, fast-acting tablet capable of reducing fear—a fear-reducing equivalent of an aspirin. The mere knowledge of being able to cope with the *effects* of fear would confer a degree of immunity to fear on the fortunate possessors of this remarkable but regrettably nonexistent drug. It would provide an antidote to *the fear of fear*. There is little doubt that many phobic people, especially those incapacitated by agoraphobic problems, would in addition experience a substantial decline in *anticipatory* fear if they knew they had the power to cope with unwanted effects, should they arise.

What we have here of course is an extension of the concept of controllability beyond the confines of ability to control the occurrence of an expected aversive event. The extension would include the ability to control the *effects* of exposure to unavoidable adversity. It is possible, indeed likely, that the second type of controllability will contribute to the first: an improvement in one's ability to control the effects of fear should reduce the fearful anticipation itself. Even if the aversive event cannot be prevented it is still possible to cushion the effects of the event when it does occur—it is perhaps the psychological equivalent of blocking your ears in anticipation of a loud noise. It is conceivable that distracting activities have the same effect. If so, this might explain why inactivity is worse than even irrelevant activities in fearful situations: it forces one to experience the full impact of the fearful stimuli. Distraction, by diminishing that impact, may help even if it has no influence on the probability of the event itself occurring.

Of course this line of argument is based on a recognition that fear and other stressful forms of stimulation have immediate effects and aftereffects. It seems that, in order to proceed satisfactorily to their next activity, people must first absorb the initial effects of these unfortunate exposures. If the effects are not absorbed, the person experiences persisting discomfort and an interference with other functions, in the form of nightmares, intrusive thoughts, autonomic disturbances, and so on.

Fear Without Avoidance, and Avoidance Without Fear

"Fear is a decisive causal factor in avoidance behavior," stated O. H. Mowrer.[6] Ever since its introduction in 1939, Mowrer's two-stage theory of fear and avoidance has had a major influence on psychologists' view of fear.

In the original statement of the theory, elaborated in the course of the next twenty years, Mowrer critically examined the contrasting theories of Freud, Pavlov, and Watson and concluded that anxiety is most accurately construed as a conditioned pain reaction. He also argued that fear can *energize* behavior and is not merely an inconsequential reaction to stimuli associated with pain. This motivating quality of fear is of central importance. Mowrer went on to add that behavior leading to a reduction of fear is stamped in—the reduction of fear acts as a reinforcement. The final part of the theory is the proposition that behavior motivated by fear is of the avoidance type and, when it is successfully executed, it leads to a reduction of fear, and hence to a strengthening of the avoidance behavior itself. In the original paper Mowrer wrote as follows: "Fear ... motivates and reinforces behavior that tends to avoid or prevent the recurrence of the pain-producing (unconditioned) stimulus."[7]

In his elaboration of these ideas throughout the next few years, Mowrer shifted the emphasis from the cause of fear to its motivating qualities. He claimed, "two causal steps are necessary ... fear in the case of both active and passive avoidance behavior is an essential intermediate 'cause' or 'variable.'"[8]

Abundant empirical support for these ideas was obtained and for a period the findings were conveniently slotted into the two-stage theory, until some difficulties began to arise in the early 1950s. The first major problem was the remarkable persistence of acquired avoidance patterns. In a number of experiments, laboratory animals continued to engage in avoidance behavior for hundreds of trials—even after the unpleasant stimulus had been withdrawn. This presented a problem for the two-stage theory, because, in the absence of further unpleasant experiences, active avoidance behavior should disappear.

The second problem is that the two-stage theory incorporates two assumptions that are no longer adequately defensible. It assumes that all fears are acquired by conditioning, and that neutral stimuli are all equally prone to be turned into fear signals. As we have seen in Chapter 11, the conditioning theory of fear suffers from major weaknesses; moreover, the presumption that all stimuli are potential fear signals is dubious. The two-stage theory was correctly criticized by Harry F. Harlow on the grounds that it exaggerates the motivating role of fear in human behavior. In his own words, "The greater part of our energies are motivated by positive goals, not escape from fear and threat."[9]

Most decisive of all, the claim that fear is a necessary causal stage in the development of avoidance behavior is certainly mistaken. A wide range of avoidance responses arise, wax, and wane—even in the absence of fear. Curiously, this obvious fact was overlooked for a long time, but there is no doubt whatsoever about its validity. Without any difficulty, one can engender, maintain, or modify complex patterns of avoidance behavior without invoking fear at any stage. Let us take some simple everyday examples. John Teasdale has pointed out that a person who takes his umbrella with him when he leaves the house on a cloudy day, is engaging in active avoidance behavior in order to save himself discomfort later in the day.[10] Going to the station to get on an early train is a way of avoiding the discomfort of congestion. Passively avoiding *sauce Bearnaise* is for some psychologists an effective way of avoiding digestive problems later in the day. Actively avoiding a muddy field is effort reducing not fear reducing.

Just as these types of everyday avoidance behavior can occur in the absence of fear, so too can fear be experienced even though it is not followed by or accompanied by avoidance. As pointed out in Chapter 1, although fear and avoidance often correspond, there is no absolute or necessary connection between them. Fear and avoidance often occur together, but not infrequently they arise and develop independently of each other.

Additional difficulties presented by the theory are discussed thoroughly by M. Seligman and J. Johnston,[11] and for our purposes it is unnecessary to state more than three of the major problems discussed by them. In their view, persuasively argued, the two-stage theory does not adequately explain the undue persistence of avoidance responses, the concomitant absence of fear, and what they refer to as the elusiveness of the conditioned stimulus. By this last criticism, they refer to the fact that it is often difficult to specify precisely what stimulus the person or animal is supposed to be avoiding.

Acting on the basis of the two-stage theory, clinicians took care to advise and encourage patients to refrain from avoiding fearful situations or stimuli—especially during treatment. It was customary to warn patients that they risked increasing both fear and avoidance if they fled from the provoking scene; that although temporary relief would be obtained, it would be at the cost of greater difficulties later. The reduction of anxiety accomplished by fleeing increases the avoidance behavior.

Although there are good reasons for agreeing that this sequence of events can take place, it is most unlikely that avoidance behavior is based solely on an escape from fear. It also follows from a three-systems analysis that fear can wax or wane independently of avoidance behavior.

In an attempt to demonstrate that the connection between fear and avoidance is not inflexible and unvarying, P. de Silva and J. Rachman[12] carried out a preliminary study on eight agoraphobic patients. They were divided into two groups, both of which received *in vivo* exposure treatment, but the instructions on avoidance behavior were varied. The patients in Group 1 were told to leave the fear-provoking situation as soon as their subjective fear estimates reached a "fear-thermometer" reading of 25—a low amount of fear (that is, they were to *avoid*). The patients in Group 2 were told that it was highly desirable for them to remain in the fear-provoking situation despite their subjective fears, and that if they left the situation while still frightened, it might promote increased fear. They were encouraged to remain until their fears subsided (to *refrain* from avoiding).

Fear and avoidance were measured by subjective estimates and overt behavioral testing—before, during, and after treatment sessions. The main findings were that the patients in both groups made slight progress. Despite our encouragement of an avoidance strategy during treatment (among the members of Group 1), neither their fears nor their agoraphobic avoidance behavior increased significantly—contrary to predictions drawn from the two-stage theory.

If it is agreed that the two-stage theory of fear and avoidance, despite its remaining powers and attractions, is insufficient, then a number of new possibilites are opened. On the theoretical side it should now be possible to explain some previously incomprehensible phenomena, and on the clinical side it will open the way for the development of new treatment techniques and a refinement of the existing ones.

From a practical point of view, some of the immediate implications to be drawn from the relative failure of the two-stage theory include the following. Clinicians dealing with patients whose problems include a significant element of fear, need no longer assume a tight connection between the subjective complaint of fear and the appearance of avoidance behavior. Patients who complain of excessive fear but refrain from carrying out what might seem to be the appropriate patterns of avoidance, are not necessarily dissimulating. Similarly, patients who engage in extensive avoidance behavior, but deny that it is accompanied by the experience of subjective fear, may well be reporting a genuine phenomenon. A revised view of the relationships between fear and avoidance, one that recognizes that they are somewhat independent from one another, corresponds to clinical observations showing that the evocation of fear during behavioral treatments such as flooding, *is not necessary* for success. Although the possibility that it might be facilitative in some cases cannot be dismissed, on the whole the deliberate arousal of anxiety is unnecessary and should be avoided. One of the unforeseen and unfortunate consequences of an uncritical acceptance of the lump theory of fear is that when the technique of flooding was introduced, many clinicians mistakenly assumed that in order to reduce fear, it is necessary first to evoke it. As a result of this understandable but entirely mistaken belief, fear was unnecessarily provoked in many already distressed patients.

Does Fear Produce Imitation?

It has been argued that fear can be reduced or increased by observational learning. Interestingly, the reverse sequence—fear producing an increase in imitative behavior—can also occur. A simple and common illustration of this sequence can be seen in the behavior of children as they enter a new social group for the first time. In these circumstances many children display overt signs of fear, tensely watching the other children, and take particular care to do as the other children do. During their first few days of attendance at nursery school, many children are subdued and imitative.

In view of the preceding critique of the claim that fear "is an essential intermediate cause" of avoidance behavior, it is worth noticing that this is an example in which fear generates behavior other than avoidance. Because of the close connections between fear and avoidance behavior, we tended to assume rather too easily that fear always generates *avoidance* behavior. Although we are far from being in a position to describe the conditions in which fear will generate either avoidance or imitative behavior, we can go part of the way by treating fear-generated imitative behavior as an attempt to cope. Avoidance and escape behavior implicitly admit defeat. The generation of imitative behavior in fearful situations is an attempt to achieve a degree of control over a potentially threatening situation.

We can interpret this imitative behavior as an attempt to acquire control through observational learning, using models as a guide. In these circumstances, exposure to a coping model can be expected to have at least three distinct effects: it may produce a direct reduction in fear, it transmits a good deal of information (and this in turn can reduce the unpredictability of the situation and increase the possibilities of control), and it facilitates the vicarious acquisition of coping behavior. If the period of observing the model coping adequately is then followed by the translation of the newly acquired skills into appropriate actions, the value of the modeling experience will be powerfully increased.

Unfortunately we do not have sufficient information about this phenomenon to go much beyond what has already been said. It can be speculated, however, that in many circumstances the display of excessive and inappropriate imitative behavior might well be an indication that the person is fearful. From that possibility one can move on to contemplate the relationship between excessive imitative behavior and social conformity. Is it possible that unduly conforming people are more fearful than their less conforming companions? And are certain kinds of nonconforming behavior indicative of comparative fearlessness?

Fear, Imitation, and Conformity

Conduct that is strongly modeled on the behavior of the majority of the members of the group in which one finds oneself is taken as a clear instance of conformity. By extrapolating from the example of fearful children showing increased imitative behavior in a novel situation, it is not unreasonable to predict that fear facilitates conformist behavior. If our definition of conformity includes the imitation of normative group behavior, in a novel and potentially threatening situation conformist behavior may well be an effective method of coping. Observation of the behavior of established members of the group is an important source of information for a newcomer: it can reduce unpredictability, reveal information about the relation between behavior and consequences, facilitate vicarious decreases in fear, and expedite the learning of coping skills. It need hardly be said that excessive conformity, or inappropriate conformity, may be much less adaptive than independent behavior—as well as being morally indefensible, as in the commission of war crimes based on the justification of obedience to higher authority.

If we pursue this speculation a little further, it is

possible to deduce that timid people are more likely to display conformist behavior and, conversely, that fearless and courageous people will display more independent behavior. As we have already seen, courageous behavior derives at least in part from perceived competence; to pursue the present argument, people with high levels of perceived competence should also display more nonconforming behavior than those with low levels of perceived competence. Although none of these deductions are particularly novel, it is nevertheless interesting that they should be reached from a novel starting point— the three-system analysis of fear.

Starting with the pioneering work of S. Asch[13] social psychologists have devoted a good deal of attention to the phenomenon of conformity, and E. Aronson recently summarized contemporary knowledge on the subject. Among the variables that increase or decrease our strong inclinations to conformity, the unanimity of the majority opinion is particularly influential: "If the subject is presented with only one ally, his tendency to conform to an erroneous judgment by the majority is reduced sharply."[14] Prior success in dealing with the task or situation also helps to reduce the tendency to conformity (thus if fear has been reduced on earlier occasions, the tendency to model the behavior of others decreases). Aronson points out that the tendency of the observer to conform is strongly influenced by the constitution of the group: he is more likely to conform if the members are experts, if they are important to him, and if they share important characteristics with him. All three of these variables have, in research on other aspects of behavior, been shown to be important determinants of modeling: we are more likely to model the behavior of experts, of people who are significant to us, and of people who share attributes similar to ours. I am not here suggesting that the presence of fear is the sole or even the major determinant of conformist behavior. Rather, I propose that the presence of fear increases the probability that a person will model the behavior of others when he enters a threatening or novel situation, and this tendency will be strengthened if the members of the group are perceived as being competent and as having characteristics that are important to the observer and similar to his own. Since we have noted that excessive or inappropriate conformity can be seriously maladaptive, it should also be said that successfully modeling the behavior of competent people is a powerful way of acquiring skilled and adaptive behavior—especially when one begins by being fearful.

Fear Reduction: Single or Multiple Processes?

In Chapter 9, the possibility of constructing a unifying theory that would explain the main fear-reduction techniques was introduced. Is such a single theory feasible, or will we have to settle for multiple explanations? For purposes of the argument, we will take into account only the major techniques of desensitization, flooding, and modeling.

Let us consider the merits of the three original contending theories—reciprocal inhibition, extinction, and habituation. The arguments for and against reciprocal inhibition have been assessed here (page 207) and elsewhere,[15] and in the absence of new information, they cannot be elaborated. Suffice it to say that the theory can cope with much information and, not surprisingly, is particularly useful in construing fear reduction by desensitization, especially when the emphasis is shifted from muscular to mental relaxation. However, the reciprocal inhibition theory does not explain and could not have predicted, the effects of flooding.

Assessment of the other two possibilities, habituation and extinction, has been hampered by the question whether the two processes can be distinguished and, if so, how? Both are decremental processes and the repeated presentation of the fearful stimulus is the central operation in both. They also share some parametric properties such as the duration of presentations, intervals between stimuli, and so on. The differences between them include the following. Habituation refers to decrements in the strength of unlearned responses, whereas extinction refers to decrements in the strength of learned responses. Habituation is said to be a temporary decrement whereas extinction tends to be stable. Only one condition is required for habituation to occur— the repeated presentation of the relevant stimulus. But for extinction two conditions are necessary: the repeated presentation of the relevant stimulus *and* an absence of reinforcement. In extinction, one has to break a link (which has been learned).

The first distinction, that between a decrement in an unlearned response and a decrement in a learned response, may be difficult to maintain in practice—partly because of our ignorance about the origin of many types of behavior. In approaching the present problem of fear reduction, we are unable to specify whether some of the important fears (such as fear of the dark) are learned or not (see Chapter 7). It follows that an insistence on this distinction between habituation and extinction would make it impossible

273

to consider any fears other than those in which a learned origin can be confirmed. In effect, acceptance of such a definition would rule out any unifying theory based on habituation. If this definition is rejected, however, we can proceed to test the value of a habituation explanation.

The second distinction between habituation and extinction is based on the temporary nature of the decrements resulting from habituation. If it can be shown that habituation training (defined simply as the repeated presentation of the relevant stimulus) never produces enduring decrements, then habituation must fail as a unifying explanation of fear-reduction techniques, because all of them frequently produce enduring decrements. But even though, in most experimental studies of habituation, such training produces only transitory decrements in responsiveness, there are exceptions.[16] Thus the distinction between habituation and extinction based on transience is not absolute, but the relative ease with which the extinction theory explains permanent reductions in fear is an important advantage for that theory.

The third distinction between habituation and extinction, the role of reinforcement, offers a useful means for differentiating the two processes. In theory, we can separate the two by manipulating the occurrence of reinforcement. Experimentally one might separate them by comparing the decrements in fear responses observed after the repeated presentation of the fearful stimulus, with and then without the presentation of the "negative" reinforcement. For example, under controlled conditions, spider phobic subjects could be presented with a spider repeatedly. In one technique this presentation would be followed by an aversive stimulus (and hence should *not* lead to extinction), while, in the other, presentation of the spider would not be followed by any other stimulus (and hence *should* lead to extinction). However, if the fear-reduction processes involved resemble habituation rather than extinction, then our prediction would be quite different. With either technique, fear should be reduced. In a fear-reduction technique based on habituation, the consequences of presenting the fearful stimulus should be comparatively unimportant, unless the intensity of the stimulus is increased to extraordinarily high levels. So a habituation theory leads to the prediction that both techniques will reduce fear; an extinction theory leads to the prediction that one technique will fail.

One drawback to an explanation of fear reduction based on habituation is the therapeutic value of flooding—can we habituate to high-intensity stimuli and/or prolonged stimulation? It had always been assumed that the answer must be negative, and the proponents of the habituation hypothesis, M. Lader and L. Wing, specifically argued that habituation proceeds best when the stimuli are attenuated and the subject is at a low level of arousal.[17] However, we now know that flooding treatment can be effective when the stimuli are not attenuated and even when the subject is highly aroused. In the Klorman experiment referred to in Chapter 12, habituation to intense stimuli was successfully accomplished. His fearful subjects showed similar patterns of rapid habituation to highly and to mildly fear-provoking film material. These results make a habituation explanation more plausible after all. Perhaps we were simply misled by the claim, quite likely to be correct in a range of circumstances, that habituation is *most* effective when stimuli are attenuated and the subject's arousal level is low. However we had no basis—and still do not—for excluding the occurrence of habituation to intense stimuli (even under conditions of high arousal).

At the same time we must acknowledge Klorman's failure to confirm Lader and Wing's finding of a correlation between habituation of the galvanic skin response to auditory stimulation and fear reduction. Although failures to confirm a correlation between auditory habituation and fear reduction are not unduly serious,[18] it is advisable to recall the importance placed on this finding in the original theorizing by Lader and Wing.

The absence of a consistent correlation may mean that there is no general attribute of proneness to habituation and/or it may reflect a difference of habituation that takes place within and between sessions. In all, the habituation hypothesis is worth reviving. The extinction hypothesis has always been able to accommodate a good deal of information but, as we shall see, it may be more obviously applicable to the avoidance component of fear than to the subjective element or the accompanying psychophysiological disturbances.

Analysis of the role of extinction is bedeviled by uncertainty about the nature of the reinforcement (or, if you prefer, the unconditioned stimulus). Until one can identify the reinforcement, it is impossible to assess its role in maintaining the behavior. The problem can be overcome in laboratory conditions (by generating an experimental fear) but this would introduce doubts about the validity of extrapolating from artificially produced fears to naturally occurring fears.

Thus far it has been assumed that fear reduction involves the modification of a single, composite component. However if we substitute a three-systems analysis, it may be profitable to consider the possibility that the three components (avoidance behavior, subjective fear, and physiological disturbance) are subject to *different* decremental processes. The physiological component may be particularly susceptible to habituation, and the avoidance behavior to extinction. The subjective component seems open to both processes, habituation and extinction, although the extinction hypothesis might not explain adequately what the relevant reinforcement is.

If we allow the possibility that at least two decremental processes might occur in fear reduction (and that these processes are not always synchronous), is there any way of disentangling the two? As proposed earlier, habituation and extinction can be teased out by controlling the role of reinforcement. Habituation should proceed irrespective of the exclusion of reinforcement. Hence, if the physiological component of a fear is subject mainly to habituation, it should decrease with repeated stimulation, regardless of the provision or exclusion of reinforcement. The behavioral avoidance component should be more responsive to reinforcement contingencies. If the contingencies are rearranged so that avoidance behavior is followed by nonreinforcement, and approach behavior by positive reinforcement, the avoidance behavior should decline in strength. There are few indications of whether subjective fear is likely to be more susceptible to extinction or to habituation.

We can now return to the original question. Do we need multiple explanations for fear reduction, or can we manage with a single theory? The answer seems to be that a single explanation is unlikely to be sufficient—but this conclusion is offered for different, new reasons. Formerly it was argued that no single theory could account for the three main fear-reduction methods of flooding, modeling, and desensitization. It is now suggested that, although the same explanation (for example, extinction) can be applied to all three methods, it is unlikely that a single explanation will account for changes in all three of the components of fear. The need for multiple explanations derives not from variations in the fear itself—conceived of as a set of loosely coupled components. These components can change desynchronously, and it is suspected that they are differentially susceptible to habituation and extinction.

In theory it should be possible to test this view by recording all three components during a treatment based on a habituation model and then comparing the results with those occurring during a treatment based on an extinction model. The key difference will rest on the inclusion or exclusion of reinforcement.

Emotional Processing

The present emphasis on habituation inevitably leads to a consideration of the nature of emotional processing. What is known about the process by which fearful stimuli are transformed into neutral ones? At present, very little. However, we have identified some of the variables that promote this process of transformation and other variables that impede it. We also have some idea of the effects that follow or accompany the process.

The transformation, or neutralization, of fear-provoking stimuli is facilitated by repeated presentations, by stimuli that have a certain minimal duration, by piecemeal presentations, by minimal distractions, and by a low level of background arousal. The transformation (neutralization) can be impeded by unduly brief presentations, excessive stimulus intensity, unusually complex, ambiguous, or large stimulus inputs, and excessively high levels of arousal. The accompanying or consequent signs of this process may include heightened autonomic activity, unusual dream activity, nightmares, intrusive thoughts, disturbances of concentration, tension, discomfort, and fatigue.

These findings give rise to the speculation that the process of transformation, at least that of the psychophysiological component, is a matter of breaking down the incoming stimulation into manageable proportions and then absorbing it over an optimal period. The process of breakdown and absorption is facilitated by the transformation variables listed in the preceding paragraph (low arousal level, minimal distraction, and so on) and impeded by effects of the other extreme, such as excessively intense or complex stimulation. If conditions that impede processing are operative when a potentially fear-evoking stimulus enters, then the moment is ripe for the onset of fear. So it is that we are more vulnerable to fear induction when we are fatigued, highly aroused, attempting to process earlier stressful stimulation, ill, confined, or confused.

Starting from a different point, the psychophysiological analysis of imagery, Peter Lang has argued that our attempts to understand emotional processing are unlikely to succeed unless we abandon the view that emotional images are "internal percepts," primitive pictures in the mind.[19] The act of imagining is not a process of inwardly perceiving or scanning a personal collection of stored images. Instead, images are regarded as "functionally organized finite sets of propositions." These stored propositions are fundamental to the emotional response of fear, and it follows that any attempt to comprehend the nature of emotional processing must include an account of these "templates" and how they are modified. It remains to be seen whether this novel approach will prove as fruitful as Lang's earlier research on the components of fear. A. Bandura's approach is avowedly cognitive and "posits a central processor of efficacy information." People regulate their behavior "on the basis of their perceived self-efficacy," which is built up as "people process, weigh and integrate diverse sources of information concerning their capabilities."[20]

Bandura argues that behavioral changes derive from a common cognitive mechanism.[21] Regardless of the particular procedure employed, improvements in defensive behavior are the results of an increased sense of self-efficacy. To put it another way, *any* procedure that improves the person's self-efficacy is bound to be effective. Although the experience of mastering the pertinent situation is the most potent contributor to the sense of self-efficacy, more remote procedures, such as the imaginary rehearsals of desensitization or the observation of someone else achieving mastery, are also effective. The main determinant of how adequately a person will cope with fear or stress is the sense of self-efficacy, and Bandura's early experiments were impressively successful in predicting the outcome of various forms of training.[22]

However, certain pieces of evidence introduce doubts about the comprehensiveness of the theory, even if it is partly enlightening. First, there are the military examples in which reported self-confidence did not correlate with fear experienced in combat (see Chapter 3 and this chapter, page 261). Although confidence and courage corresponded closely in most soldiers, some with little confidence experienced only slight fear, and others with considerable confidence experienced high levels of fear. Second, in clinical practice one encounters patients who perform fearlessly despite their repeated expressions of low self-efficacy. These exceptions could however be discounted on the grounds that they are indirect and imprecise.

The three-systems analysis suggests that psychological changes can be produced by modifying one, two, or all three components. Naturally the modification of one component—say, the psychophysiological, is likely to affect the remaining two components. Hence, directly changing a person's avoidance behavior may well produce a change in perceived self-efficacy. Similarly, directly reducing his psychophysiological responses to fear-provoking situations is likely to affect his perceived self-efficacy. Although there is good reason to expect that improvements in perceived self-efficacy are particularly helpful, there is no reason to suppose that all therapeutic changes are mediated by such improvements. This self-appraisal can be a producer of change, or a result of change. At present there seems no easy way in which this analysis can be reconciled with Bandura's emphasis on the major or even exclusive mediational influence of perceived self-efficacy.

Whether the concept of fear reduction is approached from a unitary definition of fear or a three-systems analysis, there is little doubt that the searchlight is now focused on the processes by which fear-provoking stimulation is neutralized.

Notes

1) For example, A. Bandura, *Psychological Review* **84**, 1977; C. Spielberger, *Anxiety: Current Trends*, 1972. Even if we reject the idea that the cognitive component is the *sole* indicator of fear, it is still possible to argue that it should have pride of place. It is not suggested that all three fear components are of equal weight—but their relative significance is as yet unexplored.

2) D. Bolton, personal communication, 1976.

3) J. A. Gray, *The Psychology of Fear and Stress*, 1971, p. 22.

4) W. Erwin, *Behaviour Research and Therapy* **1**, 1963, p. 179.

5) S. Stouffer et al., *The American Soldier*, 1949, p. 225.

6) O. H. Mowrer, *Learning Theory and Behavior*, 1960, p. 97. See also the original statement of the theory, in *Psychological Review* **46**, 1939.

7) Mowrer, 1939, p. 554.

8) Mowrer, 1960, pp. 48−49.

9) H. Harlow, *Learning Theory, Personality Theory, and Clinical Research*, 1954, p. 37.

10) J. Teasdale, in H. R. Beech, Ed., *Obsessional States*, 1974.

11) M. Seligman and J. Johnston, in J. McGuigan and B. Lumsden, *Contemporary Approaches to Conditioning and Learning*, 1973.

12) P. de Silva and S. Rachman, in preparation.

13) S. Asch, *Social Psychology*, 1962.

14) E. Aronson, *The Social Animal*, 1976, p. 19.

15) See S. Rachman, *Behaviour Research and Therapy* **14**, 1976; J. Wolpe, *Psychotherapy by Reciprocal Inhibition*, 1958; M. Lader and A. Mathews, *Behaviour Research and Therapy* **6**, 1968.

16) For example, H. Kimmel, in H. Peeke and M. Herz, *Habituation*, 1973.

17) M. Lader and L. Wing, *Physiological Measures, Sedative Drugs, and Morbid Anxiety*, 1966.

18) See also Gillan and Rachman's failure (1974), but Lang, Melamed and Hart's success (1970).

19) P. Lang, *Behavior Therapy* **8**, 1977.

20) A. Bandura, N. Adams, and J. Beyer, *Journal of Personality and Social Psychology* **35**, 1977, p. 137.

21) A. Bandura, *Psychological Review* **84**, 1977.

22) Bandura, Adams, and Beyer, 1977; Bandura and Adams, in preparation. (The effect that making the prediction may have on the person's subsequent performance remains to be studied.)

Appendix

Some Notes on Physiological Aspects of Fear

Are gut reactions *gut* reactions? We know from several sources (such as reports by combat soldiers, analyses of psychiatric patients, and some remarkable direct observations of a patient with a partially exposed stomach) that the stomach is affected by strong emotional experiences. Partly because research into the subject of gut reactions does not lend itself to elegant or easy experimental study, and partly because such reactions are believed to be gross indicators, comparatively little is known about them. We are however in a position to know that fear interrupts gastric activity. Cardiac responses, easy to record but tricky to interpret, are better understood. With some exceptions, heart rate appears to accelerate during fear. Clinically, one can observe the heart rate of phobic patients double from 70 to 140 beats per minute within seconds of their approaching a fear-provoking stimulus or situation. It comes as no surprise, then, to learn that one of the most prominent subjective experiences reported by fearful subjects or patients is that of palpitations. Measurements of skin conductance have featured largely in research into fear and other emotions, but it must be admitted that the return from most of this research has been meager. Early hopes that the electrical activity of the skin might provide the desired thermometer of internal emotional states have not been fulfilled, despite useful advances in the technology of recording and quantification. Unfortunately the emotional significance of electrical activity in the skin appears to be limited.

Indeed, the poor results from research on electrical activity of the skin reflect a general disappointment about the contribution by psychophysiology to an understanding of emotional states and experiences. With exceptions, such as the distinction between fear and anger, psychologists have had little success in identifying psychophysiological patterns as characteristic of specific emotional experiences. Instead it has been found that, on the whole, psychophysiological reactions accompanying subjective emotional experiences are diffuse, nonspecific, and imperfectly correlated with any particular experience or source. The levels of psychophysiological reactivity range from intense excitement along a continuum to quiescence, and at no point along this scale is any reaction peculiar to, or indicative of, any specific emotional experience. Whether this lack of psychophysiological subtlety reflects our true constitution or only the extent of our present ignorance, remains to be seen.[1]

The experience and expression of fear is closely associated with the activity of the sympathetic branch of the autonomic nervous system. The "opposite" state of calmness is associated with parasympathetic nervous activity. So, for example, cardiac acceleration, pupil dilation, increased skin conductance, gastric inhibition—all associated with fear—are mediated by the sympathetic nervous system. On the contrary, low and regular cardiac activity, high skin resistance, pupil constriction, and gastric activity are all parasympathetic functions.

As already noted, it should not be concluded that sympathetic activity is necessarily indicative of fear. There is more than one pattern of sympathetic responding. So, for example, despite some common attributes (such as increased facial temperature), the patterns that reflect fear and anger differ in the cardiac element—the pulse rate usually decreases in anger but rarely in fear.

A prodigious amount of research on animals, supplemented by clinical observations of patients, has yielded considerable information about the emotional consequences of interventions, temporary or permanent, in the functioning of the central nervous system.[2] It is, however, exceedingly difficult to link and interpret the data in a coherent model of brain function (see J. A. Gray's stimulating interpretation[3]). For the sake of convenience, the central nervous system is often conceived of as comprising three major areas: the brain stem, midbrain, and cortex.

Stimulation of the brain stem produces fragmentary, isolated emotional reactions. The stimuli that provoke these primitive reactions are limited, unchanging, and direct, while the reactions themselves are predictable, massive, and short-lived. Proceeding along the system from the brain stem through the midbrain to the cortex, the reactions become better coordinated, directed, and controlled. At the midbrain level, the fragmentary reactions are ordered into a composite pattern. Both sympathetic and parasympathetic functions are integrated here, the hypothalamus playing an important part in the regulation of emotional behavior, including fear. It is generally assumed that this regulatory function is supplemented and partly controlled by the cortex, which is responsible for the experience of emotion, Direct stimulation of the hypothalamus can, however, produce coordinated and directed emotional reactions; fearful responses are most easily provoked by stimulation of the anterior sections and quiescence by stimulation of the posterior sections. Theorists such as E. Gellhorn[4] emphasize the reciprocal nature of the balance between the different areas, and his views have been quoted in support of Wolpe's theory of psychotherapy[5] based on the reciprocal inhibition of fear/anxiety by relaxation or other responses incompatible with fear.

Research into the emotional functions of the cortex is continuing briskly, and here I will mention only two general observations. First, certain areas of the brain exert a controlling and restraining influence on the functioning of the lower centers. So, for example, damage to the frontal lobes can result in grossly disinhibited asocial behavior. Second, the cortex is vital in interpreting the stimuli that impinge on us. We have some fascinating examples of how stimuli (even when applied directly to specific, small areas of the brain) may, in certain social circumstances, produce one or another emotional reaction. For instance, direct stimulation of the monkey's brain may produce aggression in the presence of a submissive peer but little or no reaction in the presence of a dominant one.[6] Findings of this type provide a link with Schachter's writings (see page 104) on the importance of cognitive appraisal in the interpretation and experience of emotion, including fear.[7]

Damage to the central nervous system can of course have serious emotional consequences, direct and indirect. Direct damage to certain areas may diminish a person's emotional responsiveness (e.g., patients who suffer spinal cord injuries or undergo surgical operations on the frontal lobes generally experience lessened fear reactions), and damage to other areas may lead to increased emotional irritability, including heightened fearfulness.

Notes

1) W. Greenfield and R. Sternbach, *Handbook of Psychophysiology*, 1972.

2) See S. Grossman, *A Textbook of Physiological Psychology*, 1967.

3) J. A. Gray, *The Psychology of Fear and Stress*, 1971.

4) E. Gellhorn, *Psychological Review* **71**, 1964.

5) J. Wolpe, *Psychotherapy by Reciprocal Inhibition*, 1958.

6) J. Delgado, *Physical Control of the Mind*, 1969.

7) S. Schachter and J. Singer, *Psychological Review* **69**, 1962.

References

Abraham, K. *Selected Papers.* London: Hogarth Press, 1927.

Abramson, L., M. Seligman, and J. Teasdale. "Depression and learned helplessness: critique and reformation." In preparation.

Adams, J. and W. Rothstein. "The relationship between 16 fear factors and psychiatric status." *Behaviour Research and Therapy* **9**, 1971, 361–365.

Agras, S., D. Sylvester, and D. Oliveau. "The epidemiology of common fears and phobias." *Comprehensive Psychiatry* **10**, 1969, 151–156.

Aronson, E. *The Social Animal.* San Francisco: W. H. Freeman and Company, 1976.

Asch, S. *Social Psychology.* Englewood Cliffs, N.J.: Prentice Hall, 1962.

Asch, S. "Studies of independence and conformity." *Psychological Monographs* **70**, 9, 1956.

Bancroft, J. "Aversion therapy of homosexuality." *British Journal of Psychiatry* **115**, 1969, 1417–1431.

Bandura, A. *The Principles of Behavior Modification.* New York: Holt, Rinehart, and Winston, 1969.

Bandura, A. *Social Learning Theory.* New York: Prentice Hall, 1976.

Bandura A. (Ed.), *Psychological Modeling.* Chicago: Atherton Press, 1971.

Bandura, A. "Self-efficacy: Toward a unifying theory of behavioral change." *Psychological Review* **84**, 1977, 191–215.

Bandura, A. and N. Adams. "Analysis of self-efficacy theory of behavioral change." In press.

Bandura, A., N. Adams, and J. Beyer. "Cognitive processes mediating behavioral change." *Journal of Personality and Social Psychology* **35**, 1977, 125–139.

Bandura, A., E. Blanchard, and B. Ritter. "The relative efficacy of desensitization and modeling approaches for inducing behavioral, affective and attitudinal changes." *Journal of Personality and Social Psychology* **13**, 1969, 173–199.

Bandura, A. and T. Rosenthal. "Vicarious classical conditioning as a function of arousal level." *Journal of Personality and Social Psychology* **3**, 1966, 54–62.

Becker, H., and C. Costello. "Effects of graduated exposure." *Journal of Consulting and Clinical Psychology* **43**, 1975, 478–484.

References

Beech, R. *Changing Man's Behaviour*. London: Penguin Books, 1968.

Behnke, A. "Psychological and psychiatric reactions in diving and in submarine warfare." *American Journal of Psychiatry* **101**, 1945, 720–725.

Bianchi, G. "Origins of disease phobia." *Australian Journal of Psychiatry* **5**, 1971, 241–257.

Birley, J.L. "The psychology of courage." *The Lancet* **1**, 1923, 779–789.

Bond, D. *The Love and Fear of Flying*. New York: International University Press, 1952.

Borkovec, T., T. Weerts, and D. Bernstein. "Behavioral assessment of anxiety." In A. Ciminero, K. Calhoun, and H. Adams (Eds.), *Handbook of Behavioral Assessment*. New York: Wiley, 1976.

Bregman, E. "An attempt to modify the emotional attitudes of infants by the conditioned response technique." *Journal of Genetic Psychology* **45**, 1934, 169–196.

Broadhurst, P. "Abnormal animal behaviour." In H.J. Eysenck (Ed.), *Handbook of Abnormal Psychology*. London: Pitmans, 1960.

Broadhurst, P. "Abnormal animal behaviour." In H.J. Eysenck (Ed.), *Handbook of Abnormal Psychology*, Second Edition. London: Pitmans, 1972.

Bronson, G. "Fear of novelty." *Psychological Bulletin* **69**, 1968, 350–358.

Bunyan, J. "Autobiography of a Soul." In *Selected Works*. London: Murray, 1912.

References

Cannon, W. *The Wisdom of the Body.* New York: Norton, 1932.

Collett, L. and D. Lester. "The fear of death and the fear of dying." *Journal of Psychology* **72**, 1969, 179–181.

Crawford, M. (Ed.) *Psychological Research on Operational Training.* USAAF APR Report, No. 16. Washington, D.C.: U.S. Government Printing Office, 1947.

Darwin, C. *The Expression of the Emotions in Man and Animals.* London: Murray, 1872.

Darwin, C. *The Expression of the Emotions in Man and Animals.* New York: Appleton and Co., 1913.

de Silva, P., S. Rachman, and M. Seligman. "Prepared phobias and obsessions: therapeutic outcome." *Behaviour Research and Therapy* **15**, 1977, 65–77.

Delgado, J. *Physical Control of the Mind.* New York: Harper & Row, 1969.

Dollard, J. *Fear in Battle.* Washington, D.C.: *The Infantry Journal,* 1944.

Duff, I., and C. Shillin. "Psychiatric casualties in submarine warfare." *American Journal of Psychiatry* **103**, 1947, 607–613.

Egbert, L. "Reduction of post-operative pain." *New England Journal of Medicine* **270**, 1964, 825–827.

Ekman, P., W. Friesen, and P. Ellsworth. *Emotion in the Human Face.* Oxford, England: Pergamon Press, 1972.

Endler, N. and D. Magnusson. "Multi-dimensional aspects of state and trait anxiety." In C. Spielberger (Ed.), *Cross-Cultural Anxiety*. Washington D.C.: Hemisphere Publishing Co., 1976.

English, H. "Three cases of 'conditioned fear response.' *Journal of Abnormal and Social Psychology* **34**, 1929, 221—225.

Epstein, S. "The measurement of drive and conflict in humans." In M. R. Jones (Ed.), *Nebraska Sympsium on Motivation*. Lincoln, Nebraska: University of Nebraska Press, 1962.

Epstein, S. "Towards a unified theory of anxiety." In B. Maher (Ed.), *Progress in Experimental Personality Research*. New York: Academic Press, 1967.

Epstein, S., and W. Fenz. "Steepness of approach and avoidance gradients in humans as a function of experience." *Journal of Experimental Psychology* **70**, 1965, 1—12.

Erwin, W. "Confinement in the production of human neuroses." *Behaviour Research and Therapy* **1**, 1963, 175—184.

Eysenck, H. J. *Fact and Fiction in Psychology*. London: Penguin Books, 1965.

Eysenck, H. J. *The Biological Basis of Personality*. Springfield, Ill.: Thomas, 1967.

Eysenck, H. J. *Psychology Is About People*. London: Allen Lane Press, 1972.

Eysenck, H. J. (Ed.). *The Handbook of Abnormal Psychology*. 2d Ed., London: Pitmans, 1972.

Eysenck, H. J. (Ed.). *Case Studies in Behaviour Therapy.* London: Routledge & Kegan Paul, 1976.

Eysenck, H. J. *You and Neurosis.* London: Temple Smith, 1977.

Eysenck, H. J., and S. Rachman. *The Causes and Cures of Neurosis.* London: Routledge & Kegan Paul, 1965.

Feldman, M. P., and A. Broadhurst. *Theoretical and Experimental Bases of the Behavior Therapies.* New York: Wiley, 1976.

Fenz, W. D. "Conflict and stress." *Psychological Monographs* **78**, 585, 1964.

Fenz, W., and S. Epstein. "Gradients of physiological arousal in parachutists." *Psychosomatic Medicine* **29**, 1967, 33 — 51.

Flanagan, J. (Ed.). *The Aviation Psychology Program in the Army Air Forces.* USAAF Aviation Psychology Research Report No. 1. Washington, D.C.: U.S. Government Printing Office, 1948.

Freud, S. "The analysis of a phobia in a five-year-old boy." Reprinted in *Collected Papers of S. Freud,* Vol. III. London: Hogarth Press, 1950.

Garcia, J., F. Ervin, and R. Koelling. "Learning with prolonged delay of reinforcement." *Psychonomic Science* **5**, 1966, 121 — 122.

Garcia, J., and D. Koelling. "Relation of cue to consequence in avoidance." *Psychonomic Science* **4**, 1966, 123 — 124.

Gelder, M., I. Marks, and H. Wolff. "Desensitization and psychotherapy in the treatment of phobic states." *British Journal of Psychiatry,* **113**, 1967, 53—73.

Gellhorn, E. "Motion and emotion." *Psychological Review* **71**, 1964, 475—466.

George, A. *The Chinese Communist Army in Action.* New York: Columbia University Press, 1967.

Gillan, P., and S. Rachman. "An experimental investigation of desensitization in phobic patients." *British Journal of Psychiatry* **124**, 1974, 392—401.

Gillespie, R. D. "War neuroses after psychological trauma." *British Medical Journal* **1**, 1945, 653—656.

Glover, E. *On the Early Development of Mind.* New York: International Press, 1956.

Goldstein, M. "Physiological theories of emotion." *Psychological Bulletin* **69**, 1968, 23—40.

Goodenough, F. "The expression of the emotions in infancy." *Child Development* **2**, 1931, 96—101.

Goorney, A. B. and P. J. O'Connor. "Anxiety associated with flying." *British Journal of Psychiatry* **119**, 1971, 159—166.

Gray, J. A. *The Psychology of Fear and Stress.* London: Weidenfeld & Nicholson, 1971.

Greenfield, W., and R. Sternbach. *Handbook of Psychophysiology.* New York: Holt, 1972.

Griffiths, D., and M. Joy. "The prediction of phobic behaviour." *Behaviour Research and Therapy* **9**, 1971, 109—118.

Grinker, R. and J. Spiegel. *Men Under Stress.* Philadelphia: Blakiston, 1945. London: Churchills, 1945.

Grossman, S. *A Textbook of Physiological Psychology.* New York: Wiley, 1967.

Groves, P., and R. Thompson. "Habituation: A dual-process theory." *Psychological Review* **77**, 1970, 419–450.

Grünbaum, A. "Is psychoanalysis a pseudo-science?" In R. Stern, L. Horowitz, and J. Lynes (Eds.), *Science and Psychotherapy.* New York: Haven Press, 1977.

Hagman, C. "A study of fear in pre-school children." *Journal of Experimental Psychology* **1**, 1932, 110–130.

Hallam, R. S., and S. Rachman. "Current status of aversion therapy." In M. Hersen, R. Eisler, and P. Miller (Eds.), *Progress in Behavior Modification,* Vol. II. New York: Academic Press, 1976.

Hallam, R. S., S. Rachman, and W. Falkowski. "Subjective, attitudinal, and physiological effects of electrical aversion therapy." *Behaviour Research and Therapy* **10**, 1972, 1–14.

Hallowell, A. I. "Fear and anxiety as cultural and individual variables in a primitive society." *Journal of Social Psychology* **9**, 1938, 25–47.

Hamburg, D. (Ed.). *Report of an ad hoc Committee on Central Factgathering Data.* New York: American Psychoanalytic Association, 1967.

Hamilton, M. "Imitation of facial expression of emotion." *Journal of Psychology* **80**, 1972, 345–350.

Hammersley, D. "Conditioned reflex therapy. In R. Wallerstein (Ed.), *Hospital Treatment of Alcoholism.* Menninger Clinic Monographs, No. 11, 1957.

Harlow, H. "Motivational forces underlying learning." *Learning Theory, Personality Theory and Clinical Research—Kentucky Symposium.* New York: Wiley, 1954.

Hastings, D., D. Wright, and B. Glueck. *Psychiatric Experiences of the Eighth Air Force.* New York: Josiah Macy Foundation, 1944.

Hepner, A., and N. Cauthen. "Effect of subject control and graduated exposure." *Journal of Consulting and Clinical Psychology* **43**, 1975, 297–304.

Hersen, M. "Review of school phobias." *Journal of Nervous and Mental Diseases* **153**, 1971, 99–107.

Hersen, M. "Self-assessment of fear." *Behavior Therapy* **4**, 1973, 241–257.

Hinton, J. *Dying.* London: Penguin Books, 1967.

Hodgson, R., and S. Rachman. "II. Desynchrony in measures of fear." *Behaviour Research and Therapy* **12**, 1974, 319–326.

Hodgson, R., and S. Rachman. "The modification of compulsive behaviour." In H. J. Eysenck (Ed.), *Case Studies in Behaviour Modification.* London: Routledge & Kegan Paul, 1976.

Holmes, F. "An experimental study of fears." *Child Development Monographs*, No. 20, 1935.

Izard, C. *The Face of Emotion.* New York: Appleton-Century-Crofts, 1971.

James, W. *Principles of Psychology.* Dover, 1890.

Janis, I. L. *Air War and Emotional Stress.* New York: Mc-Graw Hill, 1951.

Janis, I. L. *Psychological Stress.* New York: Wiley, 1958.

Janis, I. L. *Stress and Frustration.* New York: Harcourt, 1971.

Jersild, A. and F. Holmes. *Children's Fears.* Child Development Monograph, No. 20, 1935.

John, E. "A study of the effects of evacuation and air raids on pre-school children." *British Journal of Educational Psychology* **11**, 1941, 173–179.

Jones, E. *Sigmund Freud: Life and Works.* London: Hogarth Press, 1955.

Jones, M. C. "A laboratory study of fear." *Pedagogical Seminars* **31**, 1924, 308–315.

Kimmel, H. "Habituation, habituability and conditioning." In H. Peeke and M. Herz (Eds.), *Habituation.* New York: Academic Press, 1973.

Klorman, R. "Habituation of fear: effects of intensity and stimulus order." *Psychophysiology* **11**, 1974, 15–26.

Korchin, S., and G. Ruff. "Personality characteristics of the Mercury astronauts." In G. Grosser, H. Wechsler, and M. Greenblatt (Eds.), *The Threat of Impending Disaster.* Cambridge: MIT Press, 1964.

Lader, M., and I. Marks. *Clinical Anxiety.* London: Heinemann Medical, 1971.

Lader, M., and A. Mathews. "A physiological model of phobic anxiety and desensitization." *Behaviour Research and Therapy* **6**, 1968, 411–418.

Lader, M., and L. Wing. *Physiological Measures,*

Sedative Drugs and Morbid Anxiety. London: Oxford University Press, 1966.

Landis, C. "Studies of emotional reactions." *Journal of Comparative Psychology* **4**, 1924, 447—509.

Landis, C. "The interpretation of facial expression in emotion." *Journal of General Psychology* **2**, 1929, 59—72.

Lang, P. "Stimulus control, response control and desensitization of fear." In D. Levis (Ed.), *Learning Approaches to Therapeutic Behaviour Change.* Chicago: Aldine Press, 1970.

Lang, P. "Imagery in therapy: An information processing analysis of fear." *Behavior Therapy* **8**, 1977, 862—886.

Lang, P., and D. Lazowik. "The experimental desensitization of a phobia." *Journal of Abnormal and Social Psychology* **66**, 1963, 519—528.

Lang, P., D. Lazowik, and C. Reynolds. "Desensitization, suggestibility and pseudotherapy." *Journal of Abnormal and Social Psychology* **70**, 1966, 395—405.

Lang, P., B. Melamed, and J. Hart. "A psychophysiological analysis of fear modification using an automated desensitization technique." *Journal of Abnormal Psychology* **76**, 1970, 220—234.

Lautch, H. "Dental phobia." *British Journal of Psychiatry* **119**, 1971, 151—158.

Lawlis, G. F. "Response styles of a patient population on the fear survey schedule." *Behaviour Research and Therapy* **9**, 1971, 95—102.

Lazarus, R. S. *Psychological Stress and the Coping Process.* New York: McGraw-Hill, 1966.

Leitenberg, H., S. Agras, R. Butz, and J. Wincze. "Heart rate and behavioral change during treatment of phobia." *Journal of Abnormal Psychology* **78**, 1971, 59–64.

Lepley, W. (Ed.). *Psychological Research in the Theaters of War.* USAAF Aviation Psychology Research Report, No. 17., Washington D.C.: U.S. Government Printing Office, 1947.

Lester, D. "Experimental and correlational studies of the fear of death." *Psychological Bulletin* **67**, 1967, 27–36.

Lester, D. "Fear of death in mother and daughters." *Psychological Record* **20**, 1970, 541.

Lewis, A. "Incidence of neurosis in England under war conditions." *Lancet* **2**, 1942, 175–183.

Lewis, N. and B. Engle. *Wartime Psychiatry.* New York: Oxford University Press, 1954.

Ley, P. "Doctor-patient communication." In S. Rachman (Ed.), *Contributions to Medical Psychology.* Oxford: Pergamon Press, 1977.

Lidz, T. "Nightmares and the combat neuroses." *Psychiatry* **9**, 1946, 37–49.

MacCurdy, J. *The Structure of Morale.* New York: Macmillan, 1943.

Mackenzie, C. *Certain Aspects of Moral Courage.* New York: Doubleday, 1962.

Mackworth, J. F. *Vigilance and Habituation.* London: Penguin Books, 1969.

MacMillan, H. *Winds of Change*. London: Macmillans, 1966.

Marks, I. M. *Fears and Phobias*. London: Heinemann, 1969.

Marks, I. M. "The origin of phobic states." *American Journal of Psychotherapy* **34**, 1970, 652–676.

Marks, I. M. "Phobic disorders four years after treatment." *British Journal of Psychiatry* **118**, 1971, 683–688.

Marks, I. M. and M. Gelder. "A controlled retrospective study of behaviour therapy in phobic patients." *British Journal of Psychiatry* **111**, 1966, 561–573.

Marks, I. M., and M. Gelder. "Transvestism and fetishism: Clinical and psychological changes during faradic aversion." *British Journal of Psychiatry* **117**, 1967, 173—185.

Marks, I. M., and E. R. Herst. "A survey of 1,200 agoraphobics in Britain." *Social Psychiatry* **5**, 1970, 16–24.

Marshall, S. L. A. *Battle at Best*. New York: Morrow, 1963.

Mathews, A. "Psychophysiological approaches to the investigation of desensitization." *Psychological Bulletin* **76**, 1971, 73–83.

Mathews, A., and V. Rezin. "Treatment of dental fears by imaginal flooding and rehearsal of coping behaviour." *Behaviour Research and Therapy*, **15**, 1977, 321–328.

May, M. *A Social Psychology of War and Peace*. New Haven: Yale University Press, 1944.

May, R. *The Meaning of Anxiety*. New York: Ronald Press, 1950.

McCutcheon, B., and A. Adams. "The physiological basis of implosive therapy." *Behaviour Research and Therapy* **13**, 1975, 93 – 100.

McGuire, R., and M. Vallance. "Aversion therapy by electric shock." *British Medical Journal* **1**, 1964, 151 – 152.

Melamed, B. "Psychological preparation for hospitalization." In S. Rachman, *Contributions to Medical Psychology*. Oxford: Pergamon Press, 1977.

Meyer, V., and E. Chesser. *Behaviour Therapy and Clinical Psychiatry.* . London: Penguin Books, 1970.

Miller, L., C. Barrett, E. Hampe, and H. Noble. "Comparison of reciprocal inhibition, psychotherapy and waiting list control for phobic children." *Journal of Abnormal Psychology* **72**, 1972, 269 – 279.

Miller, N. E. "Learning of visceral and glandular responses." *Science* **163**, 1969, 434 – 445.

Miller, R., T. Murphy, and I. Mirsky. "Non-verbal communication of affect." *Journal of Clinical Psychology* **15**, 1959, 155 – 158.

Mowrer, O. H. "Stimulus response theory of anxiety." *Psychological Review* **46**, 1939, 553 – 565.

Mowrer, O. H. *Learning Theory and Behavior*. New York: Wiley, 1960.

Newman, L., and R. Stoller. "Spider symbolism and bisexuality." *Journal of the American Psychoanalytic Association* **17**, 1969, 862 – 872.

Öhman, A., G. Erixon, and I. Lofberg. "Phobias and preparedness: Phobic versus neutral pictures as conditioned stimuli for human autonomic responses." *Journal of Abnormal Psychology* **84**, 1975, 41–45.

O'Leary, D., and G. T. Wilson. *Behavior Therapy: Application and Outcome.* New Jersey: Prentice Hall, 1975.

Panter-Downes, M. *London War Notes.* New York: Farrar Straus & Giroux, 1971.

Parkinson, L. "Psychological preparation of children for surgery." Thesis, University of London, in preparation.

Paul, G. *Insight versus Densensitization in Psychotherapy.* Stanford: Stanford University Press, 1966.

Rachman, S. "Systematic desensitization." *Psychological Bulletin* **67**, 1967, 93–103.

Rachman, S. *Phobias: Their Nature and Control.* Springfield, Ill.: Thomas, 1968.

Rachman, S. "The role of muscular relaxation in desensitization." *Behaviour Research and Therapy* **6**, 1968, 159–166.

Rachman, S. *The Effects of Psychotherapy.* Oxford: Pergamon Press, 1971.

Rachman, S. "Clinical applications of observational learning, imitation and modelling." *Behavior Therapy* **3**, 1972, 379–397.

Rachman, S. *The Meanings of Fear.* Middlesex: Penguin Books, 1974.

Rachman, S. "The passing of the two-stage theory of fear and avoidance: fresh possibilities." *Behaviour Research and Therapy,* **14**, 1976, 125–131.

Rachman, S. "Observational learning and therapeutic modelling." In M. Feldman and A. Broadhurst, (Eds.), *Theoretical and Experimental Bases of Behaviour Therapy.* Chichester: Wiley, 1976.

Rachman, S., and C. Costello. "The aetiology and treatment of children's phobias." *American Journal of Psychiatry* **118**, 1961, 97–105.

Rachman, S., and R. Hodgson. "Synchrony and desynchrony in fear and avoidance." *Behaviour Research and Therapy* **12**, 1974, 311–318.

Rachman, S., and R. Hodgson. *Obsessions and Compulsions.* Englewood Cliffs, N.J.: Prentice Hall, 1979.

Rachman, S., R. Hodgson, and I. Marks. "The treatment of chronic obsessive-compulsive neuroses." *Behaviour Research and Therapy* **9**, 1971, 237–247.

Rachman, S., and C. Philips. *Psychology and Medicine,* Revised Edition. London: Penguin Books, 1978.

Rachman, S., and M. Seligman. "Unprepared phobias: Be prepared." *Behaviour Research and Therapy,* **14**, 1976, 333–338.

Rachman, S., and J. Teasdale. *Aversion Therapy and the Behaviour Disorders.* London: Routledge & Kegan Paul, 1969.

Rachman, S., and G.T. Wilson. *The Effects of Psychotherapy, Second Edition.* Oxford: Pergamon Press, 1979.

Rakos, R., and H. Schroeder. "Fear reduction in help-givers as a function of helping." *Journal of Counseling Psychology* **23**, 1976, 428–435.

Rickman, J. "Panic and air-raid precautions." *The Lancet* **1**, 1938, 1291 — 1294.

Rimm, D., and J. Masters. *Behavior Therapy: Techniques and Empirical Findings.* New York: Academic Press, 1974.

Röper, G., S. Rachman, and I. Marks. "Passive and participant modeling in exposure treatment of obsessive-compulsive neurotics." *Behaviour Research and Therapy* **13**, 1975, 271 — 279.

Rosenthal, T., and A. Bandura. "Therapeutic modelling." In A. Bergin and S. Garfield (Eds.), *Handbook of Psychotherapy and Behavior Change,* Second Edition. New York: Wiley, 1978.

Ruff, G., and S. Korchin. "Psychological responses of the Mercury astronauts to stress." In G. Grosser, H. Wechsler, and M. Greenblatt (Eds.), *The Threat of Impending Disaster.* Cambridge: MIT Press, 1964.

Rutter, M., J. Tizard, and S. Whitmore. *Education, Health and Behaviour.* London: Longmans, 1970.

Sackett, G. "Monkeys reared in isolation with pictures as visual imput." *Science* 154, 1966, 1468 — 1472.

Sanderson, R., S. Laverty, and D. Campbell. "Traumatically conditioned responses acquired during respiratory paralysis." *Nature* **196**, 1963, 1235 — 1236.

Sartory, G., S. Grey, and S. Rachman. "Desynchronous changes in fear components under varying therapeutic demand." *Behaviour Research and Therapy* **16**, 1978, in press.

Sartory, G., S. Rachman, and S. Grey. "An investigation of the relation between reported fear and heart rate." *Behaviour Research and Therapy* **15**, 1977, 435−437.

Schachter, S., and T. Singer. "Cognitive, social and physiological determinants of emotional state." *Psychological Review* **69** 1962, 379−399.

Seligman, M. "On the generality of the laws of learning." *Psychological Review* **77**, 1970, 406−418.

Seligman, M. "Phobias and preparedness." *Behavior Therapy* **2**, 1971, 307−320.

Seligman, M., and J. Hager (Eds.). *Biological Boundaries of Learning*. New York: Appleton Century Crofts, 1972.

Seligman, M., and J. Johnston. "A cognitive theory of avoidance learning." In J. McGuigan and B. Lumsden (Eds.), *Contemporary Approaches to Conditioning and Learning*. New York: Wiley, 1973.

Shaffer, L. *Psychological Studies of Anxiety Reaction to Combat*. USAAF Aviation Psychology Research Report No. 14. Washington, D.C.: U.S. Government Printing Office, 1947.

Shepherd, M., B. Oppenheim, and S. Mitchell. *Childhood Behaviour and Mental Health*. London: University of London Press, 1971.

Sherman, M. "The differentiation of emotional responses in infants." *Journal of Comparative Psychology* **7**, 1927, 265−284, 335−351.

Shils, E., and M. Janowitz. "Cohesion and disintegration in the Wehrmacht in World War II." *Public Opinion Quarterly* **12**, 1948, 280−315.

Skinner, B. F. *Science and Human Behavior.* New York: Macmillan, 1953.

Slater, E. "Responses to a nursery school situation." *Society for Research in Child Development Monograph*, No. 4, 1939.

Sloane, B. R., F. Staples, A. Cristol, N. Yorkston, and K. Whipple. *Psychotherapy versus Behavior Therapy*. Cambridge, Mass.: Harvard University Press, 1975.

Smith, M. B. "Combat motivations among ground troops," In S. A. Stouffer et al. (Eds.), *The American Soldier*. Princeton, N.J.: Princeton University Press, 1949.

Solomon, J. "Reactions of children to black-outs." *American Journal of Orthopsychiatry* **12**, 1942, 361 – 364.

Sperling, M. "Spider phobias and spider fantasies." *Journal of the American Psychoanalytic Association* **19**, 1971, 472 – 498.

Spielberger, C. "Anxiety as an emotional state." In C. Spielberger (Ed.), *Anxiety: Current Trends*. New York: Academic Press, 1972.

Spielberger, C., S. Auerbach, A. Wadsworth, and T. Dunn. "Emotional reactions to surgery." *Journal of Consulting and Clinical Psychology* **40**, 1973, 33 – 38.

Stampfl, T. "Implosive therapy." In D. Levis, *Learning Approaches to Therapeutic Behavior Change*. Chicago: Aldine Press, 1970.

Stengel, E. "Air-raid phobia." *British Journal of Medical Psychology* **20**, 1946, 135 – 143.

Stouffer, S., A. Lumsdaine, R. Williams, M. Smith, I. Janis, S. Star, and L. Cottrell. *The American Soldier: Combat and its Aftermath*. Princeton, N.J.: Princeton University Press, 1949.

Suarez, Y., H. Adams, and B. McCutcheon. "Flooding and systematic desensitization." *Journal of Consulting and Clinical Psychology* **44**, 1976, 872.

Teasdale, J. "Learning models of obsessional disorders." In H. R. Beech (Ed.), *Obsessional States*. London: Methuen, 1974.

Thompson, R., P. Groves, T. Teyler, and R. Roemer. "A dual-process theory of habituation." In H. Peeke and M. Herz (Eds.), *Habituation*. New York: Academic Press, 1973.

Thompson, R. F., and W. Spencer. "Habituation." *Psychological Review* **73**, 1966, 16—42.

Ullmann, L., and L. Krasner. *A Psychological Approach to Abnormal Behavior.* New York: Prentice Hall, 1969.

Valentine, C. W. "The innate bases of fear." *Journal of Genetic Psychology* **37**, 1930, 394—419.

Valentine, C. W. *The Psychology of Early Childhood*, Third Edition. London: Methuen, 1946.

Vernon, D., J. Foley, R. Sipowicz, and J. Schulman. *The Psychological Responses of Children to Hospitalization and Illnesses.* Springfield, Ill.: Thomas, 1965.

Vernon, P. "Psychological effects of air raids." *Journal of Abnormal and Social Psychology* **36**, 1941, 457—476.

Walk, R. "Self-ratings of fear in a fear-evoking situation." *Journal of Abnormal and Social Psychology* **52**, 1956, 171—178.

Wallen, R. "Food aversions of normal and neurotic males." *Journal of Abnormal and Social Psychology* **40**, 1945, 77—81.

Watson, J., and R. Rayner. "Conditioned emotional reactions." *Journal of Experimental Psychology* **3**, 1920, 1—22.

Wickert, F. (Ed.). *Psychological Research on Problems of Redistribution, Report No. 14.* USAAF Aviation Psychology Program Research Reports. Washington, D.C.: U.S. Government Printing Office, 1947.

Wilson, H. "Mental reactions to air raids." *The Lancet* **1**, 1942, 284—287.

Wolpe, J. *Psychotherapy by Reciprocal Inhibition.* Stanford: Stanford University Press, 1958.

Wolpe, J. *The Practice of Behaviour Therapy.* Oxford: Pergamon Press, 1973.

Wolpe, J., and P. Lang. "A fear-survey schedule for use in behaviour therapy." *Behaviour Research and Therapy* **2**, 1964, 27—34.

Wolpe, J., and S. Rachman. "Psychoanalytic evidence: A critique based on Friend's case of Little Hans." *Journal of Nervous and Mental Diseases* **131**, 1960, 135—145.

Index